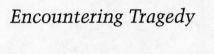

Encountering Tragedy

Encountering Tragedy

ROUSSEAU AND THE PROJECT
OF DEMOCRATIC ORDER

Steven Johnston

Cornell University Press

ITHACA AND LONDON

First published 1999 by Cornell University Press

Printed in the United States of America

Library of Congress Cataloging-in-Publication Data
Johnston, Steven.
    Encountering tragedy : Rousseau and the project of democratic
order / Steven Johnston.
        p.   cm.
    Includes bibliographical references.
    ISBN 0-8014-3596-X (cloth : alk. paper)
    1. Rousseau, Jean-Jacques, 1712–1778—Contributions in political
science. 2. Democracy. I. Title.
JC179.R9J65   1999
320'.01'1—dc21   99-21250

Cornell University Press strives to use environmentally responsible suppliers and
materials to the fullest extent possible in the publishing of its books. Such materials
include vegetable-based, low-VOC inks, and acid-free papers that are recycled, totally
chlorine-free, or partly composed of nonwood fibers. Books that bear the logo of the FSC
(Forest Stewardship Council) use paper taken from forests that have been inspected and
certified as meeting the highest standards for environmental and social responsibility.
For further information, visit our website at www.cornellpress.cornell.edu.

Cloth printing   10 9 8 7 6 5 4 3 2 1

For Judy

CONTENTS

Preface   ix

Acknowledgments   xi

1 On Tragedy   1
Rousseau's Legacy   1
Thinking Tragedy   3
The Ironic Road to Cruelty   10
Ontological Intimations   12
Virtue Wars   16
Political Incommensurabilities   20

2 On Nature   25
First Movement: Attunement   27
Second Movement: Ressentiment   32
Third Movement: Tragedy   35
Concluding with Hobbes   40
Eternal Returns   42

3 On Founding   45
Founding Paradoxes   47
Founding Violence   55
Founding Poetics   61
Founding Fictions   66
Founding Politics   71
Founding Futures   73

4 On Government   75
Governmentality   77
Government and Sovereignty   80

Government and Order   81
Government and Politics   84
The Government of Security and Liberty   89
The Government of Service and Signs   95
The Government of Life and Morality   99
The Government of Sexuality and Pleasure   103
The Government of Opinion and Culture   106
The Government of Sovereignty   114

5 On Enmity   121
Virtue and Enmity   124
Moral Enmity   128
Gender Enmity   133
Foreign Enmity   139
Civil Wars   143
On Cruelty   145
The Return of the Repressed   148

Notes   155
Index   187

PREFACE

Scylla guards the right side; implacable Charybdis the left.
Virgil, *Aeneid*

For modern thought, no morality is possible. . . . As soon as it
functions it offends or reconciles, attracts or repels, breaks,
dissociates, unites or reunites; it cannot help but liberate and
enslave.
Michel Foucault, *The Order of Things*

An aporia haunts the political thought of Rousseau—tragedy.
Nestled in the interstices of his works, it enjoys a phantasmic
life which manifests itself at untimely moments. Thus where Rousseau promises freedom, marginalization perseveres. Where Rousseau
pronounces equality, domination ensues. Where Rousseau posits
identity, difference emerges. Where Rousseau inaugurates legitimacy,
arbitrariness lurks. Where Rousseau affirms virtue, cruelty appears.
Where Rousseau promotes peace, discord is delivered. Where Rousseau presumes resolution, fragmentation is found. Where Rousseau
affords openness, closure prevails. Where Rousseau celebrates the
miracle of birth, the misfortune of life has always already begun.

And so it must be. Flaws and failings plague Rousseau's social and
political interventions at their finest. Not despite his best theoretical
efforts, as he would presume, but because of them. Given Rousseau's
penchant for rebuke and recrimination regarding the world's shortcomings, I take him to be a theorist of regret and resignation, occasionally of hope, not tragedy.[1]

A conundrum, then, animates the studies on Rousseau which follow. Given his passionate commitment to democracy and his determination to identify and eliminate domination in its various and sun-

dry forms, its nagging presence in both his real and imagined polities is striking. Accordingly, I explore the web of ontological assumptions, political aspirations, and moral pressures which might help account for this startling result.

Caveat: I will not rehearse the criticism that the vision Rousseau offers is unattainable because its standards are exorbitant or because it appeals to a world which has disappeared in modernity. The concern here is theoretical not empirical. Rousseau's conception of social and political life is impossible precisely to the extent it can be installed— though Rousseau secures something other than what he actually stipulates. It might be more frightening to witness Rousseau's rhetorical republic realized than disheartening to live without it.

Second caveat: I am not arguing that Rousseau's project is sound in basic conception but flawed in its particular manifestation. The achievement that eludes Rousseau cannot be reconstructed in a future synthesis which captures his moments of truth while leaving behind his self-defeating errors. The project itself needs to be challenged. Rousseau, then, cannot be saved by Hegel. His is a problem of success not failure.

This book, first, offers a close reading of Rousseau and, second, is a meditation on democracy and tragedy. A study of Rousseau's texts provides the occasion to explore a number of political paradoxes critical to an age celebrating the spiritual hegemony of democracy, an age Rousseau helped launch. A tragic understanding can be brought to bear on Rousseau's texts, and questions of sovereignty, government, and order, citizenship, politics, and founding can be illuminated by it. (Chapters 2 through 5 are the results of this effort.) The question of cruelty, furthermore, assumes a privileged place in the tragic analytic offered below, a place secured by Rousseau's failure to confront fully the contingent and contestable underpinnings of his thought. Armed with a newfound appreciation of limits and liabilities, the costs of Rousseau's virtuous republic, many of them hidden or muted, can be reckoned alongside its accomplishments. The wager being made here is that Rousseau himself would flinch at the entries on his ledger, as perhaps would those whose own politics are informed by his example. Insofar as the very pursuit of social and political projects is problematic, democratic theory will be impoverished, I believe, until it confronts the tragic element in its own practice as exemplified by Rousseau.

ACKNOWLEDGMENTS

Many people assisted in the writing of this book. For reading early and late drafts of selected chapters, I thank Mike Gibbons, Cheryl Hall, Alan Keenan, and Penny Weiss. I am especially grateful to the readers for Cornell University Press. The close readings they provided of the manuscript, coupled with detailed suggestions for revisions, proved indispensable in the completion of the project. The book is stronger due to their considerable efforts.

Thanks to my dad who, once upon a time, had the fortitude to read an early version of the entire manuscript and quiz me on its contents. I greatly enjoyed that particular conversation. I am also grateful to Alison Shonkwiler, Laura Healy, and Teresa Jesionowski of Cornell University Press for steering the book from submission to successful completion.

I started thinking about several of the issues pursued here while at Johns Hopkins University. The late George Armstrong Kelly and I used to meet once a week for an independent study on Rousseau. We discovered that neither of us was quite prepared for the other's understanding of Rousseau, but that made for lively conversation. Richard Flathman brought the right combination of skepticism and generative criticism to his interventions, which made for superior motivation. The manuscript would have collapsed of its own weight if not for his timely assistance.

The debt I owe to William Connolly is staggering. I have known Bill since the early 1980s, and he has been a source of intellectual inspiration from day one. The generosity, insight, advice, and candor he brought to an earlier incarnation of the book went above and beyond the call of duty. The manuscript would have been unthinkable without his unique contributions.

Late in the project I found a marvelous new friend in Kirsten Fischer. I cannot thank her enough for the encouragement, energy, and excitement she provided just when I needed them most.

Finally, I dedicate the book to Judy Gallant, my long-standing partner in crime. Her love and support over the years have been a source both of joy and wonder.

Steven Johnston

Tampa, Florida

Encountering Tragedy

I

On Tragedy

As long as I can remember, I have been a Rousseauian.
Tracy Strong, *Jean-Jacques Rousseau: The Politics of the Ordinary*

I am not a Rousseauian, nor do I know anyone who is.
Arthur Melzer, *The Natural Goodness of Man*

Rousseau's Legacy

Rousseau's contributions to western political thought, more specifically to democratic thought, are legion. Nonetheless, a periodic reminder may prove salutary. Consider the following modest sample. Parodying Locke, Rousseau offers a devastating genealogy of western social and political institutions, locating the origins of society in the most brilliant fraud of the rich who implicated the poor in their own subjection and impoverishment. The introduction of law, rather than equalizing everyone under it, as promised, froze existing inequalities and disparities into place. Usurpation was converted into right. Rousseau thereby challenges the dominant self-conceptions of European political orders and charges them with illegitimacy. Referencing state of nature philosophers, Locke again and Hobbes, he subverts ahistorical understandings of human nature which effectively close down the political enterprise before it can even start. Indicting Hobbes, he scorns regimes that resort to terror to generate the obedience and respect they cannot otherwise obtain. He scorns them for both moral depravity and strategic ignorance. Given the courses of action they pursue, they ensure their own demise. Echoing Machiavelli, he puzzles through the problems accompanying the birth of a political society and insists upon the indispensability of religion at the founding. Transcendental assistance is needed to replace anarchy with association. Even so, Rousseau rejects strong forms of Christianity for their otherworldly focus and debilitating effects on a robust notion of citizenship. Those dedicated to a world to come may not contribute fully to a world rooted in the here and now.

Rousseau, of course, does more than name names. He decries the insidious influence partial associations or factions have on the state as they relentlessly pursue their own interest blind or indifferent to the dictates of the common good. He finds it axiomatic that an extreme distribution of wealth renders dubious the advent of an order genuinely ruled by law: those of fortune are able to overcome or elude it at critical junctures while those in poverty tend to disappear before it. He denies that incentive systems appealing to self-interest can produce the kind of citizens a well-ordered society requires. A polity without virtue is no polity at all. He delineates the corrupting effects personal forms of dependence have on individual integrity and dignity. The definition of freedom as self-legislation he proposes reveals both the opportunities and responsibilities political action entails. The perpetual possibilities for enactment, for new beginnings, bring the concept of freedom to a climax and, ironically, strengthen the social compact by exposing its fragility. He identifies the causes and consequences of discord and division in the self and the order, which he then seeks to remedy. The list could be extended for pages.

Rousseau, moreover, presents his analyses and executes his critiques with a rhetorical flair which makes them difficult to resist and impossible to ignore. Rousseau's righteous anger compels, his derision rivets, his passion seduces.

Despite such signal theoretical contributions, Paul de Man identified a persistent problem in Rousseau interpretation. Critics often adopt a superior moral position from which his theoretical shortcomings are discerned and solutions for them proposed. This imperial enterprise treats Rousseau shabbily, as if he and his works were obviously defective and in urgent need of correction. Routinely the problem lies with Rousseau himself whose identity is converted from theorist to "interesting psychological case."[1] He becomes the object of diagnosis and treatment.[2] The resort to psychological reductionism is a familiar mode of misreading which brutalizes what is under its care. A rush to judgment replaces reflection and understanding.

De Man argues that the rough handling of Rousseau is part of a larger interpretive phenomenon. Granted, to concede the problematic character of language, whether literary or philosophical, has become part of the conventional wisdom. Nonetheless, efforts regularly are made to eliminate dilemmatic features of thought by any means available.[3] The tendency is accentuated vis-à-vis Rousseau who incorporates ambivalence into his philosophical ethos. De Man may have been more right than he knew. Rousseau himself, I believe, is susceptible to the charge de Man levels against Rousseau readers.

De Man's ethic of reading, featuring an admonition of respect, is pertinent here.[4] Rather than upbraid Rousseau, I seek to rethink and radicalize certain aspects of his thought: to identify prominent silences and omissions; to indicate where he falls short of ideals articulated; to highlight where, by all appearances, he fails to keep promises made, capitalize on opportunities available, follow fully the trajectory of disconcerting themes, or pursue possible implications of his thought. In short, I propose to do to Rousseau what he often did to his predecessors. And though I enlist Rousseau as an ally against himself, I recognize that the readings offered here would not be possible without his interventions and analyses. Though extended in another context, I take advantage of a theoretical offer Rousseau himself made: "Let my readers not imagine, therefore, that I dare flatter myself with having seen what appears to me so difficult to see. I began some lines of reasoning, I ventured some conjectures. . . . Others will easily be able to go farther on the same road."[5]

Thinking Tragedy

Rousseau's texts frustrate. Poised to explore the dizzying difficulties of constructing a democratic political order, routinely they retreat at the brink of theoretical adventure. While Rousseau considers himself a theorist of paradox, his commitment to it is intermittent, imperfect, incomplete.[6]

From the theogony sung to praise the goodness of nature to the epic project of founding an authentic republic capable of healing the wounds of history, from the manifold practices of government undergirding the state and providing it with the citizens it needs to the righteous reign of virtue defining the just and stable political order, the reflections pursued here trace the danger, dissonance, and denial at the core of Rousseau's vision. My aim, however, is to further the paradoxes of things political which his texts broach and then manage to skirt. To do so I elaborate a tragic perspective—tragedy as a materialization of the myriad impossibilities, infarctions, and agonies which characterize, even define, the political. Here Nietzsche can prove indispensable. His offerings on the perplexities and perversities of human life are protean.[7] Though the invitation extended to Nietzsche is mine, Rousseau's texts suggest, sometimes even insist upon, it.

In an aphorism from *The Gay Science* entitled "By doing we forego," Nietzsche articulates a mode of being in the world which recognizes, acknowledges, and negotiates the bounds bedeviling life. Situated in a moral and political context marked by the permanence of profound conflicts and fundamental animosities, he rejects moralities based on commandments or imperatives, those "whose very essence it is to negate and deny." Nietzsche favors an ethos which beckons by virtue of its own excellences—which encourages, prods, goads. An ethic of preferment prevails—as opposed to one of negation—which can affirm itself while minimizing harm. What lies behind the distinction? Nietzsche may be resisting the dogmatism he discerns in dominant moral codes, that is, their insistence on singularity and universality. For Nietzsche, to initiate a set of practices, routines, and exercises is to develop particular dispositions and habits and, ultimately, to lead a ceratin kind of life. Other possible modes of being fade from view or fall by the wayside. Not so much because they are explicitly considered and rejected due to some fatal flaw or shortcoming, but because there is no opportunity to develop them given the alternative trajectory pursued. Where moral contestation reigns, Nietzsche crafts a gentle response. The ethos he prefers does not insist on securing its own status and standing by demonizing and demolishing its opposition. Adopting a morality (or being adopted by it) flows more from an affirmation and cultivation of what it is than from hostility to what it is not—even if the affirmation is in some sense contingent or arbitrary. "Without hatred or aversion one sees this take its leave today and that tomorrow, like yellow leaves that any slight stirring of the air takes off a tree."[8] By doing, Nietzsche thus concludes, we forego. The claim tantalizes: one or more of the roads not taken may have been well worth traveling. But only one path could be pursued. While one mode of being prospers, other possible modes perish. It cannot be assumed that the path pursued was the one right path. We are in no position to assess options missed or lost. Even in retrospect, one cannot know what it might have been best to do.

When, furthermore, Nietzsche insists that "[w]hat we do should determine what we forego," he suggests that there is a price to be paid, a sacrifice to be made, for each and every doing. In fact, it may be the cost exacted which determines its value—which makes it worth doing. The experience of foregoing lets us know that the world is not at our disposal, that it is not available to us as we might like. We live in a world where equally estimable possibilities often have to be distinguished and wrenching decisions rendered.

When it comes to politics, matters become particularly complicated. Doing not only entails foregoing, it necessarily involves denying and refusing, too. The political logic at work here can be unpacked. What if, at the ontological level, any political community is an arbitrary, contingent artifact? What if it neither expresses, represents, nor embodies some essential or immutable truth about the world: not the commands of God, the dictates of Reason, the telos of History, the wisdom of Nature, the cause of Truth, the consensus of the Community, the conclusions of the General Will? If we were not meant to live one way rather than another, ruled by this set of values rather than that one, governed by this complex of institutions rather than that one, subject to this system of laws rather than that one, then any form of life will both enable and disable, engender and eclipse, foster and foreclose. To be able to overcome the resistance it generates, it must employ an element of power to complete, install, and maintain itself. To live one way, then, is to do violence—perhaps worse—to other admirable possibilities for human flourishing.[9]

Also, for any form of life, insofar as good and evil flow from the same basic sources, the fundaments constitutive of a political community simultaneously work to undermine it. In other words, that which is indispensable is also problematic, perhaps inimical—whether founding myths, basic laws, political practices, or traditional values. The sources of unity in the order will be the cause of celebration for some, outrage for others. A presumption of incommensurability, then, animates a tragic perspective. As contending forms of life vie for ascendancy and institutional expression, as irreconcilable antagonisms emerge and erupt, any settlement necessarily spawns injuries and injustices, anger and resentment.

Can an order be imagined or designed absent this maddening dynamic? The suspicion here is no. Thus social and political arrangements are inherently unstable. Any achievement is necessarily fragile. The consensus and concord emblematic of political determinations foster corresponding forms of dissensus and discord. Every political order, it would seem, is permanently poised in its very conception to subvert itself, the potential cause of its own undoing. A decent society, alert to the tragic dynamic, seeks to redress the wounds it inflicts. The effort, however, to correct one evil frequently, if not invariably, produces others. And so on ad infinitum. This dynamic can be negotiated but not negated. Injustice, arbitrariness, suffering can be displaced but not eliminated. Political achievements, then, necessarily combine features which are cause for both pride and despair, congratulation and criticism.

Now we are in a position to expand on Nietzsche's insights. If to do is invariably to deny, to do may also be to deconstruct—that is, destabilize, diminish, devalue, possibly destroy. Doing raises the specter of undoing. Doing as self-defeating—at least partially.

In a fragment from *Will to Power*, Nietzsche explores what he calls "the concept of decadence." He argues that all variety and manner of detritus "are [the] necessary consequences of life, of the growth of life." Responsibility for them must be assumed not denied. Moreover, they require just handling and treatment rooted in reason rather than reaction. Challenging a prominent ontological presumption he writes: "It is a disgrace for all socialist systematizers that they suppose there could be circumstances—social combinations—in which vice, disease, prostitution, distress would no longer grow. . . . A society . . . even at the height of its strength . . . has to form refuse and waste materials." Reversing dominant forms of assessment, a polity can be evaluated according to the by-products it produces. "The more energetically and boldly [a society] advances, the richer it will be in failures and deformities. . . . Age is not abolished by means of institutions. Neither is disease. Nor vice."[10]

Nietzsche's ontological claim (note the language of necessity) is rife with ethical and political implications. Nietzsche posits a dynamic at work in the life of any political community, not just socialist projects. Every polity produces facets and features it deplores and disowns according to its own table of values. The claim pertains to political orders at their zenith not just their nadir. Thus the dynamic he identifies is a function of success rather than failure. To imagine this fate could be circumvented would be an act of naivete.

For Nietzsche, justice cannot be provided to decadence unless and until its status is altered. Given its genesis, to demean, demonize, or deny it is not only suspect but ethically objectionable. At best. The absence of decadence cannot—and should not—be the litmus test of a properly designed regime. No polity can even conceive of itself minus what it takes to be unwanted aspects. Rather, how an order treats decadence is revelatory. Of course, from an alternative perspective decadence may assume a different countenance. It can represent opposition and resistance to dominant norms and codes. Decadence can name another way of life. Doing justice to decadence, then, might require that an order treat it with the respect it claims for itself. In effect, Nietzsche has issued a warning: efforts to remove what is intrinsic to any polity may prove disastrous to its most cherished values.

Having sketched the rudimentary elements of a tragic perspective, what of Rousseau? Given the depth and profundity of his thought, perhaps his texts evince awareness of the tragic dimension in politics while assuming that most readers are ill prepared to receive this message directly? Or is the tragic concealed from both author and audience so that a subversive reading is needed to expose it through amplification? If the latter is true, Rousseauian theory is itself an obstacle, even though his texts can suggest responses to the issues raised here. I tend to promote the second reading, though I doubt that the texts themselves allow the issue to be settled definitively to everyone's satisfaction.[11] But, to offer one piece of preliminary evidence, recall that Rousseau insists on the systemic integrity and coherence of his thought, which allows him to announce: "it is so false that the social contract involves any true renunciation."[12]

Nonetheless, since I do not claim to have cornered the theoretical market on tragedy, could some of Rousseau's works be placed within a contending tragic problematic? For example, it could be argued that the history of political thought in the west constitutes a series of heroic failures. Beginning with Plato one epic political project after another has been unable to keep the promises it made or attain the perfection it sought. The imagination always seems to outstrip the human capacity to realize its vision. Efforts to promote justice, secure freedom, find peace, and build a harmonious community have been thwarted both by assistants and assailants alike. Success, ever on the horizon, always seems to recede with approach. Given the stakes involved, failure is unacceptable. What with the expectations generated, bitter disappointment results.[13]

To some, Plato again comes to mind, failure is no surprise. For every lavish scheme devised, an ironic appreciation of limits surfaces to contest it. For every theorist who succumbs to intoxication there is another who champions the virtue of sobriety. To articulate the constituent elements of an ideal order is to reveal the impossibility of the task apparently being executed. What inferences can be drawn after such a demonstration is arguable. Should efforts be made to approximate the best regime as closely as possible, a task by definition never-ending? Should the quest be halted once and for all because of the deeds likely to be committed in its name? Neither position can reign uncontested or refute the other.

How might *The Social Contract* fit into this narrative scenario? Is not this classic text, which reveals in all its painful truth the considerable gap between what is and what might be (or what once might have been),[14] just such a tragic drama? According to Rousseau, only in small sovereign republics can freedom be actuated. "All things considered, I do not see that it is henceforth possible for the sovereign to preserve the exercise of its rights among us unless the City is very small."[15] Rousseau identified but one country capable of securing a legitimate state: Corsica. He deemed most states too large or too corrupt to permit the emergence of legitimate political arrangements. Thus precisely what is desired most is unattainable. That which must be cannot be. Surely this is a tragic fate: reach exceeds grasp, perpetual failure coupled with eternal tantalization. Tragedy, then, revolves around the goal being both thinkable and unreachable.

Likewise, the second *Discourse*, which purportedly tells of humankind's descent from the simple glories of the original state of nature to the depths of Hobbesian hell in society, must be a tragic tale. Unquestionably the human race would have been immeasurably better off if it had remained in the pure, pristine condition where human and world were one. But paradise disappeared due to a complex combination of forces and factors ultimately beyond human control (even if partly the product of human action). Subsequently whatever progress has been celebrated is more apparent than real, a desperate attempt to deny the truth that cannot be faced. "[M]ost of our ills are our own work, and . . . we would have avoided almost all of them by preserving the simple, uniform, and solitary way of life prescribed to us by nature."[16] On this reading tragedy is equated with loss the calamitous effects of which linger in perpetuity. Surely the history Rousseau recounts is a tragic one?

Perhaps. But it seems to me that neither decline nor loss nor improbability nor failure adequately defines the tragic. Granted these are prominent themes in Rousseau's writings. What makes them compelling is the recognition that things once could have been otherwise or could still be. If this be tragedy, it is basically theistic, for solace and consolation are still possible. Tragedy, I want to argue, is both more tangible and intractable. It refers to neither a distant past nor an irreal future. It denies that things could have been gloriously otherwise or might still be. It challenges dominant presumptions of what is possible in moral and political life. Inspired by Nietzsche I want to advance a notion of tragedy as inescapable, inevitable, inexorable, and—what is more—commonplace, even banal. Tragedy as an intrinsic, perhaps quotidian, feature of human being. Tragedy lies in wait, an inevitable concomitant to human exertions and projects.

Rousseau argues in the second *Discourse* that humans prepared for themselves a wretched future, in part, by taking actions the effects of which they did not and could not foresee. What is left unsaid is that if only humankind could have known what it was doing to itself, things might be different now. Alternatively, now that it is known where mistakes were made, perhaps such mistakes can be avoided in the new beginning that must be made. After all, if humankind is responsible for the course and conduct of history, can it not undo what it has done? Is not this one of the themes driving *The Social Contract?*[17]

My claim, rather, is that neither foresight nor knowledge nor experience can prevent tragedy. Just the opposite. And so, rather than theorize tragedy as an incidental, intermittent feature of moral and political life, I want to give it a more prominent location and role.[18] A tragic understanding, ultimately, must be distilled from Rousseau's texts given the presumption of resolution embedded in his terms of political discourse.[19] Rousseau does not attend to the rhetorical effects this feature of his thought produces. It operates independently of the temporal and spatial constraints Rousseau places on his ideal. Ontology trumps history. To say that Rousseau assumes his dream cannot be realized misses the point. To say that he knows in good republican fashion that political achievements *become* corrupt does too. Rousseau's texts intoxicate even if Rousseau himself appears sober. Hopes and expectations insinuated into his texts remain untouched by candid historical assessments. To insist that if only the right empirical conditions were secured institutional initiatives could fall into place may be the last theoretical illusion. I would argue that the presence or absence of preconditions is irrelevant.[20] The distinction Rousseau makes between what is humanly possible and historically probable reveals anything but sobriety—if not drunkenness at least mild inebriation.

The Ironic Road to Cruelty

Rousseau incites. *The Social Contract* subverts the political pretensions of the age. By delineating the constituent elements of freedom, it discloses the actuality of chains. If successful the reader of *The Social Contract* will be transformed by an encounter with it, experiencing more fully what was previously inchoate. The text thus does more than report a condition. It also produces a sense of unfreedom. According to Rousseau, no form of subjection is more pernicious than the personal. The indignity and insult suffered when one is exposed to the whim and caprice of another are monstrous. One is rendered less than human as will is drained from action. The social compact is designed to preclude such vulnerability.

The second *Discourse,* similarly, charts the rise of domination as nascent political society emerges. The viciousness of which humans are capable is boundless. Domination is a unique pleasure, one that surpasses all others. Once tasted it admits no substitutes. Those exercising power are exalted and exulted. Those experiencing it are degraded and debased. Rousseau observes that people will suffer any insult or injury in the hope of one day being in a position to do the inflicting. In the interim, there is no shortage of targets for selective retaliation and partial compensation.[21] Rousseau's hypothetical history of government describes a thoroughly Hobbesian world.

Rousseau, it would seem, is uniquely situated to theorize the problem of cruelty in politics. But anticipation quickly turns to frustration, especially if cruelty is defined as the systemic imperative to conquer or convert, to assimilate or exclude that which (in the self and the order) does not correspond to or harmonize with authoritative political norms and standards. Though appalled by regimes which wreak pain and suffering and deem leniency weakness, Rousseau's republic of virtue, where law expresses a truth (or will) to which one and all must adhere, tends to replicate what it abhors. Thus, while genuinely committed to the project of eliminating many extant forms of violence in political life, Rousseau's schemes nonetheless contribute to the proliferation and escalation of violence.

Contrary to Rousseau's presentation, then, violence does not abate—let alone end—with the introduction of the new republican regime. Moreover, Rousseau's politics can be ominous. The moral and political prescriptions he recommends oftentimes exceed human capacity. Form a tragic perspective, to insist upon the impossible and then hold responsible and punish those who cannot provide it is unreasonable and cruel, even barbarous. Citizens are set up for the fall they take. The pain and anguish, even humiliation, endured are undeserved, gratuitous. To imagine otherwise is to indulge the extraordinary politics flowing from Rousseau's contestable ontology. But with the seminal role Rousseau's theorizing plays, he unwittingly travels the road from violence to cruelty in search of unity (both intra- and intersubjective). Indeed he expects to meet with opposition but not to produce it himself. I believe this can account for the otherwise inexplicable presence of social and political practices that seem incongruous in a democratic order, some of which rival those in the best of despotic regimes. Among them: orchestrating the exercise of politics and reducing it to a public call for conformity; routinely converting expressions of opposition and resistance into dire threats requiring serious response; the casual deployment of the death penalty for what is designated the crime of crimes, lying in the face of the law; treating all prisoners of the regime as if they richly deserve their grim fate.

Rousseau's cruelty, I believe, can be traced to ontological insistence. Though incapable of vindication, the principal assumption anchoring his political reflections, that the world is predisposed to the successful realization of social and political projects, in effect demands that the world can conform to the heart's desire. As the political enterprise inevitably, invariably falters, Rousseau's expectation of fruition governs not only his explanation of failure but the assignation of responsibility for it and the corollary will to punish in response. The system works.

If the persistent harshness of Rousseau can be traced to the ontological framework which funds it, then it is first and foremost a
problem of faith. But given the long history of ontological intoxication
in the western political tradition, calls for abstinence will encounter
resistance. From the perspective pursued here, Rousseau's persever-
ance is not an admirable act of resilience but the obstinate refusal to
acknowledge an endeavor etched in futility. How many times must
the foundations on which he rests his political vision crumble before
they are discredited permanently and abandoned? To deny, dismiss, or
ignore the long record of interpretive failure defies rational explanation. Rousseau's reflections in *Emile*, voiced courtesy of the Vicar,
offer ample indications that the age of ontological exhaustion has
arrived. In modernity, cruelty may not be practiced directly in God's
name, but a creationist ontology enables it in the first instance and
legitimizes it in the last. Faith thus remains, however distant or removed, the condition of possibility of cruelty. Rousseau's texts teach
it. If a tragic understanding is opposed to Rousseau, it may serve to
expose violences hidden in his theorizations as well as the elaborate
cover-ups required to keep them safe.

Ontological Intimations

I approach Rousseau at the ontological level.[22] The ontological frame
which enables and energizes Rousseau's moral and political vision
comprises a number of assumptions about God, nature, history, and
humankind taken to be true. Belief in "the existence of a powerful,
intelligent, beneficent, foresighted, and providential divinity," one of
the tenets of the civil religion, forms the core of Rousseau's ontology.[23] What are the implications of this belief? Rousseau proceeds
theoretically as if God's creation affords an hospitable context within
which social and political projects can unfold. He starts with a presumption about the possibility—as opposed to the impossibility—of
both the theoretical and political enterprises. The goodness and order
intrinsic to the creation can be enjoyed in the mundane world. Consider this a divine endowment. Accordingly, Rousseau rejects the idea
that "heaven has abandoned us without resources to the depravation
of the species."[24]

Connection to God may have become tenuous, especially in modernity, but it remains intact via the creation itself. For Rousseau the

basic structure provided by God's original creative act is unaffected by His subsequent recession, exile, or death. The Vicar expresses the tension nicely: "But as soon as I want to contemplate Him in Himself, as soon as I want to find out where He is, what He is, what His substance is, He escapes me, and my clouded mind no longer perceives anything."[25] Despite the vertigo induced by contemplation, Rousseau writes: "What is there so ridiculous about thinking that everything is made for me?"[26] The Vicar suggests that the world awaits its fashioning with human hands. It is susceptible to the shape it is to be given.[27]

Rousseau's political theory, in short, is tucked within the confines of a munificent ontology the critical feature of which is a presumption of resolution: political projects can be conceived and executed according to plan, thus lacking any significant unwanted features.[28] The nature of things, including the nature of human being, allows for it. Here Rousseau shares Hobbes's assertion that when it comes to the problem of building commonwealths, "the fault is not in men, as they are Matter; but as they are the Makers . . . of them."[29]

Rousseau endeavors heroically to deliver what he takes to be the dream of dreams. Hence the governing impulse of the social compact is to: "Find a form of association that defends and protects the person and goods of each associate with all the common force, and by means of which each one, uniting with all, nevertheless obeys only himself and remains as free as before."[30]

Rousseau assumes that *in theory* such an association can be found. Confidence stems from prior ontological assurance. Ultimately Rousseau flirts with the notion that, if situated correctly, human being can attain or express that which is most essential and distinctive about it, something deposited in it by Nature or Nature's Author.[31] Realization is always a permanent possibility, for though the divine endowment is subject to humankind's ingenious powers of corruption, it is beyond its ability to destroy.[32] Thus with the advent of the social compact he speaks of a remarkable change which takes place in human being: faculties are exercised and developed, ideas broadened, feelings ennobled, and souls elevated. This is the promise which can justify the sacrifices to be made if the face of the earth is to be changed. There may be all manner of obstacles to face, but these can be overcome. And the greater the effort, the more precious the reward in the end. "To complain about God's not preventing man from doing evil is to complain about His having given him an excellent nature . . . about His having given him the right to virtue. . . . What more could divine power itself do for us?"[33] What divine power is alleged to have done helps explain Rousseau's enormous ambition, notwithstanding periodic protestations of modesty.

Despite the brittleness and essential contestability of ontological foundations, dominant political conceptions, whether liberal or communitarian, republican or marxist, secular or theistic, proudly claim or subtly presume to be able to resolve the alienation and anomie, conflict and contention, discord and dissensus bedeviling other theories and hold rival perspectives responsible for the injuries and accidents that inevitably accompany the introduction of social and political order. Opposition to truth is allegedly what prevents it from reigning. But for the perverse persistence of opposition, the rifts and fissures that other perspectives foster could be healed. This faith is fundamentalism run rampant.

Rousseau takes his place in this hallowed tradition of western thought. The Savoyard, as if surveying a long history of failure, neatly captures the upshot of centuries of ontological contestation: "Impenetrable mysteries surround us on all sides. . . . We are a small part of a great whole whose limits escape us and whose Author delivers us to our mad disputes. . . . Each [philosopher] knows well that his system is no better founded than the others. But he maintains it because it is his."[34] Rousseau is not exempt from the phenomenon the Vicar reports. Likewise, speaking of the principles of the social compact, he asserts their universality: "although they may never have been formally pronounced, they are everywhere the same, everywhere tacitly accepted and recognized."[35] Indeed, there are an endless number of ways to bring people together, but there is only one way truly to unite them. Thus Rousseau pursues the "one method for the formation of political societies." He is determined not to repeat the mistakes of previous theorists who managed only to develop "false concepts of the social bond."[36]

Ontological questions are dicey and demanding. A political project authentically committed to securing freedom and delivering justice, plausible, even compelling, within its ontological frame, may also, given a different starting point, seem deeply problematic, perhaps riddled with violence. If, for example, it is assumed that the world is created and thus inclined toward the pursuits of human beings, political initiatives can proceed confident that they can be brought to fruition as conceived. Similarly, if it is assumed that the world possesses an inherent moral bent, it follows that human being should align itself with that trajectory in order to realize what is best in itself. With an hospitable ontology, success is expected and anticipated. Nothing more need be done than following directions properly or living up to that which inheres in the design. Success was meant to be. Politics has a beginning, but also a definitive end. It can be dispensed with upon completion. Should things misfire, the explanation is already at hand and the locus of responsibility apparent. Failure, therefore, is to be attributed to readily identifiable sources which can be punished and even forced to be free, insofar as they are being pressed to behave in accordance with natural and rational expectations.

Alternatively, if we assume that the world is not created for but is indifferent—even resistant—to human initiative, then architectonic aspirations need to be reconsidered. Assumptions begin to look like demands, anticipation like wishful thinking, and proceeding as if the world can respond to the heart's desire—and blaming and punishing where it does not—begins to look like an act of unwarranted aggression. When efforts to implement the new world order fail, such failures will beget an increasingly severe series of moves to see the dream realized. Contrarily, with an assumption of indifference, infelicities and misfirings are to be expected in basic political schemes and arrangements and appraised accordingly. They are constitutive of success rather than signs of failure. This is the stuff of politics.

Nietzsche articulates the spirit of this essay succinctly: "War on all presuppositions on the basis of which one has invented a true world."[37] Hesitation and distrust can be sown not by refuting or disproving Rousseau, for his theories are never proven, but through candidly substituting one explicit instance of insistence for another implicit pattern.

Likewise, consider Foucault's skepticism, which discomfits theoretical systems that insist on cognitive tidiness. Substituting an explicit and hypothetical imperative for the implicit and putatively necessary imperatives governing so much political thought in the west, he writes: "we must not imagine that the world turns toward us a legible face which we would have only to decipher; the world is not the accomplice of our knowledge; there is no prediscursive providence which disposes the world in our favor. We must conceive discourse as a violence which we do to things, or in any case as a practice which we impose on them."[38]

Rousseau's political problems, I contend, stem from unredeemable ontological assumptions. His texts reflect the fault lines marking providential ontologies while simultaneously casting a thin veil over them. Difficulties (cruelties, exclusions, violences, injustices) arise in his republic which reveal a disturbing pattern of repetition which, ultimately, becomes predictable. Suspicion falls on Rousseau's virtue project where he fosters it himself—with evidence provided by his own texts.

A tragic perspective relentlessly applied to Rousseau might expose certain dimensions of his texts while, inadvertently perhaps, leaving some of its own presumptions in the shadows. It can live with its status openly in doubt, but it may not be able to place everything pertinent in doubt at any particular time. The value of such a perspective is in the effect it has on reading Rousseau. His ontology performs, often surreptitiously, essentially political tasks. It can immunize from inspection the myriad sites of social and political formation, consolidation, and regeneration it supports. It can also preclude from consideration alternative visions disabled by the parameters it effects. The task now is to wrestle with the implications of the lack of transcendental warrant for social and political practices and values. Rousseau's texts sparkle with signs that these are threats to be subdued. To bring them out, then, is to force Rousseau to be free.

Virtue Wars

Rousseau's republic can inspire. The promise of freedom through participation in lawmaking, where commitment to the common good rules, renders pale rival conceptions of freedom which restrict it to unimpeded motion in officially designated spaces. Moreover, his advocacy of a righteous politics is unabashed. Obviously vigor in the defense of virtue is no vice. Unless and until exacting standards are brought to bear on morality and politics, some form of Hobbesianism will prevail. For Rousseau the options are clear and distinct. Whatever price has to be paid for a genuine republic is preferable to its alternatives. Does that mean some may suffer under a republican regime? Yes, but "whoever wants the end also wants the means, and these are inseparable from some risks, even from some losses."³⁹ Could it be worse than the misery rival systems routinely inflict? Doubtful. If anything, just the opposite. A virtue politics has the best interests of its recipients in mind. Besides, to retreat before the prospect of success because success entails unfortunate, lamentable costs suggests courage and conviction cannot be combined.

The structure of a political theory of virtue may simultaneously reveal its dangers. Rousseau's virtue politics is forged through an articulation of enmity—by juxtaposing itself against alternatives both real and potential.⁴⁰ It would possess neither its sharpness nor surety without the contrast alternatives provide. The demarcations generate a sense of superiority from which it draws meaning and sustenance. It thus experiences a symbiotic relation to possible alternatives—to difference.

Trouble ensues if and when a virtue politics immerses or shrouds itself in immutable, fundamental truth, perhaps its sine qua non.⁴¹ Commonly invoked: the Order of Things, the Will of the Nation, the Claims of Reason, the Word of God, the Imperatives of Nature, the General Will. Once invoked, rivals are no longer mere alternatives. They represent the negation of the good virtue seeks. Difference becomes other—evil, sick, perverse. The conversion process buttresses the self-conception of a virtue theory of politics. It enables it to fend off doubt and appease its need for certainty. A virtue politics with a window onto truth converts what might have been an adversarial but respectful, even productively antagonistic, relation to difference into something more serious, potentially deadly. Alternatives are to be condemned: they signify the gap between the sacred and the profane.⁴²

For Rousseau virtue is to reign. The royal metaphor is apt. The conduct of politics in Rousseau's republic, rather than provide an opportunity to explore new options, contest old understandings, or revise existing arrangements, affords an occasion publicly to ratify truths already operative in the common life. A more robust conception of politics is both unnecessary and perilous. If there is conflict or dissent in the order, it is to be curtailed and contained. Since neither is to be read as a sign that basic arrangements are dubious or problematic, there is no need to provide for public accommodation where they might find expression and engagement. The truths to be revealed through politics cannot be left vulnerable to the uncertainties and vagaries of contestation. The victory of virtue calls for a series of coordinated actions which guarantee in advance the right outcome. If politics is understood to be a medium for communicating truth, it possesses little, if any, significance of its own. Granted, politics as a formal or ritual exercise may be deemed necessary, even valuable, but contingently so. It is rather unlikely to be considered or celebrated for its own sake.

Not surprisingly, then, while Rousseau anticipates resistance to the virtue politics he commends, his understanding of its genesis enables him to devalue and depoliticize it. To refuse the gift that is the republic of virtue is ultimately unthinkable to Rousseau. Anyone doing so singles himself out for reprisal. He is deemed selfish, perverse, willful, immature, evil. Responsibility lies with the one who resists. To Rousseau failure is all too predictable, for people do not appreciate, among other things, "the continual deprivations imposed by good laws."[43] Here Rousseau understands failure as a lack of success, which occurs despite the best efforts made. He does not allow for the possibility that success fosters its own brand of "failure," that his virtue politics may generate principled political opposition to it. Thus Rousseau's conceptualization of resistance is a prelude to its dismissal. For Rousseau, doing does not involve foregoing or denying.

The political character of Rousseau's republic suffers accordingly. Civic life can be curt, especially once the general will has been declared. How might Rousseau's republican regime respond, say, to permanent, pervasive challenges from one or more of its citizens? Ironically, even controlled contestation rooted in the cultivation of agonistic respect is bound to misfire.[44] To Rousseau's republic of virtue, critical agonism looks like a subtle effort to discredit fundamental communal truths. It presupposes and promotes ontological and political reciprocity and reciprocity depends on a certain willing suspension of belief, on a mutual agnosticism, if you will. Yet there is no agreement that this is a postfoundational age. Not even Rousseau's reflections in *Emile* could generate such an overt conclusion. To encourage all parties to admit to the contestability or shakiness of their ontologies, as a first step to peaceful and respectful coexistence, could be interpreted as a subtle move to fix precisely what is in dispute.[45] The fundamentalist, for instance, does not construe truth as his truth—just truth. To admit otherwise would be tantamount to conceptual self-annihilation. Agonistic respect, then, may exacerbate the tensions it seeks to alleviate, for the fundamentalist is not treated on terms he would recognize or endorse. His response would be that there is no ontological contestability. Those who insist otherwise are wrong—at best. For Rousseau, for example, "[a]ll justice comes from God; He alone is its source." Thus the presence of ontological variability does not itself constitute evidence of contestability. Moreover, to the fundamentalist ironic affirmation may be a sign that a profession of belief is insincere, just gaming, and therefore undeserving of respect. And he who does not really believe what he says is the most dangerous of enemies.[46] Regardless, Rousseau's republic treats challenge and opposition to its fundamental tenets as sources of energy through which it can consolidate and solidify itself. Resistance spurs reinforcement not reevaluation or reconfiguration.

As a result, Rousseau's republic of enmity is neatly self-sustaining. What is the logic at work here? If ours is an age of nihilism, it may be an age of horrors as well. Nietzsche writes: "Extreme positions are not succeeded by moderate ones but by extreme positions of the opposite kind."[47] For generations of fundamentalists onto-political investments have not prospered. Their portfolios are in disarray. While failed investment might lead to divestment, it may also lead to frenzied reinvestment, a redoubling of efforts to secure what has so far proved elusive. It is always possible to conclude that a long history of failure reveals not the futility of a project pursued but the inadequacy of the efforts made to date. Such a conclusion may constitute the ultimate leap of faith, but it is not unreasonable. Wars are long, wars are expensive.

Are Rousseau's truncated politics and circumscribed conception of citizenship perhaps decisive pieces of evidence regarding the presence of tragedy in his texts? Politics for Rousseau involves performing a script drawn to the last detail. The performance is exhaustively rehearsed by actors whose mission is to duplicate the script's instructions exactly. Such a one-dimensional understanding of politics, I would argue, cannot respond to the tragic forces that haunt human life. If, then, Rousseau did present furtively the themes I offer in critique of him, surely they would find institutional expression—in his conception of politics or citizenship or founding or law.

Could it be, however, that Rousseau considered politics as contestation too dangerous to be permitted? Perhaps, but Rousseau dissects and discloses the dangers endemic to mastery. Denial of a tragic con-

dition he secretly recognizes would seem to foster the very subjugation he opposes. Political benefits in the short run would fade before
long-term disaster. The lack of political space in which dialogue and
debate over fundamental norms and principles can be pursued, where
citizens can be other than right or wrong, agents of generality or particularity, good or evil, nurtures the very relations Rousseau abhors.
He proffers a prim conception of politics not because he reels before
tragedy but because a virtue theory of politics resting on a creationist
ontology conceals it from him. Politics represents a culmination for
Rousseau, the crowning achievement of elaborate institutional workings which render it a formality. An agonistic politics, after all,
may not be repressed so much as it is irrelevant or nonsensical to
Rousseau.

Granted its many successes, Rousseau's virtuous new order, I argue,
boasts significant cracks and fissures which are the result of that very
success. While a celebration of violence or cruelty may not define
Rousseau's politics, it does intermittently erupt. Wars are emotional.
At times Rousseau seems oblivious to (some of) the disturbing details
of his republican schemes. Any account of Rousseau's republic, then,
must account for these oddities.

Political Incommensurabilities

Given the multiplicity that characterizes the world (including Rousseau's idealized republic), a thoroughgoing tragic perspective presumes that moral animosities and political conflicts are ineliminable,
intractable, irreducible. It presumes, further, the indispensability of
an agonistic democratic ethos which can house them peacefully, if
not pacifically, and which can address and redress the injuries and
injustices the conduct of politics entails. The tragic opposes itself to
and resists all manner and variety of perspectives, Rousseau's republican fundamentalism included, that dismiss and disparage the prevalence and permanence of antagonism and struggle and that seek to
dominate and dogmatize the political community and normalize its
identities and institutions. A tragic sensibility privileges the promo-
tion and protection of contestation precisely because fundamental
conflicts are not susceptible of final solutions—whether based on
reason, science, tradition, a participatory ethic, or social consensus. If

they can be kept alive and held in creative tension, a dramatic art of conflict might itself elicit a mutual, ambivalent enmity and regard among practitioners, such that impasse or deadlock is not automatically experienced as a failure or a source of outrage but a noble rapprochement for a tragic condition in which we all find ourselves implicated. Respectful agonistic engagement can be conducted absent the imperative to translate into law or truth deeply held convictions on multifarious fundamental moral and political questions. The life we live in common does not obviously require elaborate and extensive codification, formal or otherwise, to ensure its viability. Tragic conflicts may betoken a need for perpetual discursive engagement more than definitive social action.

At times, of course, politics involves, even requires, decisive action. Thus all settlements, however necessary or esteemed, are to be treated as provisional and open to revision and reversal. Otherwise, critical features of social and political life start to petrify. Wounds can sediment in the bowels of an order where, even if quiescent, they affect the functioning of the republic—whether it knows it or not. Politics, then, must be considered a perpetual vocation, one that may enjoy this or that partial success, but can never actually succeed. There is always more to do, more that can be done for the recurring tragedies of politics.[48] Of particular concern here are settlements that compromise democratic understandings and arrangements, especially those offered in the name of this or that sectarian commandment or program.[49]

If contestation is to flourish, if citizenship is to combine productively freedom and limitation, and if the tragedies of politics are to be effectively negotiated, democracies must attend to the spaces of politics and the politics of spaces. Lacking a constellation of vibrant and vitriolic political locales common to citizens, the anger and resentment politics induces can metamorphose into ressentiment. Bile and poison that cannot find adequate expression fester in the subject-citizen. Ressentiment is deadly for an order such as Rousseau's, so reliant on the virtue of its people. It is not enough to inform citizens in the minority that, at best, they are wrong on basic public issues. Where, after all, is it written that the general will cannot issue multiple judgments, each equally general, on any given matter? Allowing and enabling, inviting and encouraging citizens to vent their outrage and disappointment, disagreement and disbelief implicates them in the larger life of the republic. Even when they rail against it, they also participate in its common life through actions indicative of a commitment to its practices, institutions, and norms. Pace Rousseau, unity is not necessarily endangered by dissent. Dissent, in the long run, can contribute to the unity Rousseau seeks. It can democratize democracy.

Rousseauian thought itself is not without resources to negotiate tragic dilemmas and denouements. Though conceived to prevent ambitious, powerful minorities from dominating politics, the general will proceeds in a manner consistent with a tragic appreciation of the perils of political action. Insofar as politics proceeds only where trenchant evils arise, the consequentialist ethic animating the general will embodies a discipline and restraint which more traditional forms of political action often lack. Even relatively homogeneous political communities possess heterogeneous elements, which means that the dictates of the general will could work to minimize the ability of some to impose their form of life on others. If legislation aspires seriously to treat all citizens equally, in which the benefits enjoyed and burdens shared are identical, the legislative enterprise might find itself chastened and humbled (even and especially where consensus is more or less unquestioned).

While Rousseau utilizes the general will to prevent politics from becoming legalized domination as citizens tailor law to their own narrow purposes, an ethos of generality yields its own wounds. To treat citizens in identical fashion is to protect the integrity of each of them. Yet the very success of the general will inevitably engenders new forms of domination and injustice precisely because it is willfully blind to individual distinctions. Identical treatment, that is, can also do violence, for in critical respects individuals are idiosyncratic—unalike—and cannot be reduced entirely to a common denominator. Ironically, the successful workings of the general will issue a need for political or legislative specificity to address the tragedies it inaugurates. But how can the general will incorporate the exceptional into its ethos without compromising itself? Can the general will admit that to treat all citizens identically may also violate the respect for citizens it promotes? What if the general will were to admit fully that the basic complexities of communal living tax its competence to legislate? Declarations of the general will might then become occasions to further ongoing political conversations, not just complete and conclude them.

For Rousseau, nevertheless, political action through the medium of the state remains indispensable, which also means that the general will poses its own unique dangers. How might Rousseau's state-centered politics informed by a tragic sensibility avoid the problem of political arrogance to which a generalizing will is prone? Law, Nietzsche claims, can be deployed as an instrument to facilitate and foster struggle.[50] Law that is partial, restrained, forbearing fosters contestation by recognizing and respecting (read leaving alone or unfinished) many of the mysteries, enigmas, and undecidabilities of life.[51] Law can contribute to engagement in other ways, too. Theorists from Aristotle to Nietzsche have argued that the freedom of politics sometimes requires problematic measures if freedom is to be preserved and protected. The exercise of freedom, perversely, can subvert, even eliminate, freedom itself. It can become the victim of its own success. In Aristotle, for example, citizens who might legitimately come to dominate the political by virtue of their own excellence are ostracized so that the contest of politics may continue. With Rousseau threats stem not so much from exceptional individuals, but from the people themselves. The people, though, cannot be exiled.

What structural devices might press citizens to tend to their freedom? While acknowledging its symbolic import, what if the republic made the ritual reenactment of the founding real? What if the assembly genuinely acted like a constitutional convention and basic political laws were periodically subject to explicit review? If a yearly rite is too frequent for such potential political upheaval, what if it were performed every five years? or once a decade? What kind of effect might the sheer prospect of such a recurring event have on the commitment and involvement of citizens? If it were met with horror, as is likely, its utter necessity would be proven. Ordinary lawmaking can also be designed to trigger its own disruption. The sovereign can legislate that it formally review its findings on a continual basis—the idea being that law must be actively renewed to stay in force. Suspicious of the logic of tacit consent, such a requirement, among other things, would keep defeated and minority voices alive and active—what with a reversal in fortunes now a meaningful possibility rather than a forlorn hope.[52]

The politicization of Rousseauian practices and institutions could prove convulsive to his republic. But perhaps that is what a state thrust into tragedy from birth most needs. If the contingency of the political is folded into the structure of law, contestation might be productively institutionalized. Furthermore, if Rousseau's republican ethos were informed by an explicitly politicizing constitutional faith which celebrates the principles of a democratic order and the creativity of a democratic process rather than a civil religion dogmatized by transcendental insinuation, the conduct of politics would have to look to itself for inspiration and guidance. Might not such measures energize and enliven the citizenship—and freedom—Rousseau fears will wither and die?

The chapters to follow chart Rousseau's remarkable, if unconsummated, theoretical odyssey of deliverance, redemption, and vindication. From the enduring promise of nature which shines through whatever corruption it has suffered at human hands to the wondrous spectacle of founding a legitimate republic where people can live their lives in freedom, equality, and justice; from the multifarious practices of government which embody and express the virtuous identity of subjects to the heroic struggles of citizens overcoming their manifold enemies to consolidate and solidify the way of life they were meant to live, Rousseau's political adventures and achievements turn out to be more complicated, problematic, and paradoxical than even he imagined. Hence tragedy. With the assistance of several late-modern interlocutors, Rousseau's thought can be radicalized in ways not only congruent with his interventions on nature, founding, sovereignty, government, freedom, politics, and citizenship, but oddly compelled by them. The result may be to reveal more fully, perhaps multiply, the tragedies of social and political life, but doing so can serve a full-bodied democratic politics newly capable of finessing them.

2

On Nature

The second *Discourse* . . . is a work which in every way
transcends Rousseau's conscious or unconscious intentions.
Jean Starobinski, "The Discourse on Inequality"

We all tell a story with additions, in the belief that we are doing
our hearers a pleasure.
Aristotle, *Rhetoric*

The second *Discourse* is tantamount to Rousseau's ontological
declaration of independence. Challenging both Augustinian and
Hobbesian understandings of the nature of human being, the stain of
original sin on the one hand, the specter of perpetual war on the other,
the text proffers transformative theoretical and political possibilities.

Admittedly Rousseau proceeds in curious fashion. He informs European civilization with considerable panache that its intellectual
pride and self-confidence are unwarranted, European states that their
social and political institutions are morally bankrupt, Europe's best
and brightest, rich and famous that their way of life is frivolous, pernicious. It thus resumes where the first *Discourse* concluded: it provides history to denunciation, substance to an accusation of corruption and degeneracy.

In Rousseau's hands, though, nature stands vindicated, civilization
condemned for the ills that afflict humankind. We must accept responsibility for our deplorable condition. Nature cannot be blamed. It
endures unadulterated. The *Discourse* dexterously couples ontological potential and promise with historical putrefaction and pessimism.
While the force of Rousseau's narrative fosters the suspicion that
humankind's likely fate is the eternal return of chaos and anarchy

("short and frequent revolutions"), nevertheless, ideally legitimate social and political institutions might still emerge.

Yet due to Rousseau's mixture of hypnoticism and hyperbole, the *Discourse* invites readings that applaud or attack rather than expand its findings. Rousseau's indictment juggles and balances optimism and outrage so skillfully that it obviates alternative readings of the text. Specifically, the constituent elements of a tragic politics lodged in it remain fragmented. The second *Discourse*, then, is of interest as much for what it does not do or say as for any theme articulated or analysis offered.

To this end, I argue that the second *Discourse* is animated by three thematic movements in which the affects induced in the reader are critical to its reception.[1] The essay thus presents Rousseau's *Discourse* in a way Rousseau himself did not, as part of an effort to subvert patterns of thought which inform—and inhibit—his later works. The first movement, which ponders a return to or recovery of an idyllic past, appeals to and inspires a quest for attunement. The second movement, which presumes both the necessity and virtual impossibility of moral and political redemption, signals the rise of ressentiment. The third movement reveals our tragic fate. We live in a world where political aims and ambitions invariably undermine and subvert themselves. Contingency, conflict, and crisis are permanent, prominent characteristics of social and political life even in the best of polities.[2]

The first two movements name recurrent moral and political impulses operative in polities suffering from a wide array of intractable ills. Each jostles for position and priority with the other. Neither can sustain its dominance for long. Neither can eradicate the presence and return of the other. Even as the instability of one is revealed, the hegemony of the other cannot be secured and it too recedes. Rousseau readers can find themselves stymied by these revolving options with no apparent alternative. While the first two movements are largely Rousseau's complicated handiwork, the third I plan to tease out of the *Discourse* to fulfill, if ironically, its ontological promise.

In short, I propose to capitalize on Rousseau's endeavors without giving him the last word. I argue that the second *Discourse*, with interpretive assistance, presents a range of carefully selected alternatives, narrows the field of viable options, and arrives inadvertently at a

tragic destination as if artfully concealed from those not ready to
assimilate its aporetic teachings. Rousseau included.

First Movement: Attunement

Part one of the *Discourse* devotes considerable attention to what
Rousseau calls the original state of nature. And no wonder. He intends
to destroy "ancient errors and inveterate prejudices."[3] Demolition
work requires emphatic repetition. A warning is apposite here. It will
be necessary to rehearse some familiar material, to travel some well
worn interpretive paths, before forging new ones. The paradox: it is
necessary to succumb to Rousseau's seductions in order, ultimately,
to resist them.

In the beginning, Rousseau's story goes, in its original splendor, the
earth displays immense riches and imponderable fecundity. Un-
spoiled. Untapped. It offers sustenance and protection to its creatures.
This is a world where living does not involve existential struggle. The
actions of nature demonstrate how jealous it is of its right to care for
its varied offspring. It hides things from human being that it would be
better for it not to know. The world contains danger and it must be
protected.[4]

The wondrous power of nature can be seen at work as it successfully
organizes the elements of which it is composed and the entities under
its command. Things and beings are always what they need to be.
Relations are in accord, forces proportioned. Human and world are
one.

[In] the state of nature . . . all things move in . . . a uniform manner
. . . the face of the earth is not subject to . . . brusque and continual
changes . . . there is always the same order, there are always the same
revolutions . . . the greatest marvels.[5]

Rousseau is candid about his ontological insistence. He turns to the
images of his mind's eye to find the human animal "as he must have
come from the hands of nature." Rousseau provides a glimpse of what
it might have been like to experience attunement with the world. "I
see an animal less strong than some, less agile than others, but all

things considered, the most advantageously organized of all. I see him satisfying his hunger under an oak, quenching his thirst at the first stream, finding his bed at the foot of the same tree that furnished his meal; and therewith his needs are satisfied."6

The bucolic scene finds Rousseau employing his considerable rhetorical powers. Laden with verbs expressing fulfillment and satisfaction, a sense of well-being and wholeness pervades the imagery. The human is one with its world, needs and powers are nicely balanced. At the close of the paragraph, the world is complete. Rousseau's creationist ontology is on full display here. The earth, naturally fertile, seems designed in fundamental ways to support and nourish its denizens, as it "offers at every step storehouses and shelters."7 The structure of the world and human capacities for survival in it correspond. The earth offers help; instincts enable the human to avail itself of that help. This is a world without care, regret, guilt, deficiency, or responsibility. The beings in it are not governed by a "lack." There is "concern" for nothing other than the "present existence without any idea of the future."8

There are two sources of appeal to the state of nature. One is intrinsic. If, as Rousseau suggests, the nature (or essence) of humankind endures through time impervious to the assaults of history, his imagery can touch everyone in some way.9 If properly drawn, Rousseau's state of nature can connect to that part of human being which was once at home in it and can long for its return, however unknowingly, however viscerally. This helps to explain how humans could be nostalgic for a condition that existed, if it ever did so, ages ago—as opposed to being nostalgic for a period of history within the living or recorded memory and imagination of a people.

The linchpin of Rousseau's exercise is the response of the reader. Thus particular images are judged by their power to evoke or conjure. One set of images will give rise to and fade before another more personal, intimate set. Indifference is the enemy here. Rousseau speaks in the first *Discourse* of "delighting in the recollection of the simplicity of the earliest times. It is a lovely shore, adorned by the hands of nature alone, toward which one incessantly turns one's eyes and from which one regretfully feels oneself moving away."10

Why conjure this image? As just mentioned Rousseau's trip down memory lane is complicated by the apparent want of an actual memory of the state of nature. Even assuming such a condition once monopolized the earth, veritable aeons have passed since its heyday. Perhaps Rousseau believes that a primordial scene can be glimpsed through a gaze into nature unperturbed by thought.

Rousseau's solemn recitation of the glorious beginning softly sings the praises of a wondrous, even miraculous nature and, by extension, nature's Author. Jean-Jacques's imagination seeks to capture timeless truths and eternal essences buried beneath the onslaught of time and the world. He will strip away all that has been acquired to divulge things in their pristine state. Secrets revealed. Identities disclosed. Forms unveiled.[11]

Rousseau's essay speaks to the human desire to return to a purer mode of existence where life again is lived as it was meant to be lived—and was originally.[12] Though such sentiment was hardly new-born in the eighteenth century, Rousseau must engender that which he appears to lament. Thus part of Rousseau's genius lies in his ability to crystallize inchoate sentiments and dispositions. He will incite, perhaps create, revulsion for what civilization has wrought—for what human being has done to itself. Rousseau shatters complacency. He deftly plants a seed in the thoughts of his readers to be harvested later: "Discontented with your present state . . . there is, I feel, an age at which the individual man would want to stop: you will seek the age at which you would desire your species had stopped . . . perhaps you would want to go backward in time."[13]

The primeval past is transformed into a receptacle which can be filled and refilled with innumerable contents. It is a time that is abundant, magnificent, meaningful, lush. It is somehow safer, more secure, full of trust. Whatever plagues the contemporary world and fosters the urge to flee from it is wanting in the image of the past. It embodies a world less complex, less tangled, less tortured, less violent. Absent is the specter of Hobbes. The old world beckons like a long awaited sleep, one filled with dreams, void of nightmares. It is a world without burdens or cares, duties or responsibilities, a world without claims on us. Rousseau evokes wistful sentiments through passages that compel through the implied ills negated: "Let us conclude that wandering in the forests, without industry, without speech, without domicile, without war and without liaisons, with no need of his fellowmen, likewise with no desire to harm them . . . the species was already old, and man remained ever a child."[14]

The quest for attunement involves more than a look back to an alluring yesteryear. It signifies an order approaching the future with trepidation because it seems flawed, perhaps compromised, beyond repair. In the beginning, in retrospect, the world seems wide open: horizons are vast, boundaries are few, expectations are enormous. This is a time which enables humanity now to believe in itself. Realization seems one short step from promise. Disenchantment has set in with the progress of things. Disillusionment haunts human prospects. The present and past have combined to compromise the future. Human being could have lived happily ever after in a world "best suited to peace and the most appropriate for the human race."[15] If not for the intervention of contingent events, it "would have remained eternally in [its] primitive condition."[16] Any subsequent progress was more apparent than real.

Entwined, then, in the reverie of return lies a stinging critique of progress and the enlightenment project of mastery. Rousseau lists with barely concealed contempt the impressive array of ills humans foist on themselves through their own prized accomplishments, which could have been avoided had they listened to the wisdom of nature and guarded the way of life it carefully laid out for them. Instead they indulge themselves in an orgy of consumption where the word excess loses all meaning. Hence the second source of appeal of the state of nature is comparative.

The provocations in Rousseau's work galled many of his contemporaries. It seemed to some that he was rejecting Enlightenment in toto—as opposed to illuminating certain of its problematic features that might otherwise escape notice. Voltaire appears to fall into this camp. He collapses the multiple impulses of the second *Discourse* into one: a call to primitivism, the condemnation of civilization per se. He penned a biting response to Rousseau:

Dear Jean-Jacques Rousseau:
I have read your new book against the human race. I thank you for it. . . . Never has so much wit been used in an attempt to make us [appear] like animals. . . . The desire to walk on all fours seizes one when one reads your work. However, as I lost that habit more than sixty years ago, I unfortunately sense the *impossibility* of going back to it, and I abandon that natural gait to those who are worthier of it than you and I.[17]

Why the detour through Voltaire? Despite the implicit misreading of Rousseau, he indicates that the state of nature cannot be a site of return. Voltaire senses an impossibility but does not elaborate it. He leaves the charge unsupported.

The impossible logic of Rousseau's nature story can be articulated, however. Nature lacks what culture wishes to recover. Nature thus achieves its cultural presence through a series of absences. Nature possesses what culture lacks but it is unable to know this, nor does culture have the foresight to forestall the loss of this possession. There is thus no return to nature that could fulfill the nostalgia for it, for no return could know itself to be one, to be the healing of a loss. Thus, even if one could go back, one could never be healed. One would be dumb.[18]

Indeed Rousseau preempts the accusation he assumes awaits him:

> What! Must we destroy societies, annihilate mine and thine, and go back to live in forests with bears? A conclusion in the manner of my adversaries, which I prefer to anticipate rather than leave them the shame of drawing it.[19]

Since Rousseau recognizes that his state of nature is no less fictitious than Hobbes's, his task is to supplant one compelling political narrative with a more enticing story of his own. Rousseau is equal to the task. If anything, he tells his tale so well that his political thought becomes strangely trapped in its unfolding. The problem is not so much that Rousseau comes to believe in the truth of his own fiction. The problem is that the state of nature induces moral and political effects that cannot be resisted or contained simply by refuting the idea of return. While it is obvious that Rousseau rejected the idea of a return to nature, the assessment may capture the intent better than the impact of his intervention. Perhaps the state of nature was designed as a tool to be discarded once it had served its critical purpose. But then Rousseau is a victim of his own skill and success insofar as the state of nature takes on a life of its own. The quest for attunement it names must be satisfied.

The first movement, then, succeeds in amplifying the experience of a lack or a deficiency in culture by comparison to nature, and this mobilization of energy persists even if the terms of comparison on

which it is based turn out to be impossible—as Rousseau's historiciz-
ation of nature indicates. It is now time for the second movement.

The Second Movement: Ressentiment

With the avenue of retreat blocked, the second *Discourse* simultaneously projects a brilliant, potentially boundless future. It is implicit in
the ontological characterization Rousseau provides of humankind
and in the unforgiving narrative he offers of European social and political orders from innocent infancy to evil maturity. The ills that afflict
European states are historical products rather than the inexorable
outcome of nature. Nothing is written in stone. What has been made
can be remade—at least in principle. Ironically, the evil that defines
modern Europe attests to a redoubtable human creative capacity that,
if turned to good, could alter the face of the earth.

No regime could read with equanimity Rousseau's hypothetical
history of government. Much of the second *Discourse*'s rhetorical
intensity stems from the genealogy that exposes the shabby origins of
civil society. Rousseau's anger is biblical. Fast approaching the war of
each against all Hobbes had described, human society reaches a point
in its evolution where its survival is imperiled. Action is mandated.
Law necessary. The rich have the superior motivation: since they
have everything, they have everything to lose. The product of a brilliant conspiracy of the rich at the expense of the poor, the introduction of the social contract is the remedy of choice. It locks into place
preexisting inequities and imbalances. It was the "most deliberate
project that ever entered the human mind,"[20] Rousseau notes with
grudging admiration. But it was necessary to do more than end the
war. Implicating the downtrodden in their own subjection guaranteed
the reliability of the newly formed state. Servitude was legitimated
under the auspices of freedom. The people were hoodwinked. While
the poor were no longer able to make war against the rich, the rich, on
the contrary, acquired free reign to grind the poor into dust. That is
how the strong could resolve to serve the weak.[21] The peace, independence, and equality which characterized the original condition of human being were negated utterly.

Rousseau's genealogy demystifies existing social and political institutions and relations. The facade of the old regime has been col-

lapsed. Righteous indignation is induced. The loyalty and allegiance of subjects can no longer be taken for granted. Any such claims made by actually existing states may now fall on angry ears. But the story does not end here.

To continue. The rich are unable to gouge forever their victims. A state of war may have been averted temporarily as the rich enjoy a period of ascendancy. But the new order, however ingenious, rests on unstable ground. Tension and conflict have been relieved not eliminated. The modus vivendi deteriorates over time. Those given a taste of domination soon cannot do without it and must have more and more to satiate themselves. Ultimately power becomes arbitrary and tyrannical as even the pretense of law disappears. One extreme engenders another until, finally, those who have been enslaved turn against their masters: "The uprising that ends by strangling or dethroning a sultan is as lawful an act as those by which he disposed, the day before, of the lives and goods of his subjects. Force maintained him, force alone overthrows him."[22] Yet the wretched of the earth, once doomed, are not delivered.

Not surprisingly, the sense of excitement surrounding Rousseau's intervention ultimately dissipates. Rousseau did give due warning. The potentiality that generates unbounded possibility simultaneously generates the possibility of misery and destruction. Unless allowed to unfold within a supportive social and political framework, the human animal is as capable of destruction and cruelty as creativity and kindness. Historically, appropriate context has been lacking, as the artless course of evolution depicted in the second *Discourse* reveals. While human being has been made sociable, evil has accompanied it. Can this ambiguous dynamic be broken?

Perhaps. But revolution amidst rampant corruption is likely to result only in a temporary change of masters as one form of enslavement replaces another.[23] The future is unlikely to fulfill expectations human being can have of it: corruption is too entrenched in the evolutionary order of things.[24] Change is always defeated before it starts. Hence Rousseau issues no call to arms. Energy has been generated, anger focused, but it seems fated to useless discharge, spent on nothing but its own exercise.

What happened? Did Rousseau miss an opportunity for manuever the text afforded? If so, what might account for his reticence?

Rousseau's nostalgia for the original state of nature notwithstanding, he insists that the time between the slothfulness of the original state of nature and the organized insanity of civilized society was humankind's best and happiest. That it came to an end must be considered the greatest of misfortunes, something that humankind would not have done to itself. Only some awful contingency could be responsible. Rousseau concludes that "*the human race was made to remain*" always in this period. He considers this state to be "the veritable prime of the world."[25] Rousseau's judgment betrays a longing to see time frozen into place, the flux and chaos of the world permanently tamed. Change per se, by definition, is a sign of decay and disease. Paradise lost. Again. This is the point of no return in the essay.

If only humankind had been able to reap the benefits of its ontological endowment and take advantage of its historical opportunities. What makes history especially painful for Rousseau to recapitulate is that we lost our true home in the world, made possible by nature and nature's Author, where life was lived as it was meant to be lived, not once, but twice.

Perhaps this accounts for Rousseau's silence regarding the possible transition from an actually existing corrupt state to a just republic. The corruption is too profound, too entrenched. The proof lies in the distance that has been travelled from the original condition of nature to the contemporary world. Any response other than complete condemnation and rejection would be to accommodate evil. Thus what could have been the first move, Rousseau's parody of the social compact, toward a democratic politics, lies stillborn in his hands.

Given an alternative understanding of the original state of nature, however, the center of gravity of Rousseau's narrative would shift and the sense of impotence which now dominates it would disappear. If the discord of nature were confronted, the burdens of social and political life could be negotiated rather than damned. By remaining under the spell of his own invention and mourning its loss, Rousseau yearns for what never was, for what never could have been, for what never could be, for nothing. Even as his genealogy gains an almost irresistible momentum, rather than provide an impetus for possible reconstruction, it further cements his sense of despair for what—allegedly—has been irretrievably lost. When humankind was in a position to guarantee its future, it did nothing. Now that it knows what to do, nothing can be done. Rousseau's attachment to his own fiction may render the permanent wounds of life unbearable.[26] For him. Not necessarily for us.

The Third Movement: Tragedy

It is time for the third movement.[27] A tragic perspective can provide an alternative account of the possibilities and limitations crisscrossing the political universe without succumbing to impossible reverie or angry lament. It not only refuses the dream of booking return passage to a foregone era. It challenges the very idea that there was or *could be* anything to which return might be imperative. It contests reading the second *Discourse* as a secular version of the Fall.[28] It stills the call to rendezvous in a millennial future.

The second *Discourse* might have provided Rousseau with his best opportunity to elaborate a tragic narrative. More specifically, a discussion of the relationship between passion and law calls out for one. Despite Rousseau's reluctance, his precious few remarks on law are fortuitously heuristic.

Like Hobbes, Rousseau is a theorist of law and order. A polity can neither be nor function without law. It may represent the reign of justice and the expression of right, particularly at the moment of its birth, but it necessarily relies on power to impose and organize. At its best, law brings harmony to chaos, peace and security to hostility, quiet to noise. It is ineluctably conquest.

The passions of socialized human beings, volatile and violent, know no inherent boundaries. According to social dogma, laws must be crafted to regulate and control them. Rousseau offers his own containment policy on the passions.[29] The greater the passion, the greater the need for law. The paradox is that a society where, reflexively, laws were followed and government officials obeyed would have need of neither one.

Rousseau understands that laws are often inadequate to the task assigned them. They can suffer from a variety of shortcomings. They may under- or overestimate the seriousness or complexity of things. Consequences implicit in their design may not become apparent until they have generated damage sufficient to call attention to themselves—at which point it may be too late to reverse their effects. Of course, the rule of law, however insufficient, remains preferable to its absence. "It must first be agreed that the more violent the passions, the more necessary laws are to contain them."[30] Ineffectiveness does not lessen necessity.

Rousseau's skepticism about law notwithstanding, his expectations for the vocation of politics are considerable. Even in a formulation that seems to wound mortally any undue romanticization of lawmaking, Rousseau's sense of the possible emerges: "the *very least* that *ought* to be *required* of the laws is to stop an evil which would not exist without them."[31] The work performed by the "ought" locution betrays Rousseau's ontological insistence. Thus he does not stop to investigate whether what ought to be expected of the laws can be expected of them. Though the demand is issued as part of a discussion of complex passions which can develop only in society, passions to which law is the response, the problem Rousseau identifies here is more complicated than fine-tuning the legislative craft: "it would still be good to examine whether . . . disorders did not arise with the laws themselves."[32] If this were true, think of the bind it would create. Laws, which are indispensable to society, would be inimical to it as well. Rousseau fears, apparently, that some laws may foster precisely what they are designed to prevent, correct, or eliminate. Rousseau speaks of

countries where, morals still counting for something, the jealousy of lovers and the vengeance of husbands are a daily cause of duels, murders, and worse things; where the obligation to eternal fidelity serves only to create adulterers; and where even the laws of continence and honor necessarily spread debauchery and multiply abortions.[33]

While Rousseau is troubled by what he reports, his explanation for it defuses concern. Disorders can arise, on Rousseau's understanding, because lawmakers have acted rashly, thoughtlessly. They just do not understand the times in which they live. The context of Rousseau's invective suggests that instances of transgression are to be attributed to weak-minded or weak-willed individuals who have been damaged by a corrupt society. If virtuous behavior is demanded from corrupt human beings and embedded in law, law will be routinely flouted. That is, holding the terminally incontinent to virtuous standards will

produce widespread immorality and lawlessness. Responsible behavior is likely to be the exception, punishment for failure the norm.
Accordingly, Rousseau's concern here is circumscribed: make laws
which fit their subjects. Rousseau's disconcerting observation on the
perverse effect of laws is a problem in contemporary practice, not
necessarily in theory.

But might there be a more troubling sense in which law is linked to
disorder and discord? Let us supplement Rousseau's conversation and
theorize the introduction of law per se—that is, law as the systematic
embodiment of a moral code rather than this or that specific law. Even
though Rousseau has posited a dynamic in which law can defeat itself,
it can be rendered inoperative given the right conditions. In a properly
supportive context, a just and legitimate republic, virtuous citizen
conduct is possible. It is this assumption I wish to challenge.[34]

Begin with an assumption Rousseau would refuse. If the human is
not created or designed to live one kind of moral and political life
rather than another (or made of such stuff that it could be fashioned to
so live), then the adoption or imposition of any one form of life will
engender resistance and require an element of power to introduce and
complete it. Accordingly, whatever life is led will simultaneously
provide and prohibit, unite and divide, harmonize and fragment. It
will foment the very phenomena it is supposed to trump. If, then, life
is basically amoral, the project of morality cannot escape the production of immorality. Moral codes necessarily produce behavior that
falls outside the range of what they define as permissible. These are
neither accidental nor trivial features of morality. But the captains of
moral consciousness do not see that the project of morality itself is
responsible for the evils it decries.

Rousseau's broadside quoted above is pertinent here. First, each and
every moral system generates results that are to be condemned within
its frame (debauchery, abortions, etc.). These consequences are not
symptoms of decay, signs of a moral system in need of repair. Such
results would arise even at the zenith of morality with a people uncor-
rupted by civilization. Thus exhortation to do better, to persevere in
the face of temptation or weakness misses the mark. It falls on deaf
ears, or seems hypocritical because those beating the public drums
often behave differently in private. The resort to punishment likewise
fails. Sanctions only drive offenders underground and force them to
devote additional resources to avoid detection, for this is not an iso-

lated problem restricted to a few libertines.[35] Punishment here makes for a better class of criminals. Legalized revenge might provide temporary comfort, though it is catastrophic—because self-deceiving—in the long run.

Second, the dictates of "eternal fidelity" necessarily spawn adulterers because humans constituted as they are do not and cannot necessarily operate within the confines of the marital arrangement, even if they are so inclined. While the human animal is radically incomplete outside a social frame, its constitution does not indicate a moral telos to be completed within it. Thus the frame does not fit naturally its intended recipient and yields forms of resistance to it.

If there is nothing natural about marriage, to establish a life sentence for couples places a burden on humans they are not designed to meet. Ironically, the insistence on strict fidelity, designed to strengthen and solidify marriage, can make the allure of sex outside marriage more exciting. Nothing tempts like the fundamentally forbidden, and the act of transgression itself can be an added pleasure. Moreover, the dictate of fidelity stands in opposition to a manner of living which rejects exclusivity. Without the norm of singularity, multiplicity could not emerge as a compelling alternative. And vice versa.

This is the stuff of tragedy. The cherished constructs and illustrious institutions of social and political life invariably sport debilitating, agonizing cracks and flaws. These architectural wonders combine elements sensational and deplorable, empowering and crippling, stabilizing and destabilizing. One element accompanies the other. And must do so.

Rousseau's later reflections on law in *The Social Contract* similarly deny tragic possibilities. Consider the expectations driving the logic or structure of lawmaking itself. In a republic, for law to be legitimate it must express the general will. Law is not legitimate simply because citizens follow proper procedures for its passage. Citizens cannot will whatever they want and call it legitimate. Authentic acts of legislation treat citizens as a whole and consider actions in the abstract. Legislation never addresses a particular individual or action. It does not make such distinctions. In Rousseau's words, the general will "obligates or favors all citizens equally." The mutuality of commitment is designed to preempt the resentment and rage so characteristic of Hobbesian polities. Rousseau is determined to prevent the conduct of politics from becoming an instrument of domination, from careen-

ing into the continuation of war by other means. With the general will presiding over collective undertakings, Rousseau insists on insisting that "it is no longer necessary to ask . . . whether the law can be unjust."[36]

Can the performance of the general will live up to its promise? What if a republic, in the name of external security, required two years of mandatory service in a citizen militia? Recall that Rousseau assumes a standing army poses a perpetual threat to the freedom of the state. Surely all citizens benefit equally from the military security of the state. Who does not have an interest in living free from foreign domination and intrigue? Is this not one of the preconditions for peace and prosperity? Moreover, the obligation seems identical: everyone serves for two years. No exceptions. Clearly the institution of a volunteer force would violate Rousseau's rule of obligation. Some would stay at home enjoying the benefits while those who serve provided them. Can it really be said, however, that a two-year term affects everyone equally? What if there is a citizen who objects to the taking of life? What if he or she insists on serving, at best, in a supporting role? As a file clerk in the rear? Or as medical personnel? Is the obligation now burdening all citizens equally? Similarly, does it affect a family, where a son could substitute for his father in the workplace, the way it affects a single man, whose business must lie dormant? Is it really the case that "everyone necessarily subjects himself to the conditions he imposes on others"? Any effort to resolve such quandaries seems doomed to violate one or the other of Rousseau's requirements for fairness. While Rousseau's intent may be laudable, the general will embodies denial. Indeed Rousseau wants to minimize the destructive capabilities of the law by limiting its power to general acts. But minimization is not elimination and Rousseau has implicitly confused them. Even if the object of legislation is the common good, not everyone can benefit from it equally no matter how carefully it is crafted with that end in mind. How could any society be so alike that the introduction of law would benefit and burden all its citizens equally? This only could work, to borrow two literary references used by Rousseau, for Adam in the garden (before Eve) or Crusoe (alone) on his island.

Contra Rousseau, a tragic perspective assumes that a republic, a state governed by the rule of law, cannot be conceived, let alone instituted, minus significant political opposition, conflict, and dissent based on legitimate principles and real grievances. Rather, a just political order must anticipate, perhaps even welcome, such features if it is to avoid the institutionalization of cruelty.

Now it is time to reconsider the first two movements, the ontological assumptions driving them, and the political possibilities they disable.

Concluding with Hobbes

Nietzsche and Voltaire, among others, recognize the power of the felt idea of return in Rousseau's thought. That the second *Discourse* can be read as Genesis secularized no doubt contributes to its undeniable allure. Nevertheless, Starobinski claims that despite "the seductive imaginary descriptions that Rousseau provides" of the state of nature, "[a]ll one can affirm at most is that he feels a profound nostalgia for this existence." Starobinski emphasizes, on Rousseau's behalf, that the primitive condition has been "irrevocably lost" and that "one cannot go back."[37] But to rescue, so to speak, the natural condition, one need not go back. Here a distinction needs to be made between return, which indeed is impossible, and recovery, a project which can be pursued. Merely revealing the impossible logic of return can leave its critical power intact. That is, arguing that an ideal condition such as the state of nature could never be reached leaves untouched the aspiration to approximation. Even if return is impossible in the final analysis, the attempt itself can be worthwhile, even admirable. The aim might be to return as closely as possible to the original condition. This is a task that, by definition, might never end. Despite the revelation of the impossible logic, the state of nature can still inform and inspire social and political thought.[38] Perhaps the point is to recover or recreate certain aspects of nature in the future. Rousseau's preference for the social state may conceal as much as it reveals. If anything, it may represent the culmination of his efforts to redeem nature in society. Rousseau can thus have it both ways, enjoy the best of both worlds. Starobinski, it seems to me, ignores this possibility in his rush to deny the state of nature is a "norm, that is to say, a value which it would be necessary to attempt to realize or to rediscover once again."[39]

Rather than challenge Rousseau's quest for attunement on the grounds that it can never be realized, the project must be interrogated from within. Simply put: the world is not predisposed toward human-kind and the world in the beginning names a world well lost. The second *Discourse* itself provides ample textual evidence that the peaceful, blissful idyll Rousseau allegedly discovers and celebrates is gainsaid by the details of the depiction.[40] That is, Rousseau's idealiza-tion of the state of nature needs to be compared to its own delineation. The particulars Rousseau provides in support of the argument that the state of nature is a condition of peace tend to undermine it, if re-presented. If Rousseau's state of nature is characterized by discord and destruction, there can be no fall, no descent because there is no para-dise to be lost. And there can be no sense of irrevocable loss governed by longing for a past that, for human benefit, should have endured in perpetuity.

Rousseau's own best efforts, then, defeat themselves. The nature he describes does not warrant the lyrical declarations he makes about it. As Rousseau extols the virtues of the natural condition, it becomes apparent that the world designed to house and care for human being contains any number of dangers, obstacles, necessities, violences, ap-propriations, and impoverishments that render beatific assessment dubious at best, deceptive at worst. Inter alia, the human animal must often extract sustenance from the world. It can go hungry, even starve, if the season is harsh. Other animals prey on it. Serious injury can result from negotiating its obstacles. Other humans may attack and kill it for what little sustenance it has managed to acquire. Survival is far from guaranteed.[41]

Consider, moreover, the inadvertent ability of the species to per-petuate itself. The tortured romantic longings prevalent in civil so-ciety, contributive to existential circumstances in which a person may find himself "complaining about life and killing himself," are originally absent. Rousseau depicts a "sexual" condition governed by the benevolent dictates of a nature to which humans, uniting for-tuitously, *yield* with pleasure.[42] Afterwards "desire is extinguished." The verbs deployed by Rousseau to characterize the sexual state of nature create a mood of calm. Or do they?

The encounter narrative erected, I would argue, is not so benign. Any woman may be good for any man, and vice versa, but given that coupling is random, fortuitous, "depending on occasion and desire," it must necessarily happen that these elements fail to concur. (Other-wise would not the most remarkable set of regularly occurring coincidences have to be present?) Drive and availability operate according to separate and distinct schedules. Assault and conquest are likely to be the norm. The "peace" of this condition now assumes a different coloration. Rape, if random, reigns.[43] Precisely those qualities of balance, harmony, and correspondence which are supposed to characterize nature are missing. The state of nature is Hobbesian in its own way, after all. Hence this condition is, ultimately, only "less cruel" than the civil state to which it is supposedly superior.

Consequently, despite the rhetorical power of the *Discourse*, there is no paradise lost over which to be nostalgic. There is nothing to return to in the past. There is nothing to recover in the future. The issue of impossibility is beside the point. Conflict, struggle, war are constitutive of the natural condition rather than contingent aspects of it that could be left behind. Nor are they features that develop over time as Rousseau's narrative indicates. They are always already present at its core.[44]

Eternal Returns

Attunement. Ressentiment. The first two movements rivet the text. Sermons abound on the unrelenting presence of evil in European civilization. Intimations of return, indications of revolution find voices. The more these movements insist on the truth of their vision, the greater the attraction. Faith compels. Apparently, each defies analytical defeat or historical comeuppance.

What is the dynamic between and among the movements? To pursue the logic of each of the first two movements to its conclusion is to undermine them from within as impossibilities emerge. Moreover, the first two movements are vulnerable to objections informed by the other. Each can offer something valued that the other lacks. Thus the excess of each renders the other attractive as an antidote. Ironically, they support one another in co-dependency.

Specifically, if the quest for a simpler way of life is pursued back far enough, despite constituting a trenchant attack on current ills, dumb silence is reached. Return cannot keep the promise it must make to sustain itself. As the state of nature is approached, the advantages dreamt of elude capture. Discontent must turn elsewhere.

Likewise, if perfectibility is projected to the limits of imagination, a fabulous city of angels beyond the reach of debased souls is described.

Ressentiment finds fertile ground here. The first option (return) is scorned, the second option (redemption) ridiculed. The first because of the intervention of history itself, the second because history cannot be redirected midstream. The currents are too strong.

Each movement is sustained by Rousseau's subversive genealogy of European institutions. At times evil seems so pervasive that only full retreat can exorcise it. At others the perversion shines so brilliantly that if its creativity could only be harnessed toward more noble ends, the political core of Europe could be permanently altered.

As for the third movement, it can be introduced as the demands placed on the world in the first two are exposed. As the logic of the first two movements ultimately leads nowhere, the third offer its own distinct possibilities and challenges. The expectations generated by the first two movements breed bitter disappointment, a fatal flaw. Refusing the search for moral or institutional finalization, a tragic sensibility provides space for neither resentment nor romanticism. It does not make promises it cannot keep nor foster expectations that cannot be met. It is as good as its word.

If the instability and contingency at its heart are explored, however, the temptations of the first two movements may resurface. Insofar as a tragic understanding insists that no political regime, no moral code, can be definitively secured, neatly instituted, or permanently installed despair and fatigue may follow. The tragic is inherently exhausting. It entails an affirmation of fundamental social and political arrangements as contingent, contestable, crippling. It provides no final resolutions, nor does it claim to do so. In its own way it mimics the disappointment generated by the first two movements.

Thus, if the tragic is marked by recognition that to do is inevitably to forgo, that any achievement must simultaneously trample admirable alternatives and produce its own opposition, frustration is likely to follow. As the arbitrary, fragile aspects of social and political existence are revealed as permanent features of life, the attraction of a simpler way of being in the world where these complexities are absent rises. Similarly, as the resentment that can accompany a life of foregoing mounts and its costs are rejected, the charm of a halcyon future where these complexities are to be transcended surges. A tragic understanding endeavors to block both routes by revealing them as fanciful at best, dangerously self-deceiving at worst. But insistence can be resistant.

Granted, the ethos emblematic of the tragic is difficult to sustain. The tension, even terror, of permanent struggle is difficult to affirm. Escape may eventually prove irresistible. Who, after all, is ready to embrace tragedy? Insofar as redemption cannot be found, the temptations of the first two movements may prove irresistible in a leap of faith. In short, even the introduction of a tragic perspective does not guarantee that romantic and revolutionary impulses can be silenced, no matter how incredible they may seem. Perhaps there is irony to the tragic fate that awaits us: the predicament it names cannot be countenanced and it too fosters denial, thereby exacerbating an already tragic lot.

3

On Founding

> But historical beginnings are lowly: not in the sense of modest or
> discreet like the steps of a dove, but derisive and ironic, capable of
> undoing every infatuation.
> Michel Foucault, "Nietzsche, Genealogy, History"

> The fitting of a hitherto unrestrained and shapeless populace into
> a tight mold, as it had begun with an act of violence, had to be
> brought to conclusion by a series of violent acts. . . . Such was the
> beginning of the human polity; I take it we have got over that
> sentimentalism that would have it begin with a contract.
> Friedrich Nietzsche, *On the Genealogy of Morals*

From Plato's *Republic* to Hobbes's *Leviathan*, from Rousseau's *The
Social Contract* to Rawls's *A Theory of Justice* and beyond, founding lays claim to be the quintessential political activity. It brings order
to chaos, body to apparition, substance to shadow. At its finest founding embodies the truth of God, Reason, Nature, or History. Plato
demonstrates the art of bringing a city, derived from the pre-existent
world of Forms, "into being in speech."[1] Hobbes insists that "the
pacts and Covenants by which the parts of this Body Politique were at
first made, set together, and united, resemble that Fiat, or the Let us
make man, pronounced by God in the Creation."[2] Rawls, extending
the social contract tradition, postulates an original position where
people with a disinterested rationality unanimously ascertain the
basic structure of society and its principles of social justice.[3]

Likewise Rousseau theorizes the origins of political life. With an
abyss threatening to consume the human race, founding challenges
death, even cheats it.[4] Assumed to be an undertaking beyond ordinary
human capability, founding poses the ultimate test of political inge-

nuity. If the opportunity it affords is to be redeemed, rational direction and design must prevail over spontaneity and improvisation. Otherwise the mistakes defining the history of politics, recounted in the second *Discourse*, are bound to recur.[5] A well-founded republic, however, should survive both its creators and the first generations living under it. This is its true measure.

Precisely because the founding moment is decisive, premature celebration can become a problem. For Rousseau birth determines life, natality is destiny: the principles and practices enacted at the founding will mark the republic in perpetuity. Founding must confront the ontological actuality, articulated by Plato, that whatever comes into being decays and dissolves.[6] History confirms this claim for Rousseau: if Sparta and Rome, the two political orders that shine above all others, could not overcome time, no state can. In short, even the best constituted state ultimately perishes. If the art of politics is to prolong the life of the state indefinitely, the task of founding is to give it a head start by providing it with a robust constitution.[7] Yet Rousseau's own account reveals that this event is deeply problematic. His virtuous republic is conceived in violence to which little, if any, attention is devoted. Triumphs there are, but tragedies accompany them. Founding, in short, exacts a steep price for the life and freedom it bestows.

Moreover, the tragedies attending the transition from nature to society do not dissolve as a new republic is debuted. They continue to operate even in a free and just republic forged from a people with a fortunate history. These are the tragedies of political founding, and they will haunt the contemporary life of even a well-instituted, well-run state. Could it be that Rousseau has not fully profited from the mistakes of his theoretical predecessors? That would be comforting, but here lessons unlearned is not so much the problem. The tragedy of giving birth in politics is that the necessary foundations, the core of the republic, simultaneously concoct and subvert it. Thus the new state tends to produce its own unremarked instances of domination and cruelty. And just as the state of nature could not be the condition of peace Rousseau insisted upon, so the moment of founding cannot deliver as promised the political redemption anticipated: a harmonious republic where citizens as a whole exemplify the proper balance between freedom and obedience.[8]

Founding Paradoxes

Despite debunking the pedigree of contemporary European states in the second *Discourse*, Rousseau's theorizations in *The Social Contract* are located outside of historical space and time. The introduction of an heuristic state of nature allows him to sidestep theorizing the thorny transition from an actually existing, imperfect political condition to a just polity.[9] The founding can be as clean as Rousseau believes it must be. He selects a moment in an imaginary past so that events can be relived and the thrilling prospect of original visions thought anew.[10] If *The Social Contract* is the sequel to the second *Discourse*, it is at the ontological level.

For Rousseau the phenomenon of founding encompasses two separate moments, two distinct acts. The first involves the transition from nature to society driven by the dictates of self-preservation. Here the compact itself is formed as a decision is reached to unite, to form a society per se. The second establishes a constitutional framework, a set of fundamental laws, what Rousseau refers to as "the conditions of civil association," which define social and political life. Among other things, it gives birth both to that mortal god, the sovereign, and its more material and fearsome creature, government. Initially Rousseau speaks of these monumental efforts in collective terms. Agency belongs to men[11] acting in unison. Among themselves they agree freely to form a political society in which they hold the reins of power.

Rousseau, then, gives voice to democratic aspirations. Though adamant that people ought to author the laws under which they are to live, he introduces a troubling paradox attending the origins of republics. At the hypothetical beginning of political life, Rousseau contends, the people do not possess the capacities and abilities needed to institute the political arrangements best suited to facilitate the rational interests and promote the profoundest possibilities of human being. The citizen only develops fully, if at all, within the social and political order after long, complicated educational inculcation. Besides, the insight and foresight integral to composing lasting political institutions are not to be expected in such inauspicious circumstances.[12] Rousseau insists that good laws require good citizens and that good citizens require good laws. One cannot be without the other: "the social spirit, which should be the result of the institution, would have to preside over the founding of the institution itself; and men would have to be prior to laws what they ought to become by means of laws."[13] Effect must become cause. But how? What will break the vicious circle of mutually supporting vice?

Amidst chaos and conflict, what can unite the people before they perish at their own hands? Appearing from nowhere, Rousseau's Legislator addresses the multiple paradoxes of foundings.[14] This mystical figure occupies the starring role in a tense theatrical drama where the line between success and disaster is razor thin. The Legislator brings into being the political world while remaining one step removed from it. He thus represents the ideal figure for the political realm. The Legislator has no explicit constitutional authority. That is, he possesses no legal standing to carry out his tasks. How could he? Legal authority does not yet exist. Legislation is an act of generosity first and foremost. It is a gift. Only someone exempt from passions and interests could possibly deliver an authentic system of laws. The Legislator expects nothing in return from those who benefit from his work. Ironically, then, it may be the extralegal character of constitution building that initially furnishes the order with validity and credibility.

Nevertheless, gifts can be suspected, feared. How does the Legislator avoid predictable distrust? The homelessness of the Legislator guarantees that the legislative scheme will be free from the taint of particularity and thereby able to foster allegiance. Rousseau's Legislator cannot be accused of having an interest in the constitutional result he fashions because he will not be a member of the republic. He cannot, therefore, profit from his labors. "This function, which constitutes the republic, does not enter into its constitution."[15] The people, then, can trust in the beauty and wisdom of his design without necessarily being able to understand it. They need not be concerned with hidden agendas. The grounds of suspicion are absent. If the English annihilate their freedom as they exercise it by voting for representatives, the Legislator, through abdication, dissolves chains as he imposes them. Thus what the Legislator does is not to be confused with sovereignty. According to Rousseau, it is the condition of possibility of sovereignty.

The people, of course, could execute founding assignments themselves despite a lack of wisdom culled from the ages. A politics of the common good, however imperfect or incomplete, could emerge battered but intact from collective deliberations and decisions. Initial agreement on some basic matters could provide a provisional platform from which remaining areas of controversy might then be addressed. Through an incremental process characterized by mutual compromise and accommodation, a people could gradually bring to life the permanent or final institutional structure to house it. Such a process would take generations to be concluded.

Rousseau, however, fears precisely a scenario in which the people, in the beginning, forge incomplete solutions which provide a measure of stability and solidity in a world of flux and change. He doubts that a genuine republic could ever be established in this way. Self-interest would threaten the integrity of the assembly, and the seduction of instant gratification would upset a measured approach which attempts to anticipate unintended consequences and oblique, distant evils. While the people desire the good, they lack the ability to perceive it, which means that they are torn between alternatives. They do not know what they really want. Sovereign right always remains with the people, but Rousseau brackets, if temporarily, its exercise. He wants to ensure that the (ab)use of a right now does not undermine the possibility of its future exercise when it can be more properly entrusted to the people and when they can take full advantage of it. The Legislator thus preserves the right in the long run by delaying its use. Democracy denied is democracy saved.

Rousseau wants to replace experimentation, if you will, with direction in politics. The intervention of the Legislator amounts to an admission that danger demands a response other than the uncertainty of politics. Though suspicion of a robust notion of politics prevails throughout the lifetime of Rousseau's republic, suspicion is never greater than at birth—a moment of limitless opportunity, but also of possible apocalyptic misstep.[16]

If Rousseau's concern seems exaggerated, consider the Legislator's principal empirical task. Once the social compact has been instituted, laws are needed to complete the republic. The Legislator relies on what might be called epistemological expertise. He shows a people what to will, even if he cannot provide the will itself. Success depends upon properly combining the general aim of all good institutions ("the maxims common to all") with local exigencies ("each people contains within itself some cause that organizes it in a particular manner").[17] Neither strict adherence to general principles nor blanket submission to specific, local factors suffices on its own. The former might not be stomached because of the sacrifices required ("A thousand nations that have flourished on earth could not have tolerated good laws"),[18] the latter might prove self-defeating or destructive to a republican ethic (frivolous, indulgent practices of amusement and entertainment, for example, undermine the self-discipline constitutive of virtue). Rousseau writes: "it is on the basis of these relationships that each people must be assigned a particular system of institutions that is the best, not perhaps in itself, but for the State for which it is intended."[19] Should the Legislator ignore these combinations and install a system at odds with the actualities confronting him, the state will tremble until it implodes.[20]

To complicate matters, the Legislator's role can exacerbate the paradoxes to which it is a response. He must design institutions that can function instantly without him. Given that the skills and capacities of citizens take time to develop, there will be an indeterminate interval between the departure of the Legislator and the full-blown emergence of the citizen. To borrow Rousseau's metaphor, if the Legislator invents the political machine, then the citizenry is responsible for operating it. Early on it would be handling a machine with which it is unfamiliar. An accident is all too predictable; it could prove fatal. And so Rousseau does mention that early in the life of republics, the resort to dictatorship is likely to be frequent. This may be due to emergent crises, and one such crisis could be the continued resistance of those excluded by the formation of the contract. Granted dictatorship is part of the constitutional scheme the Legislator devises. Provision for emergencies is paramount. But if dictators replace citizens early and often in the life of the republic, when will citizens assume responsibility for the conduct of politics critical to their evolution? Lacking experience, opportunity is denied. Without opportunity, experience cannot be acquired. The constitutional scheme established by the Legislator may contain its own vicious circle.

In Rousseau's hands, the pressures of the founding are concentrated and intensified. The inception of political society comes but once. There are no second chances. According to Rousseau, states do not have the luxury of establishing an imperfect but functional political system which can then be corrected for design flaws as they arise. Things must be done right the first time. If the foundation is fundamentally flawed, subsequent generations may tinker with this or that feature, even succeeding for a time, but they can only prolong the inevitable.[21] Once difficulties manifest themselves, any effort at restoration will fail unless it attends to the original structural inadequacy. Even sound additions placed on a compromised base cannot endure the vicissitudes of political life. Unfortunately, by the time fissures are ordinarily discovered, the possibility of designing effective remedies has already been lost. It is the nature of political engineering, Rousseau argues, that by the time symptoms of weakness manifest themselves, the fate of the polity has already been sealed. Eventually old foundations will have to be demolished and new ones raised, a necessity more easily recognized than executed. In the meantime, resources are diverted from other tasks merely to prevent collapse. This is the destructive cycle in which history has been trapped and which Rousseau intends to break. And so he theorizes a new start: it is "necessary to begin by clearing the area and setting aside the old materials," and then proceed by means of art rather than chance. Perhaps the design flaws fatal to ancestors can be circumvented.

If the founding is to reach, let alone fix, remote futurity, more than its constitutional merits must be cultivated. Rousseau seeks to provide the founding with the ultimate foundation. If the Legislator guarantees the republic, what guarantees the Legislator? "All justice comes from God; He alone is its source. But if we knew how to receive it from on high, we would need neither government nor laws."[22] Lacking recourse to transcendent forms of meaning and authority transparent to recipients, Rousseau apparently endeavors to simulate it. Once more, the identity of the Legislator is critical. This-worldly independence is to be supplemented by other-worldly connection. The chasm between heaven and earth must be bridged if the source of justice is to be tapped.

Everything associated with the Legislator seems to defy human talent and accomplishment. Though he is not required to design a system of laws that is the best reason can conceive, the task facing him is daunting. If anything, tailoring institutions to fit the people whom they are intended to benefit complicates an already complicated task. As Rousseau lists the attributes needed to complete the Legislative assignment, it would seem that no one could possibly possess them. The Legislator is blessed with towering intelligence which can discern both the contours of human nature and the contingencies of human behavior. He understands both the social and political problems they pose and the opportunities they offer. He is willing to attend selflessly to the project of human happiness without mistaking it for his own.[23] Eventually Rousseau remarks that to give men laws Gods would be needed.[24]

Rousseau's use of the conditional expresses both dependence and possibility. On the one hand, an authentic republic cannot emerge without the architectonic talents of Gods. We fool ourselves—to our own detriment—if we believe otherwise. On the other hand, if Gods were available, their achievements might be treated differently than mere human makings. Hence the aspiration that Law become a domain standing over and above humankind moves within reach.

Delicately Rousseau tries to carve out a place for the Legislator in each of two worlds while obscuring his presence in both.[25] Neither human nor divine, the Legislator can thus be read profitably as a textual device mediating the gulf between Heaven and Earth. He exalts the republic prior to and independent of its legitimation through the consent of individual wills: "It is a particular and superior activity that has nothing in common with human dominion."[26] Rousseau's account intimates that the architect of the republic solicits assistance from another realm even if the exact mode of transmission is unclear. The Legislator appears to be a divine (or divinely inspired) instrument or messenger.

Ironically, though, the Legislator ambiguates the republic's legitimacy and threatens its democratic credentials. Derrida's reading of the "Declaration of Independence," which covers similar terrain, can be of help here. Exploring the paradoxes of the American founding, he notes that those who signed the declaration in the name of "we the people" signed in the name of something that did not yet exist. Insofar as "the signature invents the signer," the completed signature is what actually authorizes the signer to sign the declaration, in what Derrida calls "a sort of fabulous retroactivity." The lack of authority to sign leads those who do sign necessarily to appeal "to the Supreme Judge of the world." A founding cannot give birth to itself; hence the need for an external ground to secure the enterprise. Here Derrida poses an unanswerable question: does the document declare an already achieved independence or does it create it in the act of declaration? Derrida argues that there must be "tension" between the constative and performative aspects of the Declaration if it is to "produce the sought-after effect." What is the effect sought? For political institutions to perdure in a climate hostile to the instantiation of authoritative authority.[27] But how does undecidability actually produce the necessary effect? Perhaps because it can draw on complimentary sources of authority such that the whole exceeds the sum of its parts.

How might Derrida's insights illuminate Rousseau's Legislator problem? Despite his denial that claims to rule can be grounded in nature, Rousseau suspects that arrangements founded solely on convention will not prove binding and lasting. Greater guarantees are sought to sanction political norms and forms. Hence the otherworldly intimations about the identity of the Legislator. Where even the rightful authority of the people dissipates in a downpour of doubts and defects, the Legislator can buttress it. Certainty sought is certainty found (or made). Similarly, the authority of the Legislator alone cannot hold the state and its people together. Unless people freely give law to themselves, they will come to experience it as imposition, regardless of its source. They must legitimate, at some point, the foundational work of the Legislator. Hence the assembly. That the legitimacy of the state cannot be reduced to the authority of either the Legislator or the people alone may be the key to its staying power. The sources of legitimacy are twofold and the tension between them is symbiotically productive. Each is necessary but insufficient. Each supplements the other. Neither can be erased.

How does the Legislator ultimately meet the challenge facing him, namely, to execute a task beyond human capacity with a worldly authority impotent on its face? To what magical means can he resort? Rousseau denies him recourse to force or reason. As to the first, violence cannot identify self and order and, consequently, makes for a poor system of rule. It would mimic the worst despotism (despite its laudable intentions) and despoil what it claims to cherish. As to the second, the rational exercise of mind is beyond the reach of prepolitical innocents. The language of virtue or the common good, assuming it even reached its audience, would be converted into its opposite, colonized by the calculus of self-interest. The "maxims of politics" and the "rules of statecraft," each centered on notions of beneficial sacrifice, are foreign to the people. Certain notions cannot be translated to their everyday language. If employed, the Legislator would be speaking in tongues. While not all communication is disabled, conceptual discourse is impossible. At least in the beginning. What expedient is available, then?

The Legislator, of necessity, turns to a divine source of authority. The situation in which he finds himself requires that he do so. "This is what has always forced the fathers of nations to have recourse to the intervention of heaven . . ."[28] Invoking God, of course, is no guarantee of success. A perilous proposition, it can provoke resistance as easily as it can prompt acceptance. When the Legislator speaks he must not be seen to be making a claim which the people are to consider or reject. Rather his performance must be able to compel the people spontaneously to respond. They must take for granted as he speaks that he is in fact what he cannot too overtly claim to be: the voice of God. Proclaiming oneself God's representative courts contumely. Insisting upon it would likely prove to be self-defeating. What kind of divinity proclaims itself to be one?

The Legislator credits his vision to the Gods, but they must be seen to work through him. Hence appeal is made to the people's Gods rather than Gods conveniently invented by the Legislator. How better to make them speak to the people than by adhering to their dictates as the people understand them? Since it is to "an order of authority" that the Legislator turns rather than an overwhelming power to which he resorts, the Legislator invokes what the people already recognize and accept. The recourse may be a ruse, of course, but it need not be.[29] If the resort to heaven is likely to provoke protest, heaven being the first refuge of scoundrels, would not the people reject the Legislator unless his words accord with their sentiments and intuitions? The people cannot be jerked to and fro at will. Unsophisticated they may be, but they are not children.

Rousseau insists that the Legislator's great soul is the ultimate proof of his miraculous mission. But with souls infuriatingly invisible, the only access to it can be through speech or through deed. The vision he puts forward must pack rhetorical punch if it is to "persuade without convincing." Moses doubted that he was the one to bring the word of God to the people, singling out his lack of loquaciousness, but God provided him with the "eloquence" he would need to move the people. Rousseau's Legislator must do for himself what God did for Moses. Lacking timely divine intervention, his arrival and appearance must be stage-managed with care. Timing may not be everything, but it is critical—as is setting the scene. Pomp and circumstance take precedence. The Legislator must be what Rousseau hates most: an accomplished thespian. If successful, the effect induced by the Legislator cannot be underestimated. Citizens do not hesitate to pledge allegiance to the social contract under God and indivisible: ". . . there is a great difference between remaining faithful to a State solely because one has sworn to do so, or because one considers its institution to be divine and indestructible."[30]

Despite the generous gift of the Legislator, citizens ultimately must sanction law for it to be valid. Consequently they enjoy the right to reject it as well. If they are not authors of the law in the first instance, they must be so in the last, if not at the founding, then at a more stable moment later in the life of the republic. Yet here again paradoxes abound. Insofar as the Legislator invokes another realm for the authority of his constitutional design, the substance of the people's sovereign power is diluted, for who is free to accept or reject what God wills?[31] Even if Rousseau's Legislator lacks access to Divine Justice at the fount, the power of proximity is considerable. What effect does this have on Rousseau's democratic order? Rhetorical force, the language of indisputable truth that defies resistance, can be as enthralling as its corporal counterpart. At its best, the Legislator's insinuation of heavenly command into the birth of the republic deifies the city and provides its laws with the power to impel the citizen just as the laws of nature possess the power to govern human being.[32] And even for Rousseau, that is precisely the problem.

Founding Violence

In Rousseau's hands, the social contract story is an inspirational, subversive tale. The well-being of society and the exercise of sovereign power rest exclusively with the people. He insists that the introduction of the social compact, and it alone, requires universal assent. The introduction of society names the moment of absolute self-determination. It would seem that the first generation—and perhaps it alone—can truly control its fate. Rousseau describes the formation of association as "the most voluntary act in the world. Since every man is born free and master of himself, no one, under any pretext whatever, can subject him without his consent."[33] The birth of the state must be free from taint.

Nonetheless, a fear gnaws at Rousseau and it permeates his reflections on founding. Can birth, that most glorious and wondrous phenomenon, escape the stain of illegitimacy when it comes to politics? Recall the principle: "There is only one law that, by its nature, requires unanimous consent. That is the social compact." Rousseau seems determined to avoid even the hint of impropriety. Whether he articulates it or not, his fear of illegitimacy derives in part from a paradox bedeviling foundings: society and the legal authority it fashions cannot be established legally. That would be to presuppose structures and relations that are goals to be attained not actualities that can be drawn on. Foundings are thus at best alegal. Can a republic governed by law survive such a beginning? Can it afford to acknowledge its ambiguous, problematic origins? What are the possible ramifications? For a republic to think of itself as free and legitimate, what kind of understanding of its origins must it have? Admittedly these are difficult questions.

From word one, Rousseau's contract story faces an intractable problem, one it cannot afford to ignore. It would be difficult to conceive of a contract that triggered no opposition to its introduction under even the best of circumstances.[34] The exigencies surrounding the founding, decidedly unpromising, complicate matters.[35] Beneath Rousseau's antiseptic depiction of the moment of transition from nature to society, the survival of human being itself is in doubt. Or so we are told.

Rousseau skirts potential objections to his narrative conceit by debunking the suspicion that all present at the creation could rise as one in unanimous approval. As if recognizing the (deplorable) ineliminability of resistance, Rousseau declares those opposed to the formation of the social contract excluded from it. Otherwise an act of incorporation would be tantamount to enslavement. No one can be compelled to join against one's will. But the price is steep: the contract now begins to lose its unanimous dimension while desperately trying to preserve its appearance. For some, there is no contract at all.[36] Arbitrarily assigning them responsibility for exclusion ("*their* opposition . . . merely prevents them from being included") cannot conceal the violence.[37]

Rousseau's contract myth inadvertently reveals the role violence must play in the founding. As the social compact is formed, the nature of opposition is unclear. If it is the idea of a contract per se, the exclusion seems eminently reasonable because necessary, defensive. The obstinacy of a few should not result in the termination, literally, of all. But such opposition seems unlikely. On Rousseau's account, it would be tantamount to opposing life itself. Who would prefer the state of war and extinction to (any) civil society and survival? Resistance, then, must center on specific features of the compact. Or perhaps there is disagreement that a contract is the basis of society. Or perhaps one cannot know whether to enter society, as it were, until one knows what that entails. Refusal may be based on ignorance of the details of communal life. Some may not be willing to let a majority determine the system of laws that is to govern all. Whatever the source of the opposition, it would seem to be inherently political. Interestingly, Rousseau does not specify the grounds of opposition.[38]

To preserve unanimity, participation in the agreement is ultimately restricted. The pursuit of unanimity is a luxury the would-be state cannot long afford. Quite simply, negotiation must be halted at some point if an agreement is to be reached. Speed is of the essence here. A decision must be made while it is still possible to make one. The moment of freedom is fleeting, but it cannot be otherwise. That some are excluded, namely, those who cannot silence their reservations and cling to old ways, does not belie Rousseau's inclusive impulse to make the arrangement as encompassing as possible. Since there are no established, settled procedures for resolving disputes, the closure decision is of necessity arbitrary, if not capricious, and can only be enforced through superior strength.[39] After all, there is no predisposition among contending parties to respect decisions reached because they were arrived at in proper procedural fashion. Thus those in opposition are unlikely merely to accede to a disagreeable agreement and abide by the exclusion. Too much is at stake: disasters to be avoided, dreams to be secured. Nonetheless: "opposition does not invalidate the contract."[40]

Rousseau seems to respect those who object to the contract. They are not forced into the agreement. They can just say no. The right of refusal (to join) dissolves the moment it is exercised, however, for the social compact which turns men into citizens converts resisters into foreigners among the newly formed citizens. To make them citizens would be to invite the resumption of their opposition. Sovereignty quickly discloses its absolute, territorial imperative: "once the state is instituted, consent is implied by residence."[41] The compact gives birth to more than citizens, then. The foreigner is an outsider within the order, subject to its dictates but stripped of any voice in the styling

of laws. In a Lockean moment Rousseau writes: "To inhabit the territory [is] to submit oneself to sovereignty."[42] The violence Rousseau
initially managed to sidestep can no longer be contained. But submission, for him, is unproblematic because legal. Once consent is implied, however, the status of the foreigner does not change accordingly. Residence may signify consent, but consent does not trigger
membership. Foreigners then disappear from Rousseau's account.

To enable and preserve the founding achievement, perhaps those
opposed might be expelled. An act of brute violence now could obviate the need for a repetition of such acts as the state consolidates the
triumph of the contract: an economy of violence, as Machiavelli proposes.[43] Why does Rousseau not take this route? Given the stakes of
the conflict, those defeated must harbor resentment toward the vic-
tors. One way of life has trumped another, a result not easily overlooked or forgotten by the losers. It seems safe to assume that opposition will continue, perhaps covertly. While such a force might prove
corrosive to the republic, Rousseau seems unconcerned. In fact,
though he does not acknowledge it here, opposition strengthens the
order. It is a good thing. If it did not exist, it would have to be invented.
It energizes the order—if isolated, unorganized, contained.[44] Hence
the formulation "they are foreigners among the citizens" neatly captures their status and position.[45] Unity is to be celebrated, while those
largely responsible for it are shunted aside.

The moment of inclusivity offers an opportunity, if limited, to one
and all. The summary exclusion dealt to those in opposition, however, cannot avoid the stigma of violence no matter how tacit the
consent or how "free the state."[46] A majority forges and then denies
the minority at the dawn of order and solidifies itself at its expense.
An alien presence has been established co-extensive with the inaug-
uration of order. There seems to be no mechanism for full inclusion
later.[47] Even capitulation to the contract at some future point might
be disallowed by the state insofar as its sincerity would be suspect.
The presumption (or extension) of trust has already been withdrawn.
Perhaps all of this is no accident. The decision to refuse the compact
amounts to political paradise rejected. Rousseau's text looks past this
exclusion. The state can be unified, and the unity derives from division, that is, exclusion.

Rousseau tries to defuse the tension by granting the right of abdication to any individual at any time. He even makes exceptions for a

series of contingencies that might bind in place the individual determined to leave: family pressure, lack of economic resources, no place to go, coercion. "[T]hen . . . sojourn alone no longer presupposes his consent to the contract or to the violation of the contract."[48]

If flight is designed to shirk responsibilities, however, judgment shifts. Should someone flee from the order while it is under siege, he runs headlong into desertion not freedom. The state is generous but not foolish. Considering the deeply constituted nature of citizens theorized by Rousseau, however, the formal right to relocate may not be so magnanimous after all. If Socrates would rather face execution than death by exile, Rousseau's citizen would probably rather succumb to the dominant will than lose the only world to which he is suited.

Moreover, perhaps the greatest test of an order's commitment to its professed values occurs precisely at a moment of crisis. To practice magnanimity when the potential consequences are minimal or nonexistent hardly proves commitment. An order might say: yes, flight is permitted even during a state of war. We are confident that none will choose to depart.[49] Should any choose to leave, rather than sanctioning them, we wish them well. Rather than spark anger, the decision could become a rallying point for those who remained. What might appear damaging could be converted into an opportunity for binding the order. The possibility seems to find no voice in Rousseau.

Founding sets precedents. The problem of violence engulfs succeeding generations, too. Despite the contingency of the contract, it is not easily voided. Though unanimous consent was required to bring it into being, similar agreement is not required to sustain it. According to Rousseau, while the terms of the contract require that all citizens be present at an assembly calculated to void it, "common agreement" is sufficient to determine its fate. The principle of majority rule may seem reasonable here, but can the legitimacy of the state survive it? In effect, the founding moment has been artificially recreated. Should not unanimity again prevail? Over time the republic consists of more than the founding generation. Rousseau insists that one generation cannot impose its will on the next. But do succeeding generations have meaningful recourse if they find themselves in opposition to basic arrangements? Principle demands that the constitutional structure as a whole be sustained even if a sizeable minority deems it undesirable. How can the republic possess legitimacy if not everyone has sanctioned it? Why, morally, should the criterion of unanimity apply only at the "original" founding of the compact? Why should not every generation be required to endorse it? Failure to endorse would then result in its expiration. Why is not the opposition of one citizen sufficient to terminate the contract?

And what of ordinary lawmaking? After the compact has been introduced, the principle of unanimity is shelved. Majority rule obligates citizens. Rousseau claims this arrangement "is a consequence of the contract itself."[50] Logic and expediency demand that majorities govern. Otherwise the state would suffer political paralysis. But this merely conceals the violence that majorities routinely practice via the imposition of their political will. Even if citizens agree to this arrangement—or are resigned to it—this means they have admitted and agreed to the necessity of submission. Majority rule, though, does not lessen the violence legally carried out in its name.

Why cannot Rousseau confront the necessarily violent, problematic character of the founding? Why the elaborate conspiracy of silence? Of what is he afraid? Contra Rousseau, Nietzsche argues in the *Genealogy of Morals* that political origins are necessarily horrific, that the beginnings of even the greatest of accomplishments involve the expenditure of considerable amounts of blood. His claim does not correspond to more popular accounts that tend toward the celebratory. For Nietzsche, of course, nothing is objectionable simply because its origins are problematic. The nature or value of something is not to be equated with its inception.

If founding itself generates resistance and opposition, and if the act of creation is and must be preceded or accompanied by an act of destruction, why does Rousseau persist in denial?[51] What is it about even creative violence that cannot be countenanced? In Rousseau's moral economy, estimation of the republic is complicated. The very fiber of the state, the values it embodies and performs, cannot be separated from the manner in which its foundations were laid. This is its first test. The means employed can compromise the end product. Crimes cannot be the prelude to the just republic. How could social and political life then succeed on its own terms? Crimes committed at birth become coextensive with the life of the republic. It would be a temporal conceit to confine a crime to the moment of its commission, as if afterwards it were merely a part of history. Effects linger. Indefinitely. And if those crimes are unreported and unacknowledged, has not a second set of crimes been committed? A cover-up? Obstruction of justice? Are these crimes not embedded in the institutional life of the republic?

Founding Poetics

The figure of the Legislator receives illuminating treatment in the *Government of Poland*. As if determined to ground his reflections historically, Rousseau salutes three luminaries of antiquity who embody the perfection to which founding always aspires: Moses, Lycurgus, Numa. Their accomplishments stun. They designed lasting institutions and thereby acquired corresponding greatness. To succeed each employed means which modern theoreticians would, Rousseau presumes, consider laughable, frivolous even.[52] But such an assessment would be sheer folly. The disciplinary devices and mechanisms of the ancients can be appropriated and brought to bear in the modern era—Poland is but one example. Ostensibly Rousseau's intent is pedagogic. Nevertheless, the narrative construction of Legislators and of Foundings, noticeably selective in its emphases and celebratory in its conclusions, needs to be unpacked, for there is a politics to Rousseau's storytelling. First, the story.

According to Rousseau, the work of Moses can be distinguished from his legislative brethren on at least one count. Moses confronted circumstances unlike anything his counterparts faced. He did not have the luxury of attending to the niceties of preconditions. Moses forged a "great nation," a "free people," from an aimlessly wandering horde of strangers, veritable nomads, who had not "a single inch of ground to call their own."[53] While Moses was blessed with possession of the Word, it did not neatly translate into successful results. Bringing together must not be mistaken for genuinely binding-as-one (especially for creatures whose habit it is to roam). Moses provided "a swarm of wretched fugitives" with an institutional stability which has withstood a history of persecution, occupation, and dispersion. His achievement borders on a second act of creation. Given the unpromising matter available to Moses, he had to resort to extraordinary means. On Rousseau's account, Moses redeemed what was otherwise the refuse of history. These beings were closer to animals than people, traveling about in a pack. They apparently lacked any qualities that might suggest suitability for transcendent designation. Rousseau, in fact, defines them by what they lacked: arts, arms, talents, virtues, courage.[54]

Now, if the authority of Scripture is acknowledged, Moses was not simply a political legislator who fashioned order out of chaos from earthly resources, but a divine messenger bringing the Word of God to the children of Israel: "And God said unto Moses, I AM THAT I AM: and he said, Thus shalt thou say unto the children of Israel, I AM hath sent me unto you."[55] Rousseau's Moses, however, appears secular. His relationship to God passes without comment.

Machiavelli fastened onto Moses' unique identity and respectfully dropped him from a consideration of notable Founders: "And although one should not discuss Moses, because he was merely an executor of what had been ordained by God, yet he should be admired even if only for that favour which made him worthy to speak with God."[56] Moses finds himself one link, however privileged, in a chain of command. Moses did not design the system the erection of which was ultimately his responsibility. The people receive from Moses the commands of God they are obligated to follow. There is no opportunity for creative genius but "only" for skillful implementation.

How does Rousseau explain Moses's remarkable accomplishment? The children of Israel were designed to live according to the laws Moses delivered on God's instructions. Moses completed and perfected what was waiting to be finished in the form he delivered. That is why the passage of time can neither "destroy" or "even . . . alter" his work. More specifically, Moses "gave them customs and usages incompatible with those of other nations."[57] Thus difference gives birth to identity. The citizens of this nation are to be "forever strangers among other men."[58] As Rousseau observed in the eighteenth century, the people Moses forged and provided with a lasting identity continue to flourish, "although the national body has ceased to exist." Five thousand years later, they are free still because they are unique, individuated, chauvinistic.[59] Moses negotiated the politics of identity and difference with consummate skill. His people endure not just despite a history of hatred and persecution, but because of it. Moses understood enmity.

Rousseau's presentation of Lycurgus differs slightly. Recall the reference to him in the second *Discourse*. Rousseau pinpoints the mistakes of the many wise legislators who brought government into being. Unfortunately, they proceeded by chance rather than art and found themselves endlessly mending and repairing institutions flawed at inception. Rousseau congratulates Lycurgus for having the temerity to tear down the old before raising the new. No futile expenditure here. Unlike the virtual creation from nothing of Moses, Lycurgus confronted an already established people. According to Rousseau, he transformed a people degraded by the vices of slavery, a feat deemed impossible in *The Social Contract*.[60] Requiring greater creative destruction than Moses and operating without direct divine assistance (he had neither word nor tablet), Lycurgus's deeds elevate him one notch above the founder of the Jewish people.

In addition to the kind of public rites and ceremonies Moses employed, Lycurgus broke down any distinction between the public world shared in common and life in the home unique to the family. Sparta was to be seamless. Repetition anchored Lycurgus's intervention. Citizens cannot be made overnight; it would be self-defeating to try. Patience is required. Thus he "kept the fatherland constantly before their eyes" (even in their loves) and "never left them an instant for solitary relaxation."[61] The demands placed on the Spartans were duly compensated. Initially Lycurgus built a city, but eventually Sparta "gave laws to the whole of Greece, became its capitol, and made the Persian Empire tremble." In short, he raised the citizens of Sparta to a divine plane, or so Rousseau suggests: "And out of this perpetual constraint, ennobled by its purpose, was born that ardent love of country which was always the strongest, or rather the sole, passion of the Spartans, and which turned them into beings above the level of humanity."[62]

The separate accounts of the Founder offered by Machiavelli and Rousseau are linked through the theme of will to power, the will not just to imagine the world differently but to organize it accordingly. For Machiavelli the world confronts the Founder as that which must be challenged, overcome, mastered—at least to the extent fortune allows. Founding provides a test of virtu. Ideally, therefore, it is coupled with adverse circumstances, the more trying and taxing the better. Therein lies the road to glory. Difficulty adds to the stature of the achievement: "If their deeds and careers are examined, it will be seen that they owed nothing to luck except the opportunity to shape the material into the form that seemed best to them."[63] Resistance is thus not a sign of possible design flaw, but a creative spur to the full introduction of the Founder's vision. Glory can be secured quickly by Machiavelli's political actor.

Rousseau's accounts similarly fascinate: they betray aspects of founding that blemish its countenance. The very greatness of the deeds means they cannot be recounted in terms that do not simultaneously belie the lyricism of the Founding. What makes it a political tale worth telling are the odds overcome, obstacles surmounted, forces deployed, enemies defeated, lives risked and lost. What Rousseau wants ideally to be simple and clean must be complex and filthy.

While Rousseau acknowledges that Moses' gift "overburdened" and "inconvenienced" its recipients, the violence that must have been deployed to form this national identity finds no explicit place in his account and is concealed through the narrative deployed. Thus the presence of violence in Rousseau's account looms large by its virtual narrative absence. Rousseau's language portrays legislation as a gift unrivaled in its generosity, which is remarkable not only for what it overlooks in the Old Testament, but surprising for an admirer of the author of *The Prince* and *The Discourses*.[64]

Machiavelli, on the other hand, argues that the astute reader of the Bible will recognize that Moses was compelled to "kill a very great number of men" in his effort to make God's Word into Law.[65] Capital crimes include striking a parent, bestiality, working on the sabbath, worshipping other gods. The range extends from the relatively trivial to the titanic.[66] Perhaps the enormity of the benefits promised encourages blindness to the brutality of the measures enacted to secure them. Those who oppose or transgress that which is sacred are justly put to death. So God has ordained. The severity can be explained, perhaps, by the nomadic circumstances Moses had to negotiate. Lacking institutional stability and solidity, severity was an expedient. This aspect of Moses' mission does not trouble Machiavelli overmuch. Elsewhere he pardons Romulus for questionable acts given his actual accomplishments. In a passage enabling some Machiavelli readers to transform his name from proper noun to derogatory adjective, he writes: "For it is the man who uses violence to spoil things, not the man who uses it to mend them, that is blameworthy."[67]

Before concluding that Rousseau lacks the noted candor of Machiavelli, Rousseau's understanding of history needs to be considered. It offers clues to the purport driving his narrative intervention.

In *Emile*, Rousseau attacks historians. Initially he excoriates them—much as he lambasted playwrights in *Letter to d'Alembert*, who celebrate vice at the expense of virtue—for having a prurient interest in their subject matter. Disasters and calamities—revolution,

war, assassination—fascinate these intellectual voyeurs: "We know
. . . only the bad; the good is hardly epoch-making. It is only the
wicked who are famous; the good are forgotten or made ridiculous.
And this is how history, like philosophy, ceaselessly calumniates humankind."[68] Rousseau's displeasure does not stop here. Next historians are criticized for distortion, for re-presenting history without
acknowledging it.[69] They specialize not in truth, but the art of lying.
As if unaware of the paradoxical character of the formulation, Rousseau insists that historians fail to provide an "exact portrayal" of
events. He claims that the perspective of the historian is decisive.
Which means that there are as many histories as there are perspectives and that history is more like novel writing.[70] For Rousseau there
is and can be but one true history.

Rousseau's critique loses force if the assumption on which it is
based proves to be untenable. The very notion of history in and of
itself, prior to and independent of narrative representation, is conceptually problematic. On Rousseau's own understanding, the historian
cannot place himself fully in context. He cannot be everywhere and
see everything. There is no Archimedean vantage point available. Full
knowledge of any event is beyond reach. If, then, everything is partial,
is it not necessary to choose among the competing "lies" Rousseau
laments? Rousseau criticizes historians for changing "the facts." But
the criticism presupposes the possibility of something that he fails to
establish, namely, history as it really was. Rousseau's charge of count-
erfeiting misses the mark insofar as there is no one original to be
privileged. He writes indignantly of the many faces that can be given
to history (governed by the frame selected), but he never offers an
alternative to this supposedly unhappy state of affairs. What else
could there be but a multiplicity of perspectives given the paradoxes
of the historical enterprise itself?

In short, how could an historian do otherwise than provide a per-
spectival account? History is mediation. The specifics of Rousseau's
criticism of history writing reveal the impossibility of providing anything other than a partial, interested account. It follows that "conjecture" is the best that can be produced. And Rousseau finds himself
trapped in the cage he inadvertently discloses.

"History in general is defective," Rousseau concludes. Regardless
of the relative merits of Rousseau's assessment, one must wonder
about the purpose of his disquisition since what he calls the "truth of

morals" ultimately is to prevail over the dictates of history. The past makes no difference to the present except insofar as it proves useful. Notions of fidelity and faithfulness are to be abandoned in the historical enterprise. Utility trumps truth. And thus Rousseau's Moses and Machiavelli's Moses diverge.

Founding Fictions

The Legislator troubles Rousseau's readers.[71] How can a figure who emerges from nowhere dealing in irresistible truth deliver democratic institutions from on high without traducing the people's sovereignty? The Legislator personifies values at odds with a democratic ethos. Even if he offers selfless service in the best interests of his intended beneficiaries, he privileges imperial pronouncement, clever manipulation, and sudden imposition at the expense of collective deliberation and consensual self-determination. The people seem to be anything but self-legislating. Rather than author the laws to which they submit, people submit to unauthorized laws. Have the principles grounding and animating Rousseau's republic been sacrificed at the altar of expediency? or necessity?

Not surprisingly, Rousseau's Legislator, introduced as a deus ex machina to solve founding riddles, engenders further enigmas. Recall Rousseau's description of the legislative vocation. Forced to silence doubt and overcome opposition, it exceeds human capacities both psychological and intellectual. To constitute a republic "is a particular and superior activity that has nothing in common with human dominion."[72] Given the veritable impossibilities of the legislative enterprise, Rousseau insists Gods would be needed to found a system of laws. Yet Gods are notoriously unavailable, dwelling in the distant heavens. Hence the transcendental assistance of the Legislator, a substitute second to (n)one. While it might seem that the Legislator emerges from the ether, his origins can be deciphered. If Gods are needed to give men laws, in Rousseau's political universe myths are needed to give men Gods.[73] And since men give themselves myths, ultimately men give to themselves both Gods and laws. But the giving process is complicated. To delineate it is to suspect that the Legislator as presented by Rousseau is a fiction, a conceit, a product of the collective cultural imagination. There is no actual Legislator in the beginning, some godlike being who pronounces: "Let there be law." There cannot be. Not on the terms Rousseau provides, that is. Similarly there are no Foundings at the founding of states. It, too, is a fiction and emerges only in retrospective moments in the lives of states. It provides, after the fact, the beginning that would have been needed to ground the present. It ontologizes the order.[74]

At the beginning of his account of Legislators in *Poland*, Rousseau remarks that he feels enraptured when reading about the political giants of yesteryear. The affect is so powerful that he feels transported to another world. Some may suspect that historians have played a trick on them. Surely they have either invented or exaggerated the histories they report. Rousseau himself finds it hard to believe that these titans ever lived.[75] The wizardry of the disciplinary mechanisms the ancient Legislators employed astounds. They were masters of identification, craftsmen of order. Rousseau's amazement stems, first, from the immensity of the deeds themselves but also from a comparative judgment betraying a certain envy: "How can we, who feel that we are so small, believe that there were ever men of such greatness? Such men did exist, however, and they were human beings like ourselves."[76] Rousseau's comments could be cause for suspicion since the question of their heroic standing really cannot be an historical one for him.

Consider Rousseau's Legislator. In *The Social Contract*, he is the protagonist of history. By constituting a republic, he secures a glory that will accrue to him well after his death. Unlike mere mortals, he is able to "work in one century and enjoy the reward in another." Why must the reward wait? Only through time can his genius, if any, be assessed, let alone appreciated, because it can only be known with the passage of time whether a political community has lasted and thus whether a founding indeed took place. The Legislator as such, then, can emerge only long after the actions that define him were allegedly performed. If so, the godlike identity of the Legislator does not enable his founding deeds. Events at the time of the founding lend themselves to the subsequent formation of such an identity. Given the role the Legislator is to play in Rousseau's republic, however, the construction of his identity demands that so-called founding actions be interpreted in divine fashion. As a result, the Legislator emerges over time in the telling of tales about him, and then he is projected back in time, as it were. Speaking of Moses, Lycurgus, and Numa, Rousseau writes: "All three achieved successes which would be thought impossible if they were not so well attested."[77]

The ambiguity of this passage serves Rousseau well. It softens his earlier insistence that such men did exist and reveals the queer status of Foundings. It could be read in one of two ways: the deeds would have been thought impossible had they not actually occurred—which cannot be definitively established in any case; the deeds are needed in retrospect but never occurred. On the second reading, well attested, given Rousseau's theorization of history, may well mean testified to repeatedly. What may or may not have actually happened is lost in the mists of time.[78] Verification, after all, is unavailable. If the successes of Founders naturally provoke political skepticism, to what can the suspension of disbelief be attributed? To the power of redundancy? Though Rousseau writes as if the epic actions of the Founding govern the shape of the subsequent memory, do not accounts of the origins of society, told and retold, facilitate the contingent, piecemeal construction of the myth itself? The myth can then be serviced by succeeding generations according to the requirements of their times. This would provide an alternative explanation for Rousseau's disparaging remark: "I look at the nations of modern times. I see in them many lawmakers, but not one legislator."[79] Of course Rousseau sees only lawmakers. Since the Legislator cannot exist except in retrospect, he can see nothing else. Though the lawmakers Rousseau does see could become Legislators one day. So he may well be looking at what he cannot now see. There is no way to know.[80]

If Rousseau's Legislator is indeed a Founding fiction, might it nevertheless be a necessary invention? Perhaps all states are in need of myths about their origins? If so, we should examine how exactly Rousseau's splendid artifice functions, and what its implications might be for a democratic republic.

The myth of Rousseau's Legislator operates at two levels. One names what he accomplished, the other marvels at the virtuoso fashion in which he accomplished it. First, the accomplishment. The Legislator miraculously snatched life from death's clutches. People were poised at the edge of the abyss about to plunge and perish from their deranged pursuit of self-interest and survival. If not for the Legislator, nothingness would reign. Having brought a halt to perpetual war, he proceeded to build a political community with lasting foundations. The Legislator delivered just and free institutions, ordained by the Gods, where citizens could enjoy the advantages of nature without suffering its detriments. This was no mere Hobbesian accommodation with evil. He gave life and then gave it meaning. Second, the style. The Legislator perpetrated these wonders in wondrous fashion. He possessed no authority. Denied the lethal weapons of war and the linguistic weapons of statecraft, the Legislator had to do the impossible with nothing. Somehow he persuaded the people of the wisdom of his offering without convincing them of it. Though he appealed to the Gods, others before him had done likewise. They failed. He did not. Thus, no one really knows how he prevailed, but the founding itself is evidence of his success. If anything, that his success defies explanation testifies to his greatness. He must be of divine inspiration. Certainly his political gift was the blessing for which people were looking.

Rousseau recommends to republics that the Founding and other key moments in their histories regularly be celebrated. Spectacles are to be staged which remind a people about its roots. As the ebb and flow of history is recounted at these august occasions, as history is recreated on stage, the citizen can imaginatively engage the world of his ancestors. By putting himself in their place he can experience with them, as it were, their trials and tribulations. As he cheers their success, as he mourns their losses, he identifies with them and—for Rousseau—becomes them. Citizens present and patriots past merge into one. Through well-choreographed productions, then, citizens are to be implicated in the republic they have inherited. They will come to regard as precious what their ancestors created for and bequeathed to them. They will learn to care about and for it. And for those who left it to them. As citizens invest in their past, they invest in themselves too. As they honor the gift of their ancestors, it honors them. They must be worthy to have received it, to have been worth the sacrifice of flesh and bone it required.

At such public celebrations, a frank accounting of the republic's origins would be misplaced. Ordinarily, tampering with myths is not appreciated. To speak of the excluded, the vanquished, the losers would spoil the festive mood. Besides, with the passage of time, nothing but the accomplishment remains.[81] Controversies slip from the collective memory and fade from view as do minority voices and those who lost out. Nothing keeps them alive.

For Rousseau's republic, one master Founding narrative is requisite.

While there may be variations from this festival to that spectacle, from this teacher to that parent, these variations derive from the univocal original. The story of the Legislator is unambiguously good. A singular rendition handed down from generation to generation contributes to the unity of the state.

Here Bonnie Honig's encounter with Arendt and Derrida on foundings is pertinent to the question of necessary fictions. Derrida suggests that no founding on its own possesses what it needs to succeed. The paradox, thanks to Sieyès, can be stated succinctly: those who combine to form a new constitutional order have no authority, no legal standing, to do so. To break this vicious circle, Gods, whether theistic or secular, are needed. Founding thus turns to a source external to itself for the guarantees it requires to work. According to Derrida, this is a structural or systemic feature of founding. The aperture plaguing every act of founding is always filled by some constative. It cannot be left open because the founding enterprise that generates it also demands that it be filled.

Rousseau, remarkably, does not seem to understand quite how serious is his legitimacy problem. He assumes and insists that the people who are forming an association have the right to do so.[82] The Legislator is introduced to address the political—as opposed to legal—deficiencies of the people. They are simply incapable of designing a system of laws. That they have every right to design it Rousseau does not explicitly question. It is in the same context (of capacity) that he talks about Gods being necessary to give men laws. Ironically, it is because he introduces the Legislator to solve the expertise problem of the people that he turns to Gods. The Legislator lacks authority, not the people.

Following Honig's and Derrida's lead, Rousseau's Legislator is a stand-in for God, and he plays the constative role in *The Social Contract* whether Rousseau recognizes it or not. The Legislator thus helps conceal the necessary violence, rhetorical and otherwise, at the formation of the compact.

Yet must not Rousseau's Legislator fail in its constative task? Must not all constatives fail? How, in other words, can Sieyès's vicious circle be broken if the guarantees assigned the demolition work beg the question, if they actually trigger an infinite regress? In short, what legitimates the legitimators? To borrow from Derrida, possible circle breakers are performatives masquerading as constatives. That is, founding anchors are contrivances, fictions, what Derrida considers fables. There may be a pretense that the founding, by turning to an external source, has resolved the dilemma it engenders, but it is still a fabulation, however imperative it may be, is it not?

As Honig points out, deconstructing or exposing the founding dynamic does not end the constative quest. The dynamic is self-sustaining. Honig treats "Derrida's insight that *all* acts of founding are necessarily secured by a constative" as an opportunity for political intervention. Here the constative moment of founding is not denied, but neither is its claim to irresistibility conceded. This is the space of and for resistance, for politics.[83]

But what might it mean to deny the constative moment of founding? If the status to which Founding traditionally aspires is divulged to be an impossibility, a nihilistic projection, is that not a form of denial? What happens to Founding once its pretense has been punctured? Can it survive the deflation? Can fictions, however necessary, sustain themselves once rendered transparent? If fictions govern the order, are not those appealing to constatives particularly mischievous, especially dangerous? Is not this precisely what a democratic ethos can and should work to deny? Pure performatives can also be despotic, but better a nontheistic than a religious conflict.

Founding Politics

On matters Founding, civic festivals work hand-in-hand with political institutions. Despite mantras about the perpetual possibility of democratic recreation, the official conduct of politics centers around the Founding. According to Rousseau, the sole purpose of the annual assembly is to reaffirm the social treaty.[84] It is not to legislate. It is not to engage critically the conventions that govern collective life. Maintenance rather than innovation defines the political sphere. Action here is symbolic: reaffirm the arrangements established in the beginning by the Legislator.

Rousseau's annual assembly, then, is notable for what it omits rather than what it includes. The sovereign does not reenact the forming of the compact in order to enliven the principles it embodies or to include those who might have been excluded previously. The people do not come together to decide again, as it were, if they want to promise themselves to one another. They decide secondary questions relating to government.[85] Should the current form of government be retained? Should the current administration be renewed? These questions always open the assembly. There is to be no prospect of dissolving the union in the background to this august occasion. And no wonder. If the people had no role in enacting the system of laws under which they live, how can there be a reenactment? The discrepancy might call attention to the fiction that governs the polity. The power of the people in the beginning is in name alone. The sovereign people is a myth inside a ritual wrapped around a fabulation.

Ordinarily, then, the discourse of Founding in contemporary politics is perforce designed to obviate disruption and struggle. A Founding story provides an outlet for contemporary frustrations and recurrent dreams. It alleviates the first and stimulates the second. Founding allows a trade of innocence for cynicism, hope for despair, birth for death. It offers a fount of lasting wisdom which can be creatively brought to bear on the contemporary world while its more disturbing elements are buried and forgotten. Founding as trump card. It stands for the belief that things were done right in the beginning. If matters have gone awry, deviation from the original is the reason. The founding legacy has been forgotten. It must be recaptured and restored.

Nevertheless, Founding rites, rituals, and recapitulations are deeply problematic. Designed to celebrate and unite, they can also foment discord and disunity. Efforts to honor and respect the founding accomplishment will be received by some citizens as an act of acknowledgment and recognition for what it achieved, but experienced by others as an act of obliteration and refusal for the costs it tolled. What is glorious to some is merely gory to others. Success, then, breeds demise. The more effectively Foundings unite, the more likely they are simultaneously to divide.

If the Founding rituals generate opposition and resistance, the Founding itself can become a site of politics unanticipated by Rousseau, a politics of interpretation. Stories can always be retold. Traditional understandings contested. Alternative meanings pondered. New details added. Old shibboleths deleted. Controversial aspects uncovered. Buried truths discovered. Intentions altered. Other possibilities projected. Founding involves dangers not seen by Rousseau.

Likewise, privileging the assemblies as ceremonial and celebratory may foster antagonism in later generations as well. It might appear to citizens as if basic institutions were designed to preempt or coopt political opposition. Institutions that might provide an outlet, an opportunity, for debate and dissent have been reserved for other purposes. If citizens are deprived of a place to turn for a serious redress of grievances, the reflective allegiance the state relies upon may be jeopardized. Citizens who are denied the respect to which they deem themselves entitled may withdraw it. For a virtue politics, such withdrawal is tantamount to death.

Founding Futures

What if we concede, again, that republics need their own unique Founding myths? Earlier I presented Rousseau's myth as he might have done so himself. How might it appear from a tragic perspective? As articulated by Rousseau, the Founding stands in opposition to the centrifugal thrust of the modern age. Rather than establish a framework able to anticipate, facilitate, or respond to change, the Forms sanctified by the Legislator erect a bulwark against it. Subsequent efforts focus on preserving the originary deed as truth overshadows sovereign will. As the Founder's Legislative truth congeals over time, the oldest laws become the best laws—not so much because the republic implicitly affirms them by not repealing them when it is free to do so—but because they embody the timeless truths of the great Legislator, bearer of the Word. What of democracy's fate? While the people retains the right to change any laws, even the best laws, this right is at odds with the unwritten injunction that calls for obeisance to divine will.

Myths thus remind. They also portend. What kind of future awaits the republic? While the Founding is supposed to prepare it to meet a variety of challenges, has the republic actually been provided with the resources it needs for its solo venture? What happens, for example, when it faces, as inevitably it will, an emergency or a crisis? Must the people await the second coming of a Legislator, because only a divine figure can be trusted to handle constitutional contretemps? Here the past does not inspire. It renders passive citizens who are now on their own.

The Founding ambition may itself encourage expectations that it should not and cannot meet. As I mentioned above, Rousseau warns that it is dangerous for citizens to think that they can once sanction a body of fundamental laws and then retreat or retire from political life confident that right has replaced violence and nature has been subjected to rule. Yet Foundings intimate that such illicit aspiration's can not just be entertained but enjoyed. Founding successes make politics unnecessary because the truth has won out.

Precisely what distinguishes the Founding, then, may ensure the eventual demise of the polity. Absent a more robust practice of politics ready to negotiate between past and future, the price of birth may turn out to be a premature death. While Founding is supposed to provide a system able to endure storm and stress, it may become a scaffold that strangles political innovation and dissipates democratic freedom.

Regardless, in the wake of the founding achievement, if its successes are to survive the birth process, an extensive network of social and cultural practices and arrangements must correspond to it. Otherwise the gift of life provided by the founding will be squandered. It is with this in mind that I turn to the art of government.

4

On Government

Sovereignty is far from being eliminated by the emergence of a
new art of government . . . on the contrary, the problem of
sovereignty is made more acute than ever.
Michel Foucault, "Governmentality"

This treatise deals with the grand *politics* of virtue. It is intended
for the use of those whose interest must lie in learning, not how
one *becomes* virtuous, but how one *makes* virtuous—how virtue
is made to dominate. I even intend to prove that to desire the
one—the domination of virtue—one absolutely must *not* desire
the other.
Friedrich Nietzsche, *The Will to Power*

Rousseau democratizes sovereignty. Unless and until a people leg-
islates for itself it cannot be free, despite what the Hobbesians of
the world claim. *The Social Contract*'s rhetorical commitment to
freedom is undeniable and impressive. Rousseau, again to counter
ancient prejudices, reiterates his democratic principles seemingly at
every opportunity. The conception of sovereignty he offers is thrilling
because exacting. Few bodies politic, if any, could meet its standards,
thus confirming their fitness.

Nevertheless, with Foucault's assistance, I plan to reexamine Rousseau's theorization of a democratic sovereignty suspicious that Rousseau may turn out to be a dangerous ally. Government cannot be the
minion of sovereignty in a Rousseauian universe. The art of government renders obsolete the master-servant relation Rousseau hopes to
fashion between them. While the centerpiece of Rousseauian theory
might seem to be the preservation of sovereignty from the machinations of government, an ethic of governmentality has already ex-

ecuted a coup d'état. Thus Rousseau's texts dethrone sovereignty even as they announce its reign. Curiously Rousseau insists on the indispensability of sovereignty precisely to the extent that it has already been lost. In short, sovereignty emerges as an effect of government.[1] The remarkable hopes and dreams the initial contract situation projects fade beneath the nitty-gritty of forging a viable political order. *The Social Contract* is a tough text. And, given Rousseau's material focus, it would be imprudent to approach him principally as a theorist of moral injunction. Sovereignty does not float in the clouds. It is structured into the tactics of governmentality.

Here the *Letter to d'Alembert, Political Economy, Considerations on the Government of Poland*, and *Constitutional Project for Corsica* will be emphasized. Situating the last two texts within Rousseau's corpus might be relatively simple if his advice were followed.[2] Responding to flattering invitations from abroad seeking his expertise, Rousseau, as luck would seem to have it, is presented with a pair of opportunities to apply his theoretical notions to concrete political locales: one on the island nation of Corsica, where the conditions of possibility for legislation are deemed favorable;[3] a second in Poland, where the bête noire of modernity,[4] the cumbersome size of states, renders conditions less than auspicious.[5]

Despite appearances, these essays pursue fundamental questions of government; they do not promote the suzerainty of politics. Rather than read *Letter to d'Alembert, Political Economy, Poland* and *Corsica* in light of the juridical or contractual principles delineated in *The Social Contract*, and then conduct textual examinations for discrepancies and discontinuities, compromises and contradictions between sentences,[6] I propose to reverse the order of textual priority. What if we think about the political dicta of *The Social Contract* in terms of the principles and practices of governmentality that permeate these other works? The temptation to erect a grand normative edifice with a theory of sovereignty as its centerpiece then recedes before the actualities constituting civil and political life.[7]

Sovereignty in Rousseau is best understood, I believe, as the crowning achievement of an order masterfully engineered from below at innumerable points through a plethora of techniques and instrumentalities of power. Sovereignty becomes a dull denouement to Rousseau's unique brand of republic building. After reconsidering Rousseau's understanding of sovereignty, the concept of politics which

prevails in his work may lose much of its fantastical character and actually seem rather unremarkable. The reading offered here hopes to tame the seductive rhetorical powers of *The Social Contract*. The costs to sovereignty can then be assessed as the strains in the inner workings of the contract are discerned. Sovereignty does not disappear in Rousseau's republic, but it is decentered.

In short, Rousseau's success may once again betray itself. Nevertheless, the liberty the sovereignty problematic prizes can be invigorated, however imperfectly, if practices of government are treated as sites of politics. Consequently, rather than repress or deny, erase or evade tragic conflicts, they would be diffused across the republic. Government might then contribute to as well as complicate the political values it supposedly serves.

Governmentality

The reconstruction of Rousseau's sovereignty problematic is indebted to Foucault, more specifically to his examination of the art of government and the rationality animating it, what he calls governmentality. Foucault's incipient reflections on this art, sufficient to redirect our theoretical gaze, impugn key political and juridical assumptions critical to Rousseau's imagined republic. Features and facets of his democratic project otherwise overlooked or unnoticed now come to the fore.

In "Governmentality," a 1978 lecture later published, Foucault extends his investigations into the actualities of power. Linked to his efforts to demystify and displace the role of the state and sovereignty in political phenomena and explanation, he explores a literature devoted to the art of government, an art that focuses on questions of governmental rationality.[8]

The fundamental concern informing this literature is the introduction of economy into the general running and management of the state and society. Though public economy cannot be reduced to the model of the family, its origins lie here. Government involves bringing perspicacity and solicitousness to the state equal to what the father exercises toward his family and its well-being. Though the operational principles suited to public and private economy differ fundamentally (because a father is best advised to heed the voice of nature, his heart), similarly detailed tactics of surveillance and techniques of control are to be applied to the inhabitants of the state.[9]

Foucault argues that the art of government literature is separate and distinct from both the princely rule associated with Machiavelli and the discourse of sovereignty. The prince literature centers on efforts to maintain control of a principality. Having acquired it by hook or by crook, the prince does not form part of his principality. He is external to it, which means that the connection between them is tenuous at best. Hence the obsession with identifying threats and dangers to this connection and the continual negotiations with violence to ensure his survival. The sovereignty literature concerns itself with securing the common good or general welfare, which, says Foucault, invariably amounts to obedience to law, whether god- or man-made. The end of sovereignty, then, is submission to sovereignty itself. Its essential aim is circular.

The new art of government, on the other hand, does not concern itself with subjecting people to law, with or without Machiavelli's advice. Government is concerned with a much broader complex of forces and factors immanent to the state. "Government is defined as a right manner of disposing things so as to lead . . . to an end which is 'convenient'" to them.[10] Government, then, pursues a multiplicity of objectives, for there is an end that is appropriate to each of the things to be governed.

According to Foucault, "things" refers to the interrelationships, interconnections, and interdependencies of people, resources, production, geography, culture, behavior, health, and well-being. The art of government surveys the entire state. Nothing, a priori, is off limits to it. Whatever ends need to be serviced, it can service. If not now, then later, as it continues to develop and expand. The art of government embodies an instrumental ethic where success breeds extension. The world of things stands ready to be disposed.

Unlike the exercise of sovereignty, through which people are required or ordered to do this or that, government eschews coercion. Disposition is accomplished through tactics, the modus operandi of governance, rather than law. Government encompasses an expanding, shifting set of instrumentalities which it seeks to intensify and perfect. Government thus utilizes manifold tactics, law included, but the importance of law fades in the governmental optic. Foucault writes:

"law is not what is important." People are guided, steered, directed toward a desired end—by tactics which are effective because they result in people moving themselves to the wanted end. If successful, to govern obviates potential opposition insofar as the actions taken are free. Thus governance can be self-concealing. As Foucault remarks, while the people may know what their interests are and what it is they want, they may not know what is being done to them.[11] A gentle art, governance can be invisible.[12]

Governmentality is an ambiguous phenomenon. It names a kind of power that forms and shapes lives and identities in innumerable, oftentimes insidious, ways. While many of the accomplishments of the art of government are substantial and undeniable, what merits concern is that this manifestation of power is unrelenting in its organization of life, in its imperative to convert everything before it into something suitable for some convenient end. In the governing process, things are rendered reliable, predictable, measurable, calculable as they become the resources they are. Thus things, including people, are treated first and foremost in terms of an instrumental calculus. They are resources for disposal.[13] As governmentality spreads more pervasively in the state and society, the character of life in it shifts. Life is governed by an economic rationality rather than a social or political ethos. Government tends to convert everything into a resource, real or potential, with value determined by the ends that are served. Value becomes a function of convertibility.

According to Foucault, Rousseau's Encyclopedia article entitled *Political Economy* falls into the art of government genre. He argues that Rousseau endeavors to provide "a new definition of the art of government." Indeed, there is evidence to support the claim. Discussing law and order, Rousseau comments, for example, that "the greatest talent of leaders is to disguise their power to make it less odious, and to manage the State so peacefully that it seems to have no need for managers." Yet, pace Foucault, Rousseau understands his art of government to be derived—and necessarily so, to be legitimate—from his theory of sovereignty. Moreover, his meditations on government self-consciously concern themselves with obedience to law. Armed with what Rousseau calls the "executor's power," government's first duty is to ensure that the laws are observed. Law (and order) is what is important. For Rousseau the introduction of economy into the re-

public is unproblematic both conceptually and politically for his theory of sovereignty—and thus the proper balance between obedience
and freedom.[14]

Government and Sovereignty

Contra Hobbes and Locke, fellow members of the social contract fra-
ternity, Rousseau defines freedom as obedience to self-prescribed
laws. No substitution can suffice. This definition is repeated in one
formulation or another throughout the text. Consider the following
instances. "Laws are properly speaking only the conditions of the civil
association. The people that is subject to the laws ought to be their
author. Only those who are forming an association have the right to
regulate the conditions of the society." "[A] people is always the master to change its laws—even the best laws." "Sovereignty cannot be
represented. . . . Any law that the people in person has not ratified is
null; it is not a law." "[T]here is no fundamental law that cannot be
revoked, not even the social compact."[15]

Rousseau's emphatic distinction between sovereignty and government, where legislative power resides with the people and executive
power lies with an administrative apparatus, no doubt threatened the
existential security of contemporary European regimes.

> It is apparent . . . that there is not, nor can there be, any kind of
> fundamental law that is obligatory for the body of the people, not
> even the social contract.[16]

Rousseau emphasizes the contingent relationship between sovereign and government. He makes it clear that the government exists
at the whim and caprice of the sovereign. The mission it is assigned,
law enforcement, is "nothing but a commission." It can be canceled at
any time. Cause need not be given. However necessary its function,
there is no contract between the sovereign and the government.

Though indispensable to the republic, the government also menaces it. Rousseau deems it intrinsically dangerous. While the sovereign needs the government as its sword of justice, the sword easily
can be turned against its rightful owner. Given the institutional resources necessarily at its disposal, the government has the power to

plunder and pillage the republic. And sooner or later it will do so—as
it develops a corporate will of its own. Subsequently, it neglects and
ignores the common good which should be its sole focus. As if pos-
tulating a law of political history, Rousseau writes: "[T]he government makes a continual effort against sovereignty. . . . That is the
inherent and inevitable vice which, from the emergence of the body
politic, tends without respite to destroy it."[17]

Rousseau's reflections on government resonate across time and
place. Complaints against a distant and disinterested government unfamiliar with and uninterested in the needs and wants of the people
are unexceptional. Unfortunately, the government is uniquely placed
to take advantage of the people it allegedly serves. It can come to
confuse a power entrusted to it with an inalienable right to exercise
that power. It can come to confuse its own good, which must be taken
into account if it is to fulfill its function, with the good of the republic.
Once these confusions surface, government can be found routinely
invoking the common good and the happiness of the people, which
serves as the perfect cover for its nefarious activities. And though the
government acts in the open and is accountable for those acts, it
nonetheless enjoys a certain invisibility as it conducts its daily business. Hence the need for vigilance, where the government is under
regular, close scrutiny, a need not easily realized. "The difficulties lie
in organizing this subordinate whole within the whole in such a way
that it does not change the general constitution by strengthening its
own . . . and . . . that it is ever ready to sacrifice the government to the
people and not the people to the government."[18]

The sovereign/government distinction apparently provides the axis
around which Rousseau's institutional system rotates. The character
of the sovereign is invariable, the form of government relative and
almost incidental: "I call every State ruled by laws a republic, whatever the form of administration may be."[19] But can the distinction
Rousseau proposes be maintained? If not, what are the implications
for the republic of freedom? Has Rousseau really identified the singular vice which threatens to destroy the body politic?

Government and Order

Rousseau's emancipation proclamation, "man is born free," which
opens *The Social Contract*, places the problem of liberty center stage.

The flip side of the celebration of freedom, though, is the challenge of order. Rousseau's proud birth announcement signals, inter alia, that humankind is no longer safely ensconced within a divine scheme of things where everything and everyone has a clearly defined place. Henceforth human being will have to provide and secure its own moral and political foundations. Precisely because the world wants for cosmic comfort and control, the need for new groundings is conspicuous. The ambiguities characterizing the modern world are many. Among others: while it offers unprecedented, previously unsuspected possibilities, it simultaneously contains newfound dangers. While human being is in greater need of regulation and restraint, at a glance it seems less agreeable and available to both.[20]

Even after the Legislator provides the constitutional underpinnings and basic institutions of society, gargantuan social and political tasks remain. The reach of the Legislator, after all, is limited. He can only do so much. Late in *The Social Contract*, Rousseau remarks that countless exigencies may arise unimagined by the Legislator. Despite the astonishing gifts of this figure, "it is a very necessary foresight to realize that one cannot foresee everything."[21] Otherwise the republic will not endure despite the efforts of its founding genius. If the Legislator, so to speak, paints only with broad brush strokes, what is to fill in the details and complete the work he began? If Rousseau's texts are read carefully, I would suggest, the prominence of law and politics recede somewhat and the importance of government surges.

Rousseau, to repeat, offers relatively unsophisticated, commonsensical counsel on the question of government as an arm of the state. The sovereign needs an entity to execute its will. By itself it is impotent. Once allocated the force it requires to meet its tasks, however, government constitutes a deadly threat to the very existence of sovereignty. And the threat is permanent, built into the very fabric of the order. On Rousseau's understanding the government will eventually transgress the boundaries established for it and usurp the sovereign prerogative. This political phenomenon is as inevitable in history as old age and death are inevitable in life. Responsibility may lie with the evil designs of a prince drunk with ambitions. Or responsibility may lie with an exhausted, apathetic populace distanced from political life. Given the energies required of the political vocation, even devoted citizens may shy away from their obligations, perhaps assuming that once a body of laws has been passed they can devote their lives to other, more important tasks. Either way the result is the same. As is the (temporary) remedy. Require the people regularly to gather and present themselves in a ritual display of vigilance, thereby signalling to the government that the sovereign is alive, well, and in command.

Yet, as the relationship between sovereignty and government is theorized, there is another factor to consider which seems beyond political recourse. The modern age, with its humongous states, does not lend itself to the pursuit of republicanism. To illustrate the point, consider book three of *The Social Contract*, where Rousseau's algebra of order reaches its apogee in the simple manipulation of population figures. His mathematico-political logic is impeccable, and the relevant equation, if hypothetical, is straightforward. Below a certain population threshold, meaningful citizen participation is conceivable as the state conducts its business. The citizen can make his voice heard in the assembly. As the state grows exponentially, however, the ratio of sovereign to subject increases accordingly. The voice of the citizen, moving in lockstep, has softened: it is now one out of countless many. It may well be inaudible.[22]

Rousseau's numbers haunt a participatory ethic. The process of legislation suffers as identification of the citizen with the law that it wills slackens. As each citizen's influence on the formation of law diminishes, it no longer seems to emanate from the will. It becomes difficult, as it were, to see oneself in the product of one's deliberation. How can the citizen perceive the influence that his voice has when it is muted, if not silenced, by the sheer force of numbers? As the state grows, politics becomes a site of domination rather than freedom. Rousseau is succinct: "the larger the state grows, the less freedom there is."[23] With this cause and effect formula, Rousseau reveals the inevitable rise of government and the fall of sovereignty.[24]

As the spontaneous grip that the law has on each citizen loosens, the question of order through other means, including the transfer of sovereign privilege to government, hovers on the horizon. Rousseau's formulation menaces: "the more numerous the people, the greater the increase in repressive force should be."[25] The ineluctable power of mathematical reason fills the space that might otherwise be occupied by an art of politics: Rousseau's calculations call for the augmentation of government. Force relations within the state are determined by a self-correcting formula. Rationality triumphs over politics, though the conquest may not be quite complete: "Now the less relationship there is between private wills and the general will . . . the more repressive force should increase. Thus, in order for the government to be good, it ought to be relatively stronger in proportion as the people is more numerous."[26] Here the politics of numbers breeds an unforgiving calculus of control.

Rousseau's freedom problem is magnified and exacerbated by his truncated understanding of politics. If every political order creates the citizens appropriate to it, how is this achieved in Rousseau's republic? Politics might have provided the answer. After all, the benefits associated with participation are well known. On the one hand, as citizens collectively discuss and deliberate on common matters as a prelude to drafting and enacting legislation, they are drawn out of their solipsistic worlds and forced to encounter others. They learn that the wider world shared with others provides the necessary framework within which they pursue their own lives. They learn that their self-interest does not define the world. They learn that others have needs and interests as valid as their own and that they too must be accommodated (even if they learn also that they hate their neighbors). They learn that by contributing to the common good, they also benefit themselves and those nearest and dearest to them. Moreover, the polity has been entrusted to them temporarily and they must pass it on to the next generation in optimum condition. They learn the virtues of discipline, restraint, tolerance, generosity. They come to identify with the order to which they contribute, which they have helped nurture, shape, create, change. Political participation, then, provides a wonderful education, one that cannot be procured through other means. But there is no such conception of politics in Rousseau. At least not in *The Social Contract*. If politics is not the agent of citizen-making in the Rousseauian community, what is? Furthermore, even as Rousseau's calculations call for the augmentation of governmental force, he excoriates repression both for its moral repugnance and political ineffectiveness. What is to be made of the conundrum?

Government and Politics

On Rousseau's terms, in the modern age there can be no truly effective solution to the danger government poses to public freedom. Given the size of states, the sovereignty of the people is indeed a figure of speech. Thus in *Poland* Rousseau can be found proposing a scheme of representation, something he rejected in *The Social Contract.* What if Rousseau's Faustian pact is in vain? What if, that is, the threat to freedom posed by government is other and more serious than Rousseau apparently recognizes? What if he has short shrifted, even misconstrued, the nature of the relationship between sovereignty and government?

Rousseau begins the third book of *The Social Contract* by warning readers that it must be read meticulously, what with the inadequacy of previous theoretical treatments of government: "let us try to define the precise meaning of this word, which has not yet been very well explained."[27] Despite Rousseau's best efforts, I would suggest the idea of government requires a third look, so to speak.[28] Even he does not indicate fully the role it comes to play in his social and political arrangements.

Admittedly Rousseau grants government unique efficacy. It is the agent of change, the site of action. Early in *The Social Contract*, it is true, he writes that while a fundamental treaty gives birth to the body politic only the legislation subsequent to the treaty provides it with "movement and will." Later in the text, however, while discussing the act which institutes government, he writes that this commission is "indispensable for giving *life and motion* to the body politic."[29] Strictly speaking, of course, Rousseau cannot have it both ways. Which is progenitive: legislation or government? If the latter, what are the implications for thinking about practices of freedom? Further, what would it mean to say that government is the heart and soul of the republic?

Rousseau's conception of government may seem pedestrian, at times barely discernible, beneath a fog of mathematical equations. Though Rousseau speaks of the government as lieutenant to the sovereign, throughout his texts government as a practice encompasses more than the enforcement of law through the application of sanctions. Indeed Rousseau speaks often of adjusting what he calls the repressive force at the disposal of the government to ensure the obedience of subjects. But while Hobbesian rhetoric can make for formidable proclamation, as a tool of rule it is counterproductive. At best. If threats must be escalated and retaliation relied on, the chance for law to be respected and obeyed has already been lost. Government must concern itself with themes and problems outside of law so narrowly

construed. Moreover, institutions outside the state's immediate bai-
liwick inevitably play major roles in the organization and direction of
society.

In Rousseau's texts the art of government unveils a pincer movement across the breadth and length of the state. The systemic approach is reflected in Rousseau's vocabulary. In *Poland* and *Corsica*,
the objects of inquiry include, inter alia: questions of state; the public
welfare; the public good; the order and tranquility of the state; the
population at large; the maintenance of individuals in a state of peace
and plenty; the power and prosperity of the state; the strength of
citizens; the increase of the nation.[30] It is also reflected in the terms of
discourse: things must be so arranged; the state must be managed
such that; the administration must be ceaselessly careful; society
must be well-regulated; citizens must lead better regulated lives; the
organization of the state must be attended to with diligence.

Rousseau assays everything from agricultural production to military preparedness; from the hygiene of cities and their inhabitants to
the moral bent and health of citizens; from the most solemn of public
rituals to the secret preference each citizen accords himself; from the
games children play to the pleasures and entertainments of adults;
from the natural movements of populations to the public motions of
esteemed officials; from the fertility of rural women to the suicide
rates of city dwellers. No thematic is too large, no detail of life too
infinitesimal to escape the governmental optic. There are "an infinite
number of administrative and economic details left to the wisdom of
. . . government."[31]

Rousseau's practices of government employ fine-tuned instrumentalities. Government alone can provide the intimate, sustained attention that the body politic warrants. Thus, a caveat is issued at the
beginning of the Polish manuscript. The art of government must be
thoroughly familiar with its object of inquiry. A "detailed familiarity
with the local situation" is indispensable if an accurate rendering of
the condition of the state is to be provided.[32] Empirical data must be
incorporated and regularly updated.[33]

Rousseau's ambition to institute effective governance is far-
reaching. Law and order is to be brought to "all the parts of the republic." No dark areas are to remain. How can this be accomplished?
Consider the criteria of success Rousseau provides. Assume laws are
publicized and followed. Assume peace and tranquility characterize

the mood of the state. Assume citizens are in their proper places and walking the line throughout the republic. These achievements are not necessarily cause for reassurance. Rousseau insists that for the republic to thrive, for the law to be truly respected, obedience is insufficient. Rousseau writes that "the government will have difficulty making itself obeyed if it limits itself to obedience." What concerns Rousseau here? Obedience can be more apparent than real. In the absence of virtue, it is not always a reliable sign.

> If it is good to know how to use men as they are, *it is better still to make them what one needs them to be.* The most absolute authority is that which penetrates to the inner man and is exerted no less on his will than on his actions.[34]

Rousseau invokes the guiding spirit of antiquity as he theorizes the art of government. Once upon a time, the story goes, governments shaped citizens with care through continual exercise in a web of regulations, routines, mores, maxims, rules, and rituals. Even the most venal of ancient statesmen attended solicitously to such administrative tasks. According to Rousseau, modern government has failed to follow their example. Content with the collection of revenue to fill the state's coffers, contemporary magistrates do not appreciate the complexity of the project of order. They suffer not only from a narrow bureaucratic focus, but a failure of imagination. They fathom neither the possibility nor the necessity of fashioning a suitable subject.[35]

In short, Rousseau seeks to restrict the moral and political identities available and appropriate to his virtuous republic. Moreover, while will masquerades as a property of the sovereign realm, government assumes responsibility for its actual formation and maintenance. Government, that is, produces the artifact of will sovereignty draws upon.[36] "It is certain that *people are in the long run what the government makes them.* Warriors, citizens, men when it so pleases; mob and rabble when it wishes."[37] Here the subject-citizen is disclosed as the contrivance of power—an artifice to be constructed more than an essence to be realized. The art of government rather than the exercise of sovereignty is responsible for its manufacture.

Though prepared to overcome whatever resistance it encounters, government as a practice is not mere imposition, nor are subjects conceived of as unwilling recipients. To govern is to manage, to conduct, to control, to regulate, to incline, to dispose, to orient. Concurrently, to govern presupposes that the subject of government is active in the processes which mold, shape, and manipulate it into appropriate form. Government requires that subjects themselves act in specified ways at appointed times. Subjects are to be made so that they can conduct themselves in prescribed fashion. Government presupposes the full implication of the subject to be governed. Dutiful compliance must be active. If it is to be successful, that is.

"On the Right of Life and Death" in the second book of *The Social Contract* provides further clues to the art of government in its rise to prominence. Here the parameters regulating punishment in a republic are shifting. Granted, the absolutist pretensions of the King have been transferred to the sovereign people, but a different calculus is at work. Punishment conceived as a deterrent to future criminal activity is suspect. Such intervention is insufficient. It offers too little, too late. Moreover, an order routinely employing the sword of justice can be sure that whatever number of offenders it apprehends many more escape its carceral net. Those who have only punishment to fear find means for circumventing laws for which they have little or no regard. Talents of evasion will be developed. Those caught will no doubt regard punishment, corporal or otherwise, as a small price to pay, part of the economy of crime. Moreover, Rousseau is hypercritical of the frequent recourse to corporal forms of punishment. It signifies a failure of governance, a laziness in the state apparatus, and a dearth of virtue. Scorned by Rousseau as a resort to terror by leaders who have failed to generate respect, it is a "despicable trick" thought up by "small minds" who parade its use as a maxim of state.[38]

Thus, the spirit of indignation and revenge which fuels calls for the death penalty for crimes against the state begins to fade (though it flares up occasionally for exceptional acts). State executions become more of a scandal than a triumph, an admission of defeat rather than the restoration of glory. Rousseau's texts privilege production and abhor waste. They foster life: "There is no wicked man who could not be made good for something."[39] The subject is conceived as potential future resource (rather than current criminal drain) which can be folded back into the community as a contributing member. The policy announced represents not an act of generosity or forgiveness but an expression of confidence in the art of government.

Governmental confidence, then, reaches its apogee in the three manuscripts to be examined below, each of which exhibits the effects generated by Rousseau's governmentalization of the state. In *Poland, Corsica,* and *Letter to d'Alembert,* the practices of government, isolated, may seem unremarkable, but in combination they enable subject-citizens to function properly, productively, reliably. These normalizing practices operate throughout society. They tend to overlap, complement, augment, and reinforce one another with results that are coherent, convergent, constructive. Ultimately, Rousseauian practices of government presuppose and engender relations of reciprocal subjugation more than autonomous determination.[40]

Ironically, while Rousseau's republic looks to be a victim of its own success, success may portend its own demise. Indeed, the art of government fosters effects detrimental to the primacy and purity of the sovereignty problematic as obedience and docility tend to overwhelm freedom and self-creation. Nevertheless, though Rousseau conceives of government in terms of prepolitical preparation or postpolitical consolidation, it also names plural sites of politics outside of the state's formal institutions of power, possible sites of contestation and disruption, resistance and tragedy. As can be seen in the sections to follow, the art of government, for all its sophistication, cannot simply deliver the convenient ends Rousseau posts. His republic constructs and—ipso facto—deconstructs and reconstructs itself from the ground up. If not imminently, eventually. In the meantime, any peace and quiet government might secure are deceptive.

The Government of Security and Liberty

Rousseau assesses Poland's strategic situation within the European ensemble of states. The facts are bleak. Poland is surrounded by imperial states of considerable military capability that it, suffering from a combination of internal disorder, inadequate defensive systems, and depopulation, could not possibly resist.

Thus Rousseau concentrates on Poland's military system, a central facet of Polish life. The defense establishment is the single greatest strain on Poland's treasury. If performance past is a barometer, the return on investment will continue to be woeful.[41] Future expenditures and expectations must be calculated accordingly. Economy, in short, must be brought to the military. Here the apparent end of governance is security.

Rousseau argues that Poland's professional army is incapable of adequately defending its territory. Poland finds itself surrounded by belligerent, aggressive powers possessing experienced, disciplined soldiers which can easily overwhelm it. Even under optimal circumstances, should Poland choose to compete with its imposing neighbors, the best it could hope for would be resource exhaustion. A more likely outcome would be military, followed by civil, destruction. Thus we have Rousseau's strategic assessment, which frames the text, of the prevailing balance of forces.[42] Poland must turn inward. It must have a domestic rather than an international focus, though the former is refracted by the latter.

Simultaneously, Rousseau launches a critique of the standing army. In Poland "[r]egular troops, the plague and depopulators of Europe," will do nothing but "bind and enslave citizens." A standing army invariably exceeds its designated military role. It may do so on its own initiative or at the invitation of prominent political players. For example: the military, exaggerating the importance of its role, may think itself entitled to take responsibility for the direction of the state; or the sovereign may turn to the army to enforce its will; or a faction in the state may conspire with the army to seize power and silence its opponents. Rousseau writes: "the spirit of regular troops . . . is never favorable to freedom." The mere presence of soldiers constitutes a menace. Constant monitoring, supervision, and subordination is mandated. Trained soldiers "should be nothing but blind instruments."[43]

Likewise, the size of the army must be limited, its capabilities tailored narrowly to predetermined tasks. If the military were to pursue expansion projects abroad, it would turn that same power inward, either to establish its domestic presence or stifle resistance to its initiatives: "Anyone who wants to be free ought not to want to be a conqueror."[44]

In short, the Polish army fails on two counts: it is useless abroad and a menace at home. It neither guarantees national security nor embodies the liberty of the republic.

On the basis of this analysis, Rousseau designs a military structure suited to Poland. (Later he claims it would be suitable to any republic.)

A link between the introduction of a militia and the overall health of the polity is posited.

> I should like [Poland] also to be different in [its] military organisa-tion, tactics, and discipline. . . . [O]nly then will [it] be all [it] is capable of becoming, and draw forth . . . all the resources [it] is capa-ble of having.[45]

The professional soldier is to be replaced by the dutiful soldier-citizen. The true defenders of a city are its citizens. Citing the Ro-mans and Swiss as precedents, Rousseau finds the substitution suita-ble for Poland: "A good militia, a genuine, well-drilled militia, is alone capable of satisfying" security needs.[46]

Economy demands this recourse as well. The cost to the republic is minimal. The militia is ready to defend the homeland at a moment's notice, and it performs its duty eagerly, for the fate of the Polish nation hinges on its grit and determination. Insofar as each branch of the national militia is organized locally, citizens are defending their homes as well as their homeland. The personal is the political and the good secured is palpably visible to one and all. Thus Rousseau ob-serves and advises: "In no position to hire an army sufficient for [its] defence, [Poland] must find that army, when necessary, in [its] inhabitants."

The militia, formed to protect the nation's liberty, does not itself contribute to the republican ethic. Witness Rousseau's treatment of serfdom in Poland as he considers the militia's composition. While the serfs as a whole represent an impressive reservoir of potential recruits, their indentured status renders them unsuitable for military duties. Serfs are a risk: "arms in servile hands will always be more dangerous than useful to the state."[47] One aspect of serfdom no doubt makes serfs quite fit for militarization. They have been trained in fatigue and servitude. Another aspect of that life, the resentment that festers from being ground into the soil, makes them a threat to the order. They are an explosion waiting to happen. To arm serfs, Rous-seau suggests, would be tantamount to providing your enemy with a weapon, your grave digger with a shovel. Further, arming serfs in the short run is likely to divide the collective force, setting one element of it against the others. Do not arm the serfs. Postpone their emancipation. The day it comes may be a "happy" one, but that day has not arrived.

Does the exclusion of the serfs negatively affect the condition of the state? No. The state flourishes insofar as the country possesses well-stocked cities from which the necessary manpower can be drawn cheaply: "Poland teems with cities, and their inhabitants, if conscripted, could in time of need furnish numerous troops whose up-keep . . . would cost the state nothing."[48]

As long as the citizen remains in his hometown he need not be recompensed by the state, for his military service does not unduly interrupt the rhythms of daily life, work in particular. If anything, the discipline acquired in one domain accrues to the other. By this regionalization and economization, "no one is allowed to send another in his place" with the result that "each may receive training and . . . all may see service."[49]

The training specified for Poles bespeaks precision. Given the permanent vulnerability of the nation to rapid intervention and occupation, the militia must be able to conduct prolonged guerrilla warfare. The dictates of retaliation demand a militia characterized by coordination, flexibility, speed, maneuverability, organization, discipline, continual readiness.

Switzerland provides eighteenth century testimony on matters military. Each Swiss citizen performs military duty in his home district. He is outfitted with the national uniform (which doubles as a costume for festive occasions),[50] requisite weaponry, and other standard accoutrements of soldiering. Training is conducted at regularly scheduled intervals: summers, Sundays, holidays. The troops are partitioned into successively larger units (squads, companies, regiments) with proficiency at one level the prerequisite for advancement to the next.[51] Once the totality has achieved readiness, it is broken down into its constituent parts and taught the fundamentals of infantry: drills, maneuvers, exercises, etc. The division of the corporate body is proceeded by the dismantling of each individual body. Each body must be taught to manipulate its own elements, and its movements must be coordinated with the like motions of the bodies surrounding it.

Rousseau suggests that Poland reject the construction of fortresses placed on its borders or strategically located throughout the country. Such architectural devices ultimately serve only Poland's ene-

mies. They will be occupied and provide logistical support for offen-
sive operations. Leave the borders open, therefore, and punish after
penetration.

Manpower is thus the linchpin of the state and Poland is rich in this
resource. In fact, Rousseau envisions military service for Poles every
twelve to fifteen years, and lauds the unobtrusiveness of the schedule.
Yet the rigors of perpetual mobilization and the necessary inter-
changeability of each part of the militia dictate that training never
end. Actual service may be sporadic, but military preparation is constant. Such is the cost of a citizen army in standing reserve. Rousseau
prescribes the following:

> Let these brave noblemen learn how to drill in formation, to perform
> all sorts of maneuvers, to recognise military discipline. . . . I should
> like them above all to practice for lightness and speed, learning how
> to break off, disperse, and regroup without difficulty or confusion.[52]

The threat of guerrilla warfare is Rousseau's deterrent to foreign
intrigue. Poland must convince neighboring states that invasion
would entail such costs that conquest would prove self-defeating.

While plans for retaliation and resistance may inspire the nation,
implementing them would be quixotic. Should deterrence fail and
invasion come, implementation becomes pointless. Deterrence is a
bluff. Once it has been called, its purpose has been defeated. A response, as a matter of logic, would merely aggravate destruction. Perhaps the military does not train principally in defense of national
security, narrowly construed, after all?

Rousseau insists that regardless of Poland's empirical fate, liberty
can endure. Even if subjected by a great power, freedom can live on in
the hearts of the people, at once its sanctuary and citadel. How are
hearts to be won? The intensity of military training in and of itself can
incite and instill patriotic fervor—if properly situated in the larger life
of the republic. Panoptic technology informs Rousseau's approach to
patriotism. Make military life transparent. Conduct routine exercises
and drills before the eyes of the nation. Its gaze will prove inspiring to
citizens as they pursue expertise in arms—which is one of the qualifi-
cations for the selection of officers. (Equal opportunity governs military careers.) Patriotism wanes in the modern era. It can be resusci-
tated, even raised to a fever pitch, if citizens can be made to feel

themselves "constantly under the public eye," where success and advancement depend on public esteem and approbation. Transparency as a tool can be "infallible in its effects if properly executed."

Rousseau concludes the reformation of the military by remarking that the panoptic pressure deployed on it should serve as a model for any career in public service. Officials should start in subordinate positions and work their way up the ranks based on conduct and performance that is scrutinized and recorded at every step. The dossier compiled on officials, who can opt out whenever they so choose, "will influence the whole course of [their lives]."[53]

What if Rousseau succeeds in transforming the military culture of Poland? What would be the result? Consider his own summary of his recommendations: "In the plan I envisage . . . all Poland will become warlike in defence of [its] liberty against the undertakings no less of the Prince than of [its] neighbors."[54] Here military discipline turns political; its principal purpose is domestic not external. It forges subject-citizens who will keep the prince, the greatest threat to liberty, in check. The passage just quoted, however, possesses a troubling ambiguity. Remember Poland cannot control its geopolitical fate, but liberty can survive intact if the nation is one and united. Thus the reference to neighbors may point to Russia and other states, but it can also refer to internal threats to liberty (aside from the Prince, that is). Say, to those deemed domestic enemies. The standard ploy of the Prince, recall, is to substitute its will for the general will. Citizens similarly threaten the state with their private wills. If anything, the danger citizens pose is more deadly because more insidious. Yet the response to each is the same. The martial spirit Rousseau rouses eliminates threats by making its presence known and its commitment to freedom felt. While an aggressive, even truculent, posture may be appropriate toward the state, what about toward other citizens? Does a warlike sensibility make for a free state or an undeclared civil war? Or both? Rousseau may deem invasion inevitable, but is a warlike ethic compatible with the spirit and practice of liberty? Like the standing army, is a militia a threat to freedom too? Does it promote "the spirit of military government" as well as a republican ethos?[55] To be warlike is to be eternally vigilant, permanently on guard because perpetually under siege. Given the indispensability of solidarity to the military and political projects, opponents can be converted into enemies and traitors, disagreement or dissent can be transformed into acts of subversion and sedition. (What if a Polish citizen, in the face of the Russian threat, were to challenge the advisability of Rousseau's scheme?) If so, the republic may soon resemble a garrison state as citizens do to themselves precisely what they feared from foreign conquerors and military strongmen. Thus the context that makes the militia imperative also makes it dangerous—to other states which would be punished for incursion after the fact, to other citizens who would detract from the common security purpose. Does Rousseau's plan for saving Poland's liberty simultaneously sabotage it? Yet, can it be otherwise?

The Government of Service and Signs

Military renewal complete, Rousseau's governmental intervention turns to the economy. Once again, Poland can follow the rest of Europe, seek self-aggrandizement, and hope to win the praise of philosophers and poets. But Rousseau ridicules the state of contemporary Europe. It flounders in a decadent sameness in which the pursuits of money, luxury, and excess obliterate national distinctions and lead peoples to subject themselves to any master—provided the immoderation imperative continues apace. The abject example of Europe lies before Poland.

> If your only wish is to become noisy . . . [c]ultivate the arts and sciences, commerce and industry; have professional soldiers, fortresses, and academies; above all have a good system of public finance and make money circulate rapidly.[56]

Money is the quintessential instrument of social fragmentation. Rousseau's economic prescriptions initially focus on it. Not only does it foster the servility of those who worship its possession; not only does it lend itself to, even encourage, surreptitious undertakings and corrupt transactions; as a medium through which myriad relations are conducted, it severs and alienates subjects from the structures into which they should be integrated. Money forms the linchpin of an economic system that "will create a scheming, ardent, avid, ambitious, servile, and knavish people, like all the rest" of Europe.[57]
Rousseau received numerous suggestions, all rejected, for the reconfiguration of Poland's economic institutions.[58] They fail to make

the distinction between wealth—which is invariably fleeting, mercurial, more apparent than real—and prosperity—which is a reflection of solidity, permanence, reliability, depth. The sign of wealth is money, of prosperity, men. Appealing again to the presence of the past, he writes: "The governments of antiquity did not even know the meaning of the word finance; and what they accomplished with men is prodigious."[59]

The reconstruction of Poland depends upon a sound economic system rooted in public work.[60] This enables inhabitants of the state to be incorporated into the economy as fully as possible. Corvées lie at the heart of the republican project. "Personal services" is one of the "wholly different methods" of social regeneration Rousseau recommends.[61] The bodies of subjects are to be implicated. To Rousseau's readers corvées would no doubt evoke images of work gangs and forced labor crews detailed to public works projects. Corvées traditionally comprised vagabonds, misfits, paupers, delinquents, criminals, the incapacitated, the malfunctioning, the recalcitrant, the marginalized. Now, however, one and all are to be pressed into "duty."[62] Putting a new twist on a critique of representation, he writes: "As soon as public service ceases to be the main business of the citizens, and they prefer to serve with their pocketbooks rather than with their persons, the state is already close to ruin."[63] Men reach for their rifles and shovels, not their purses.

> In a truly free State the citizens do everything with their hands and nothing with money. . . . I am very far from commonly held ideas; I believe that corvées are less contrary to freedom than taxes.[64]

The subject-citizen is forged, in part, through service in the corvée. Identity here is performative. Simulating the republican political ethic, where those subject to laws author and thereby identify with them, so Rousseau apparently hopes for identification in the product of social labor. If citizens can see themselves in a law, why not an edifice? Service may then instill a conservative inclination: what one builds, one cares for, and is less likely to neglect. Or let others do it harm. While the size of states makes communal lawmaking impracticable, no state is too large for social service. Just the opposite. The example of Rome is apposite here: "the extraordinary levies imposed on the people were corvées, not money taxes. Its onerous public works

cost the state practically nothing; they were the labor of those redoubtable legions which worked as they fought, and were made up not
of riff-raff but of citizens."[65]

As part of a public economy of signs, service entails maximum
visibility. Exemplary behavior must be witnessed. If it goes unnoticed, its value has been diluted, if not quite wasted. Rousseau
appreciates the novelty of his proposal for social calisthenics and anticipates little enthusiasm for it. Formerly, service constituted a form
of social control, an outlet for surplus individuals. It organized the
remainders of society and fixed their status—gave it official im-
primatur. Service in corvées involves the construction of roads,
bridges, fortifications, public buildings; in short, it attends to the
needs of the state. Tasks unpleasant, demeaning, or backbreaking—
ordinarily allocated to those on the lower rungs of the social or class
order—have been revalued and redistributed. Rousseau proclaims service "the least onerous" form of national payment. Subject-citizens
are crafted who expend energy, contribute to the strength of the state,
and are strengthened in turn, which redounds to the benefit of the
state. By recovering the corvée, Rousseau redefines citizenship and
provides citizens with a common denominator: equal service. "Do
not let the word corvée frighten republicans!"[66] No longer a device to
administer potentially disruptive elements on the outskirts of the
order, or put to productive use those who might otherwise constitute
a drain on society, the corvée symbolizes what it means to be a member of and a participant in society. Of corvées, Rousseau writes: "nothing is easier among a simple and virtuous people, and nothing is more
useful in keeping them so."[67]

Military training and public service nicely complement one another. Perhaps this explains why Rousseau analogizes the organization of the State to the formation of a battalion.[68] The ethics are
connected. Consider the latter. Each soldier is assigned a particular
duty; rigorously trained so that he can execute it smoothly; strictly
subordinated to the requirements of the whole; and easily identified
by the bearing and manner, as well as the uniform, which names and
shapes him. The subject-citizen must be implicated in not one but a
multitude of common projects. Service is to be an intersubjective,
never an individual, phenomenon: "each citizen is nothing, and can
do nothing, except with all the others."[69]

Paralleling his reflections on public work, Rousseau proposes a semiotics of public service. The remuneration of administrative officials provides the occasion. Government personnel are not to be compensated financially. Rousseau deems such compensation insulting to its recipients. Public officials deserve better treatment. Rousseau thus plants an ethical seed he hopes will sprout. The core of his objection, however, lies elsewhere. Having previously located responsibility for any number of evils with money, he now indicts it for what it fails to do. Once again, its faults can be traced to its subterranean circulation. Financial reward stands accused "of being insufficiently public, of failing to make a continuous impression on the minds and hearts of men, of disappearing as soon as it is awarded, and of leaving no visible trace to excite emulation by perpetuating the honor which should accompany it."[70] Money can be decidedly unmaterial, too.

Rousseau recommends that public officers be distinguished by dress. This would separate (but not alienate) them from ordinary citizens. To distinguish officials from one another, they would be clothed according to office held, rank attained, or commendation achieved in the course of state service. "[E]xternal signs" of distinction enable administrators to acquire maximum visibility and serve as paragons of right conduct: "no public figure would ever be allowed to go incognito."[71] Continually functioning and circulating as a sign allows others to orient themselves to communally sanctioned standards, and it requires and requests the bearer to sustain the identity of which he is the designated embodiment. Official dress is heavier than it might appear on the surface.

In sum, public service matters to the state because of its performative character. It can create anew, complete what is inchoate, consolidate what is already established. Rousseau plans to multiply the number of governmental practices so subject-citizens eventually can function in whatever slot they are assigned. Admiring Switzerland, Rousseau writes of its citizens: "They are soldiers, officers, magistrates, laborers, *anything* in the service of the state."[72] Subject-citizens are made ready and able to fill whatever role is required by the state whenever it is required. They are on call, disposed to pay with their persons rather than their purses.[73]

Via public service, whether in the military or the corvées, subjectivity is formed through disciplinary processes centering on the regulation of bodies in public space. Granted new capacities are born, and there is a corresponding increase in productive powers, but has there been a companionate enhancement of citizenship or freedom? At its best, service in corvées expresses the unity of the state, but is it a practice of liberty? Insofar as social service depicts a regime of behavior more than an ethic of political action, how does it contribute to the ability of citizens to rule themselves democratically? Indeed, Rousseau concedes that liberty exacts a price, many times a dear one, but such an admission here prevents him from considering fully the ambiguity of a practice he elsewhere describes as "contrary to freedom."

Ironically, Rousseau may have underestimated the governmentality of service. The problem lies in part with governmental rationality itself. It may generate illusions specific to it. Practices are designed to achieve certain ends. Finding the right means is the prerequisite. Once found, the end can be secured. But what if no practice can be tailor-made to fit the desired end? What if the effects of practices are wild? What if all governmental practices are subject to the same self-defeating dynamic as laws? Service may well backfire. There is a difference, for example, between mandating that subject-citizens embody their membership in the state and inducing commitment and allegiance by virtue of the political practices and principles operative in the republic. What symbolizes freedom to some may represent imposition or coercion to others. Rousseau admits service is a form of taxation and taxation readily antagonizes—perhaps uniquely so. The shift from rightful contribution to resented extraction can be slight and slippery. What happens if and when subject-citizens refuse military service? What happens if and when citizens refuse to serve in corvées? Service places demands on citizens they may deem unwarranted, even outrageous, when actually faced with them. The claim to loyalty service presupposes cannot simply be redeemed by the service itself. If service is not enforced, will that encourage others to balk? If service becomes optional, what happens to the egalitarian ethic that grounds the order? If service is compelled, will it generate additional opposition and resistance, including a response from citizens initially uninvolved in such questions? Do tragic conflicts await the implementation of these practices?

The Government of Life and Morality

Foucault argues that government as public economy was liberated from the stultifying model of the family thanks to the emergence of population as a problem. Witness *Corsica* and its theoretical concerns.

Rousseau's account of the Corsican state also specializes in the specific, the contemporary, the local, the empirical. They must be marshalled to provide an accurate reckoning of Corsica's condition. Only then can it be furnished with that "government which will keep [it] healthy and vigorous."[74] The facts can be set aside only to the detriment of Corsica.

The Corsica facing Rousseau, like Poland before it, suffers from a number of maladies which require immediate diagnosis and intervention: debilitating fatigue resulting from forty years of continuous warfare; the concomitant poverty, devastation, and depopulation; the recurrent military threat from the imperial Genoese navy and the Barbary Pirates. Wherever Corsica turns calamity confronts it, actual or potential. It is exposed on all sides. As with Poland, Corsica is about to be overrun. The immediacy of the text, then, stems from the recent experience of occupation and the threat of its resumption. Sounding like a military planner or strategist, Rousseau advises the Corsicans to:

> make use of their own people and their own country as far as possible; to cultivate and regroup their forces; and to pay no more attention to foreign powers than as if they did not exist.[75]

A broad statement of principle indeed, but Rousseau hardly ignores foreign states. In fact, articulation of the maxim is followed by its abandonment. Rousseau contextualizes Corsica's constitutional project by evaluating precisely the European balance of forces and identifying Corsica's position relative to it. He advocates self-sufficiency and diplomatic recession, but the subsequent inward turn by no means suggests indifference to power considerations. As with Poland, meddlesome foreign powers govern the recommendations to be made.[76]

The first step on the road to recovery centers around agriculture. The crop of choice, however, does not spring immediately from the soil. Corsica must do what it can do best. "The island of Corsica, being incapable of growing rich in money, should try to grow rich in men."[77]

Rousseau cultivates the wellspring of population, insisting that the power "derived from [it] is more real . . . and more certain in its effects" than the power generated by the ephemeral machinations of finance.[78] First, to promote population growth, nutritional necessities must be augmented.[79] Second, people must be made to inhabit the length and breadth of the territory and induced to make it bloom.

> For if the sterile places were not peopled by industry, they would remain desert; and so much would be lost for the possible increase of the nation.[80]

Besides augmenting the health of the nation, the quotidian life of cultivation fosters identification with a rural/agricultural way of life. Ideally, Corsica's inhabitants would not be able to imagine another mode of existence for themselves.[81] Once it is experienced fully, Corsicans themselves will endorse it. What stands in the way of this experience? What alternative does Rousseau target? The life of the city; an urban existence where idleness and immorality prevail; a form of life anathema to the real Corsica. Corsican identity, then, is to be univocal. The political and military threats hovering about the text assist the project.

The benefits of a taste for agriculture accrue to the nation. Population multiplies not only because the food supply has increased but because the form of life created by agriculture is itself "conducive to an increased birth-rate." Rousseau is a political demographer with a moral eye:

> In all countries, the inhabitants of the country have more children than city-dwellers, partly as a result of the simplicity of rural life, and partly as a result of its severe working-conditions, which prevent disorder and vice.[82]

Featuring sublimation, an agricultural ethic is to be devised favorable to breeding. *Corsica* descends deep into the everyday practices of a population. Rousseau becomes an obstetrician of order. An administrative rationality, based on statistical compilation, the accumulation of lists, files, and dossiers, comparative analysis, and causal explanation begins to unfold. In the passage below, Rousseau targets the sexual and reproductive realms. This is not just moral prudery.

> For, other things being equal, those women who are most chaste, and whose senses have been least inflamed by habits of pleasure, produce

more children than others; and it is no less certain that men ener-
vated by debauchery . . . are less fit for generation than those who
have been made more temperate by an industrious way of life.[83]

Rousseau assumes that those consumed by self-indulgent pursuits
cannot be bothered with propagation. It would be self-defeating. A life
devoted to pleasure must attend to its own perpetuation, too.

The agricultural ethic dominates the Corsican text. Besides its impact on population growth, Rousseau focuses on its political aspects.
Agriculture develops a physiognomy of persons conducive to a well-
ordered state. The routinized motions and repetitive gestures of field
work mimic the disciplines perfected by the Polish military. The body
is made taut; energy is harnessed; strength is augmented; output is
increased; austerity is championed; reliability is secured. "[T]he true
education of a soldier is to work on a farm."[84]

For Corsica, Rousseau dictates a life of uniformity in which people
become absorbed in a seamless web of self-regulating, self-perpet-
uating practices, rituals, habits, customs, and experiences. Agricultural work produces a subject whose constancy and firmness make
it amenable to extensive utilization: "Tilling the soil makes men
patient and robust." Without this cultivation, people "cannot bear . . .
fatigues. . . . [They] break down."[85] Rousseau is an agrarian me-
chanic, a farm engineer.

Accordingly, the state, too, must diet selectively.[86] If it habitually
ingests that which is unhealthful and impedes easy and sure circulation, it will be unable to perform its basic tasks. Obesity, for example,
will render it sluggish and clumsy. A well-regulated, balanced nutritional regime, on the other hand, will energize and catalyze the state.
Finance, according to Rousseau, vitiates the body politic. State service
will provide the necessary sustenance:

I want to see a great deal spent on state service. . . . I regard finance as
the fat of the body politic, fat which, when clogged up in certain
muscular tissues, overburdens the body with useless obesity, and
makes it heavy rather than strong. I want to nourish the state on a
more salutary food, which will add to its substance; food capable of
turning into fibre and muscle without clogging the vessels; which
will give vigor rather than grossness to the members, and strengthen
the body without making it heavy.[87]

The life of a state reflects the ordinary course of an individual life. For the sake of longevity, the state must exercise and eat right. With discipline, it reaches its prime gradually; the decline to follow is slow and steady, the "state of decay" not as enfeebling. Both person and population receive cradle to grave care, cultivation, and concern. The forces of each are optimized and totalized in and through the other.

Here Rousseau's normalizing republic reaches a crescendo. For Corsicans one form of life receives official sanction. It is privileged as the norm against which alternatives, actual or potential, are defined and barred. The physiological lexicon assists Rousseau as he promotes this identity as natural, inherently right for the island people if they are to attain moral and political health. As if to deny the constructed, relational character of Corsican identity, Rousseau advises that "[e]verything foreign to the constitution should be carefully banished from the body politic."[88] The warning is chilling.

The Government of Sexuality and Pleasure

"[T]here ought to be many . . . entertainments in a republic," Rousseau announces grandly in *Letter to d'Alembert*. His recommendation, however, does not translate into amusement for amusement's sake. He is serious about fun. Entertainments are to have a social function.

Rousseau recommends a plethora of public festivals. Though he does not provide much detail about these proposed bacchanalian occasions, he does elaborate one ceremony, obviously admiring its architectural features and feats: the balls for "young marriageable persons."[89]

According to Rousseau, the coming of marriage is an occasion for singing and dancing, for the celebration of what nature intended: man and woman joined together in perpetuity. But this dionysian moment is principally didactic, an opportunity for instruction. In this mandatory ritual, the conjugal norms of the order (which reflect the political norms) are revealed and performed. The spectators in the ceremony (composed of parents, grandparents, and magistrates), track the couples' interactions through their watchful eyes. They are stand-ins for God, and the marriage festival itself is a divine institution. Rousseau's panoptical architecture is operative here. Transparency reigns. In this setting young men and women learn how to orient themselves to one another and to the larger community. Men and women are unable to "deceive as to their person."[90]

How does Rousseau's gaze function? It simultaneously encourages and discourages, inclines and disinclines, prompts and prevents. In the marriage festival, would-be couples actively seek to model themselves after an imagined (but no less real) ideal. They do not just experience passively a constraining force. An image initially external to the couple must come to rest within it. To be successful the image has to be one with which the couple can identify. Ultimately, the couple must appear worthy to itself from the vantage point of the spectators. Unless and until this is so, the gaze will operate more through a form of intimidation, thereby lessening its reliability. The positions of spectator and performer, finally, are to be interchangeable. "[L]et me be instructed as to where young marriageable persons will have occasion to get a taste for one another and to see one another with more propriety and circumspection than in a gathering where *the eyes of the public are constantly open and upon them, forcing them to be reserved, modest, and to watch themselves most carefully?*"[91]

Rousseau's rhetorical question ("Let me be instructed . . .") betrays the fear driving it. Afraid of what youths tend to do in private, Rousseau advises that public allowance be made for the enjoyment of certain pleasures. Better to permit dancing in public than have young people seek illicit thrills behind closed doors.[92] Hiding induces a sense of guilt which, in turn, leads to temptation and surrender (as if to justify the guilt). Rousseau rejects a zero tolerance policy toward the gathering of the sexes in public not only because it is counterproductive, but because it constitutes an "intolerable tyranny" contrary to nature and reason.

Self-surveillance and -restraint are induced through the technology of a gaze at once familial, neighborly, communal. This technology finds vivid expression here, taking into account the resistance it must overcome—though the language deployed to describe it downplays it.[93] The marriage festival discloses the inner workings of Rousseauian power and the subtle manner in which it installs communal values: interiorization. What could be more economical? The official norms of the order are folded into the subject with its aid and abet. The more firmly they are lodged, the deeper they go. The festival may not be spectacular in terms of pomp and circumstance, but it is effective: "the spectator *imposes* a *gravity* out of which [couples] would not *dare* to step for an *instant*."[94] The truth the festival expresses, via God's representatives, presents itself as irresistible. Hence the posture of awe, respect, even terror Rousseau anticipates the festival is to produce.

The production of visibility in the marriage ritual presupposes and induces regular habits of inspection and control, habits the effect of which are felt beyond the confines of the festival. Hence the festival is a critical ingredient in "the training in law and order."[95] If successful these optical techniques contribute to the realization of an order familiar, uniform, predictable. The subject can then meld into the whole, one anonymous face among many. Ideally, there is nothing irregular or remarkable in the order. It is seamless. Deviation or difference becomes prominent. The marriage festival folds the couple into the communal whole which embraces it. The festival is but one of many governmental practices in which the subject-citizen is regularly in the public eye and raised to police others reflexively. Not incidentally, as all polities do, and even require. But aggressively, self-consciously, relentlessly.

Festivals function as training grounds, but they involve more than the harmonization of conduct with norm. They produce a mystification as well. Those implicated are both directed and diverted. Rousseau insists that disaffection from the order of things stems from an imbalance, namely, the disjunction between needs and desires on one side and powers and abilities on the other. The polity comes under assault when the former exceeds the latter. Unrequited love breeds envy and resentment, forces that rot away the foundations of sociability. Any good polity strives to reconcile these elements so that satisfaction is achieved and frustration averted. But what if the gap between the two cannot be bridged? "Nothing, if possible, exclusively for the rich and powerful! Have many open-air spectacles, where the various ranks of society will be carefully distinguished, but where the whole people will participate equally."[96] Festivals, opportunities for joy and lightness, contribute to the balancing process. They are designed to increase the likelihood that each subject will accept its "station in life" and decrease the likelihood that it will "[crave] a sweeter one." Entertainment is part of an economy of order.[97]

Yet to some, the balls themselves, occasions for sexual correctness, will be experienced as "intolerable tyranny." Once life is known to be the product of convention, if traditions such as the marriage festival are not subject to the will of the people, they may well be experienced as malicious constraints. Rousseau's festival is designed to conquer or convert any resistance it might encounter. Subjects, it would appear, drift from calculated observance to habitual obedience to unthinking adoption. The panoptic architecture preserves the aspect of freedom while compromising its exercise.

Briefly, then, festivals may not produce specific political outcomes but they function to align the will with existing conventions. Are not citizens accustomed to bringing their convictions and conduct into line with established norms and practices in common social settings more likely to be predisposed to harmonization in the assembly as well? Is that the training in law and order of which Rousseau speaks?

The Government of Opinion and Culture

Rousseau's *Letter to d'Alembert* is known for its analysis and critique of theater. The essay also displays a wider theoretical concern with the formation of public opinion. Pace Habermas, who focuses narrowly on *The Social Contract* and argues that "Rousseau wanted democracy without public debate," that the general will "was more a consensus of hearts than of arguments," and that public opinion "derived from . . . the citizens assembled for acclamation and not from rational-critical public debate of a public éclairé,"[98] Rousseau does envision a reason-driven dialogue which would be routinely and vigorously conducted. Pointedly, he scorns royal regimes for their inability to abide vibrant public spaces for gatherings and conversation—especially insofar as the occasion for gathering and the possible object of criticism is the regime itself: "It is only the fiercest despotism which is alarmed at the sight of seven or eight men assembled, ever fearing that their conversation turns on their miseries."[99]

What space does Rousseau allocate for dialogic encounter? In *Letter to d'Alembert*, he applauds the Genevan social clubs known as circles. Rousseau knew of these clubs from childhood. His genealogy reveals the following: initially they were called societies and "their form was not so good nor so regular."[100] Annual military exercises; numerous occasions for festivals and prize giving; a predilection for the hunt common to Genevans; all this and more regularly brought citizens together. Thus were formed "dining societies, country outings and, finally, bonds of friendship."[101] The site of these rowdy, joyous get-togethers was ordinarily the tavern. Place and purpose corresponded. The pursuit of pleasure gave birth to the societies.

Genevan political upheaval, however, mandated that these societies take a serious turn and convene more frequently in order to confront, calmly, coldly, the crises plaguing the city. From a dubious beginning to a worthy end: "[T]hese tumultuous societies [were] changed into more decent associations. [They] took the name of circles and, from a very sad cause, issued very good effect."[102] Born amidst civil discord, the circles came to serve civil concord. Thus Rousseau understands the circles teleologically. They cannot be separated from the ends they serve. Ostensibly taking his cues from Machiavelli, institutions and practices are to be assessed by the consequences they generate. If the circles become sites of instability or insurrection they will have outlived their usefulness. In other words, the circles are theorized first and foremost in terms of the production of a well-ordered society.

The circles conceived by Rousseau are segregated by sex. The clubs for men are semi-public institutions, rented, furnished, and supplied at the members' common expense. Women, on the other hand, meet in each other's homes to play cards (men gamble), serve refreshments (men drink), and gossip endlessly (men discuss politics).

In the men's circles manly activities can be pursued "without restraint." When talk turns to civic affairs, manners fade and conversation becomes extemporaneous, genuine, thoughtful. It is facilitated by the consumption of alcohol. Drinking may be a failing, but drinkers themselves are cordial and forthright. With considerable energy and emotion expended, language may become coarse, even obscene, but to Rousseau this is more a sign of discursive health than a breach of social etiquette. Only now do "reasons take on more weight; [men] are not satisfied by jokes or compliments." The circles represent the triumph of substance over style, content over form, purpose over pretense. Candor, despite its hiccups, is preferred to the production of fine phrases in desegregated social situations where "the two sexes mutually seduce one another and familiarize themselves in all propriety with vice."[103] Conversation that is polished, poised, and practiced betrays the sure signs of deceit.

Beneath the placidity of Rousseauian political forms, then, storms brew and erupt. Recall the description of the circles as "the most reasonable, the most decent, and the least dangerous" form of social relations in which people come together.[104] Rousseau may frown on democratic tumult, but its formal absence in the assembly does not belie its concrete presence elsewhere.

Conversation begins to resemble action on a battlefield. Attacks are launched, positions defended, forces joined, passions in full play. The point in such conflict is victory, to defeat the enemy. "[I]t is thus that the mind gains precision and vigor."[105] Not surprisingly, voices of alterity are likely to be lost or silenced, unable to withstand the relentless barrage from the conventional wisdom of the general will which frames political discourse. As in the marriage festival, in Rousseau's rhetorical republic pressures are weighted toward aligning individual opinions with the established social consensus. The circles prepare citizens by educating them to common norms, habituating them to traditional practices, exposing them to societal convictions and understandings, thereby enabling them to execute expected political routines.

The normalizing practices operative in the circles prefigure the formation of the general will. Recall the procedural steps of sovereignty. When the votes are counted in the assembly, the declaration of the general will is determined by the majority. Those in the minority, it turns out, were mistaken. It is, perhaps, to the circles that the error can be traced. Those who mistook their private will for the general will did not weed out the private will. Since this cannot be accomplished in the assembly, where, if not the circles? Rousseau insists that for the general will to be forcefully articulated, each citizen must "give only his own opinion." To the circles falls this responsibility. They are also to ensure that these opinions are one and the same since there is but one right answer to the problems and evils the general will addresses.

The circles, moreover, are ideally suited to isolate and contain the possible disruptions of speech. Not only does the citizen regularly purge himself of any anger and resentment he may feel toward the republic. Once he concludes his discursive outburst, rather than advance to the assembly to continue and widen the enagagement and give publicity to his voice, he heads home for dinner.

Again, like the marriage festival, the circles contribute to Rousseau's sexual politics. With regard to republican virtue, Rousseau fears nothing so much as the transformation of men into women and women into men. He speaks obsessively about the baleful influence that women have over men whenever the two are brought together in a common setting. Dilettantish women represent the potential undoing of the masculine identity that Rousseau constructs on, in, and around the male as well as the feminine identity of the female. His concern is reflected in the binary oppositions deployed to define and demarcate the privileged identity of each. Man is strong, woman weak. Man is hard, woman soft. Man is restless, woman sedentary. Man is rational, woman emotional. Man is serious, woman frivolous. He speaks of matters of common interest, she gossips endlessly about friends and acquaintances. Man is public, woman domestic. He is complete, she is partial.[106] Rousseau's virtue politics aims to reverse the sexual trends of contemporary Europe. Speaking on behalf of men, he writes: "As for us, we have taken on entirely contrary ways; meanly devoted to the wills of the sex we ought to protect and not serve, we have learned to despise it in obeying it, to insult it by our derisive attentions; and every woman at Paris gathers in her apartment a harem of men more womanish than she. . . . [I]n a republic men are needed."[107]

The circles see the need is fulfilled. Rousseau notes with delight that the circles of Geneva reflect the sexual separation of the ancients.[108] Men are to be left alone. Once in their own company, they no longer feel compelled to distinguish themselves in trivial matters at the expense of friends and associates, as they commonly do in front of a female audience. Rather, they "can devote themselves to grave and serious discourse without fear of ridicule."[109] Discussion can focus on the fundaments of la patrie rather than the latest fashions in dress or the current trends in dining.

Granted, women have their own societies, but Rousseau largely ignores them—with one notable exception.[110] Women brought together invariably gossip, it seems. Women engaged in the talk of the town act as de facto censors.[111] Knowing that women gossip, citizens would rather subject themselves to propriety than risk the scorn and ridicule which emanate from these circles. Those tempted to transgress will think twice before doing so. Apparently the mere prospect of a campaign of whispers is deterrent enough. Just the thought that one may be the object of criticism or ridicule behind one's back gives pause. Rousseau converts an informal habit into a mechanism of social control. The specter of gossip disciplines. The circles, too, contribute to the transparency of the state. Behavior ordinarily privileged as private is ripe for gossip, which often starts with a revelation by an intimate—spouse, friend, associate. Vice may love the dark, as Rousseau never tires of repeating, but the light loves vice, since it rarely remains hidden for long.

To skeptics who find much about the circles problematic, Rousseau cautions against abolishing them. Not because they define the republic's commitment to political conversation and contestation. Not because they are indispensable to freedom in a world characterized by plurality and difference. Not because they have proven their historical contribution and value to the city. He counsels keeping them because it is uncertain what would take their place. Under the right circumstances, of course, Rousseau is ready to dispense with them.

Aside from the many positive contributions the circles can make, Rousseau is sanguine about the abuses which might arise from them. Though certain forms of unrepublican behavior are possible, the police can easily monitor them from a discreet distance, inspect their activities up close as the need arises, and repress any serious disorders that might develop. These tasks would be less comfortably, less tastefully accomplished if the (men's) circles met in the home.[112] "In a word, these decent and innocent institutions combine everything which can contribute to making friends, citizens, and soldiers out of the same men, and, in consequence, everything which is most appropriate to a free people."[113]

The speech practices of the circles reflect Rousseau's injunction regarding the use of violence to mold public opinion. This art "has nothing to do with violence."[114] At best, coercion can induce outward conformity or a false profession of belief. It has no hold over the mind. In the realm of ideas, the resort to violence is an admission of failure. If public opinion is to be administered effectively, even the hint of violence must be eliminated from its governance.[115] But opinion must be governed because in Rousseau's republic it is opinion that reigns. And for it to reign, it must imperceptibly penetrate to all parts of the republic with subject-citizens themselves the agents of transmission. Public opinion is panoptic in its own way.

The governmental efforts of the circles may prove tragically self-defeating for Rousseau's republic—especially if they work as planned.

If a consensus-cum-conformity of opinion is secured and maintained, dominant values and institutions are likely to become stale (because so familiar) and stagnant. The rough and tumble of the circles merely plays at being political: a robust politics with risk has been displaced. Secure, content, citizens can become complacent and overlook the need for a public involvement that challenges and disputes hegemonic identities and institutions. The republic can also suffer from peace and quiet, and neglect is frequently a by-product of a community comfortable in its consensus. Thus the governmental practices protecting and insulating the republic may also damage it.

While the circles pass constitutional muster, the theater does not. In the *Letter to d'Alembert*, Rousseau objects vehemently to the proposed introduction of theater into Genevan life. Let us compare the beneficial and benign activities of the circles to the allegedly pernicious and perverse happenings of the theater.

The essay expresses an urgency and stridency reminiscent of the first two *Discourses*. Why does the introduction of the theater into Genevan culture generate such consternation in Rousseau? A republican way of life hangs in the balance. It is composed of a number of delicately calibrated elements that, if tampered with, could easily implode or collapse. Rousseau's criticisms of the theater tend to focus on the content and effect (each subversive) of the plays shown in it; and on the theater as a public institution or space in the republic (it is dangerous, disruptive, degenerate).

The *Letter to d'Alembert* investigates the public entertainment or amusement enjoyed by a people. Rousseau is unconvinced that typical amusements are either necessary to the life of the individual or integral to the viability of the order. He deems the sojourn of human beings on earth too precious, too fleeting to permit wasting it on foolishness. Besides, Rousseau insists that "the state of man has its pleasures which are derived from his nature and are born of his labors, his relations, and his needs."[116] The husband-father-soldier has responsibilities the fulfillment of which provide a sense of excitement, satisfaction, and completion which no mere pastime could approach, much less duplicate. Once met, they can stifle inclinations toward idle diversion. Or so Rousseau says.

In the modern age, however, people are fragmented. Customary duties are resisted, traditional obligations are neglected. An abundance of spare time prevails. As the simple, natural things in life are forgotten, "foreign amusement [becomes] necessary." What is it about amusement that concerns Rousseau? From experience he knows that the theater targets dominant norms and values—precisely because they are dominant. Given that the traditions, customs, habits, and opinions by which people live are the product of convention, they are susceptible to critique, vulnerable to disruption, certain to meet with resistance. Rousseau, accordingly, vilifies the theater.

More specifically, the theater, it is alleged, educates citizens in the art of dangerous practices. It constitutes a classroom in the school of an incipient criminality and immorality. The actor, doubling as teacher and role model, stylishly embodies skills in treachery which others could well convert into positive attributes and employ in other walks of life. Rousseau writes: "it is not even true that murder and parricide are always hateful in the theater."[117] He points to Pheadra, Syphax, Horatias, Agamemnon, and Orestes as dramatic figures to be maligned for their textual actions, but who, through clever portrayal in the theater, "arouse sympathy" after having violated the moral order.[118]

Rousseau also fears the theater because of its impact on the passions. The themes of love, lust, jealousy, revenge, betrayal, infidelity, incest that it explores subject patrons to a pendulum of emotions. At the very least they are invigorated and it is Rousseau's suspicion that "the passions . . . degenerate from being too much excited."[119] Rousseau insists that the several passions are intimately connected: to excite one is to agitate them all. The synergistic quality is what renders them so menacing, vulnerable to explosion, and impervious to the voice of reason. Rousseau scorns those who advocate combatting one passion with another. Such an approach will not produce mutual negation but trigger an eruption. Passions feed on one another. All get high together. "Is it possible that in order to become temperate and prudent we must begin by being intemperate and mad?"[120] Moreover, reason, the only force capable of successfully combatting the passions, is not available in the theater. Given that "one cannot be self-controlled in everything," temptations must be minimized.

How does Rousseau envisage, exactly, the dynamic of the passions unfolding? Taking an example from the ancients, he cites the Roman Manilius who was expelled from the Senate for kissing his wife in front of their daughter. Rousseau admits that in and of itself this particular gesture was not objectionable. It "even gave expression to a laudable sentiment" between man and woman. [121] The kiss was transmogrified, however, by the presence of the daughter and the open

setting in which it took place. Rousseau concedes uncertainty as to
the impact of the kiss on the young girl, but nonetheless worries that
"the chaste flames of the mother could inspire impure ones in the
daughter. Hence an example for corruption could be taken away from
a very decent action."[122]

If the logic of possible social impregnation is pursued relentlessly,
the asceticism required of public life can know no boundaries. Any
action can unwittingly generate effects opposite those principles it
would seem to embody. Even purity of motive or intent is insufficient,
and no amount of self-surveillance can be sure of its thoroughness or
reliability. Henceforth public performances must be scripted, but potentially inflammatory scripts must not be performed. As for a theater
which specialized in trumpeting established values, it would suffer
from redundancy. No one would bother to attend.

The theater names prime institutional space where values are challenged and contested, complicated and ambiguated. It could become a
site of politics—unpredictable, volatile. After Molière, for example,
would the bedroom be safe? What then of the republic's precious
equilibrium? Contrary to Rousseau's claim that the theater isolates,
people do come together in it, and perhaps that is what troubles him.
Anything can and does routinely happen in the theater. Perhaps Rousseau would prohibit the theater precisely because it is not susceptible
to the art of government. It cannot be made to serve convenient ends:
virtue, for one; order, for another.

Ultimately, the theater represents the threat that the meticulous
work done on the subject-citizen making him fit for republican life
could be unraveled. The theater, in short, is noxious in its effects on
the sociability of the subject. A play's impact, for example, does not
remain at the theater at the conclusion of the performance. It travels
home with the patron, who is now a carrier of effects that may not be
felt or spread until some later time. If practices constitute people,
then their effects cannot be added or subtracted capriciously.

Rousseau attributes enormous power to the alternative (read: subversive) perspectives displayed in the theater. They threaten the
viability of a republican way of life. Rousseau would rather demonize
than engage alternatives which challenge dominant values. What
does this say about those values? He insists that the duties and obligations of life overflow with pleasures of their own. Yet he prefers at-
tacking alternatives to affirming his own vision, which could be read
as a sign of weakness and defensiveness, not strength and confidence.

As troublesome as the institution of theater is on its own, its players pose a threat of contagion as well. Rousseau thus dissects in detail the figure of the actor. On his reading, the actor betrays a quintessentially modern form, displaying the peculiar maladies which plague the enlightened subject. He is masked, unreliable, deceitful, impenetrable. For Rousseau, the actor represents the refusal of identity with boundaries fixed and stable, clear and precise.

The acting profession is itself problematic. The actor prostitutes himself in the world of commerce, performing whatever role the public will pay to see. He pursues his craft for money and applause, that is, for reasons of vainglory. The actor is "counterfeit." His identity changes from line to line, scene to scene, act to act, script to script: whatever character he needs to be; whatever thoughts he has to think; whatever words he needs to speak; whatever emotions he needs to display; none of which are his own. He trades in and on appearances and masks, not reality, not truth. There is neither firmness nor fixity to this chameleon character. The actor virtually annihilates himself as he practices his profession.

Furthermore, he is dependent upon and subordinate to the whim and caprice of a theater-going public which pursues first one taste then another. Much like a slave, he is determined by a disparate collection of forces external to him. The cultivation of his trade renders him incapable of being a citizen. He does not possess the independent spirit or integrity necessary for mature participation in communal life. The actor, it would seem, has come to represent the collective evils of the modern age, bringing together the horrors of commerce, vanity, slavishness, and insincerity. The actor and the theater represent the Other, threats originating from outside the community of Geneva. They are urban, foreign, Parisian, instances of infection, disease and contamination that must be excluded from the community. Rousseau may hate actors because they can be indistinguishable from citizens in a virtuous republic.

The Government of Sovereignty

From the militarization of politics in the militia to the mandatory expression of honor and respect in the corvées; from the optimization of productive and reproductive energies in the body and the body politic to the moralization of leisure and entertainment; from the policing and enforcement of an austere code of moral and sexual conduct to the filtration of disruptive and dangerous forms of speech; practices of government define, demarcate, and distinguish Rousseau's republican structure.

To what result does the governmentalization of the state tend? More specifically, what happens to the precious exercise of sovereignty emblematic of a free republic? Can it survive a world where the governmental arts proliferate? To explore these questions, Rousseau's understanding of sovereignty must be fleshed out.

Laws constitute, they make possible, society. Rousseau insists that people must author the laws which rule them. They alone possess this right. Observed, freedom reigns. Violated, slavery ensues. "The principle of political life lies in the sovereign authority."[123] It must be free to do as it alone determines.

Through law the sovereign declares what it wants. Once passed, a law remains in effect unless and until the sovereign revokes its declaration. If silence prevails, the law still holds where the sovereign power is intact. Tacit consent can be safely presumed under such circumstances. This is why long-standing laws are accorded such veneration. Only their continual reaffirmation could have preserved and protected them over the generations. Otherwise, the sovereign would have retracted them. By not doing so it reconfirmed them.

For the right, let alone the exercise, of sovereignty to be meaningful, then, the possibility of creating something novel, contingent, maverick must be presupposed. (A fortiori, a public space where sovereignty can be conducted exempt from external pressures that predetermine the outcome must also be presupposed.) Otherwise the right is empty, and the assembly becomes nothing but a site of conformity and uniformity. Or so Rousseau suggests when he writes: "there is no fundamental law that cannot be revoked, not even the social compact;" "[A] people is always the master to change its laws—even the best laws;" "it is contrary to the nature of the body politic for the sovereign to impose on itself a law it cannot break."[124] Sovereignty at its unpredictable, unprecedented best produces outcomes unanticipated, unimagined, perhaps initially unwelcome, by citizens as they arrive at the assembly. Decisions emerge from the discussions and deliberations attending complex negotiations in which citizens regulate the conditions of their civil association.

Yet Rousseau's depiction of the actual conduct of politics disconcerts. Is the sovereign assembly a site of robust action calling to mind
the heroics of Rousseau's beloved ancients? Where great speeches are
delivered and spine-tingling deeds are performed? Where the stuff of
lore unfolds? Or perhaps the assembly witnesses a different kind of
courage? Where nameless and faceless patriots take charge of the republic's affairs and receive little thanks or recognition for doing vital
drudge work? None of this is to be found in Rousseau.

What, then, informs the legislative enterprise? Judith Shklar notes:
"The sovereign does very little."[125] If so, what is the little it does do?
Rousseau writes that the "only object [of the assemblies] is the maintenance of the social compact."[126] People resolve to abide by the
principles of the civil association in which they live. Politics ideally
becomes a mechanism for collective affirmation. Intermittently,
however, new initiatives are required. (They may simply be unavoid-
able.) Whatever the case, "[a] State governed in this way needs very
few laws. . . . The first to propose them merely states what everyone
has already felt, and . . . resolved to do as soon as he is sure that others
will do likewise."[127] Even when the sovereign is called to active legislative duty, its tasks are minimal. Politics is the occasion for articulat-
ing publicly truths or understandings already embedded in the common life.[128] Politics now becomes a mechanism of confirmation.

Accordingly, one of the curious features of Rousseau's assembly is
that within it silence reigns. Partly Rousseau is concerned with insulating politics from the seductive and hypnotic rhythms of speech.
Recall his conspiracy narrative in the second *Discourse*. The fraud
perpetrated by the rich culminates with a beautiful (but baleful)
discourse extolling the principles of the social contract. The speech
that cements the fate of the poor by implicating them in their own
legal imprisonment is a lie. Promises were issued by the rich which
sounded too good to be true. And they were. But the poor were un-
prepared for a world where words and meanings diverge radically.
Elegant, fine sounding phrases were enough to dupe those who might
otherwise resist and resent the new world order then forming. "All
ran to meet their chains thinking they secured their freedom."[129]

Rousseau prefers that citizens "have no communication among
themselves," supposedly guaranteeing that each citizen will offer
nothing but his own opinion on matters of state. Rousseau hopes
thereby to ensure the purity of expression of the general will.[130]

Though counterintuitive, why would speech be necessary when fundamental decisions have already been made before the citizen even reaches the assembly? Indeed people can act capriciously, but the arts of government are supposed to remove the elements of chance and surprise from politics. Rousseau largely drains politics of drama as the official site of politics, the assembly, emerges from below, conditioned by the arts of government.

Contrary to appearances, sovereignty does not portend a public space where citizens convene to deliberate and enact. Thus what could be interpreted as a sign of a vigorous public realm Rousseau identifies as a symptom of decay. The exercise of politics does not involve, rather it obviates and denies, challenging established practices or contesting settled conventions. It is the official opportunity for expressing unity of sentiment, singleness of purpose, concentration of vision, and generality of will. Each signals the achievement of a well-ordered society.

> But long debates, dissensions, and tumult indicate the ascendance of private interests and the decline of the State.[131]

In the *Geneva Manuscript*, while discussing tacit consent, Rousseau acknowledges the importance, the necessity of citizens being able to speak and speak in full freedom when gathered together in the assembly. The maxim is deleted in *The Social Contract*. The peculiar quality of the communal "conversation" indicates that dialogue and deliberation are not germane to its proceedings: "Thus the law of public order in assemblies is not so much to maintain the general will therein as it is to be sure that it is always questioned and that it always answers."[132] The general will names a mellifluous, seamless monologue in which discordance is mechanically interpreted as a manifestation of private interests—and thus dismissed.

If Rousseauian sovereignty is plausible, if politics can be a capstone, credit is due to the detailed preparatory work which ensures that politics is reduced to mere formality—at long last. Rousseau dreams of citizens rushing to assemblies, the sign of a healthy polity.[133] But only citizens of whom nothing is expected would so rush—ironically to leave the assembly as soon as possible to resume what is primary: life outside politics. But not life outside of government.

Rousseau admits that "each citizen, taken separately, performs no function of sovereignty."[134] Citizens combine forces momentarily to execute predetermined assignments. These same forces unravel after the mandatory communal exercise. Their ephemeral fate is of no consequence given the circumscribed character of politics. There is consummate preparation for the role each citizen is required to play, and it is the preparation rather than the performance itself that is exhausting. Maximum effort beforehand enables minimal public display at the appointed time. Insofar as politics aims at the common good alone, its rhythms and motions are to be choreographed in advance. Rational direction conquers spontaneity. The citizen returns to his private world of home and family after the assembly has concluded its business, not to rejuvenate himself after an exhilarating but draining performance, but to resume training for the next time he is summoned to the assembly. Again, Rousseau's regime is primarily one of behaviors, not actions.

The art of government produces citizens. From the circles they acquire the right political opinions. From the marriage ball they adopt the proper moral, even bodily, postures. In the corvées they send patriotic signals. With the militia, they embrace the discipline of drill. Governmentality permeates every aspect of society, including the consciousness of subject-citizens—who come to think of themselves principally as subjects who are obedient and docile and therefore free. The art of government forges subjects by continually and correctly directing their movements and channeling their energies. Yet the form that citizenship takes is passive, inert, submissive. Are such citizens really capable of sovereign responsibility? Of changing entrenched laws, whether the best or the worst? Is it any surprise that in times of crisis or emergency, the laws are suspended, citizenship is held in abeyance, and a dictator is lawfully appointed to conduct necessary affairs of state?

Sovereignty needs the arts of government to be. It is a dangerous institution. Rousseau worries that the people may pursue self-destructive courses of action. But "who has the right to prevent it from doing so?" While the question is rhetorical, the governmentalization of the state is designed to preempt the need for an answer. Rousseau claims that the most important kind of law is unwritten. As such, it lives "in the hearts of the citizens"; it is not carved in "marble or bronze." Rousseau refers to customs, opinions, and what he calls mores—precisely what the various arts of government address. Rousseau writes that "when laws age or die out" the unwritten law "revives *or replaces* them . . . *imperceptibly.*" Force of habit replaces the public authority. This is the true foundation of Rousseau's republic. Yet the replacement process Rousseau describes is deeply problematic since the republican ethos installed in citizens has been effectively removed from challenge by the normalizing structures which excessively produce and monitor it. It presents itself as a fait accompli to which subject-citizens must adjust and align themselves.[135]

As formulated by Rousseau, the practices constitutive of government ensure that sovereignty cannot be the site of individual or communal freedom as he initially advertised. The practices integral to self-determination, in other words, subvert self-determination. Too rigidly they fix in advance what is supposed to be undecided and open-ended. If the ubiquity of government is the sine qua non of Rousseau's republic rather than sovereignty, has not Rousseau concealed this result, in part, by naturalizing and thereby depoliticizing the practices of government?

5

On Enmity

A further triumph is our spiritualization of *enmity*. It consists in
profoundly grasping the value of having enemies. . . . In politics,
too, enmity has become much more spiritual—much more
prudent, much more thoughtful, much more *forbearing*.
Friedrich Nietzsche, *Twilight of the Idols*

The high points of politics are simultaneously the moments in
which the enemy is, in concrete terms, recognized as the enemy.
Carl Schmitt, *The Concept of the Political*

Man the master, ingenious past all measure
past all dreams, the skills within his grasp—
he forges on, now to destruction
now again to greatness.
Sophocles, *Antigone*

In Rousseau's state of nature narrative, the creation of the social
compact represents an unprecedented, unparalleled, unrivaled
achievement.[1] With the human race on the verge of extinction (ironically from the pursuit of self-preservation), an original political order
emerged. Ostensibly freedom was to be the hallmark of Rousseau's
republic. Yet security receives priority in his account of its introduction. "Find a form of association that defends and protects the person
and goods of each associate with all the common force."[2] Given the
adverse circumstances of birth, the emphasis on security may be unsurprising, even appropriate, but it should also give pause, for the
fundamental character of the polity is at issue.

From the founding moment the republic is thrust into impossible
positions for which the creation of the republic itself is responsible.
As Carl Schmitt argues, the fundament of politics is conflict or strug-

gle. The formation of a political community names an act of coincident inclusion and exclusion. Every "we" entails the production of an "other," a political process repeated ad infinitum throughout the life of the state.[3] Even in the best of all possible worlds, then, threats to the republic perdure. And they flow from within its confines. Enemies real and potential are widespread, and enmity is essential to Rousseau's republic of virtue.

Curiously, in Rousseau's republic while those who once ruled the face of the earth with impunity have much to fear from the new world emerging ("I would say that as long as a people is constrained to obey and does so, it does well; as soon as it can shake off the yoke and does so, it does even better"), apparently the once downtrodden also have much to apprehend. Be careful what you wish for, Rousseau seems to advise.

What, though, lies behind his trepidation? In a sobering moment in the dedication to the second *Discourse*, Rousseau analogizes freedom to rich foods and robust wines. For the inexperienced each is as attractive as it is potentially deleterious. Rousseau laments that freedom often is mistaken for "an unbridled license which is its opposite." Given the misconception, people who remove their tethers often suffer an even greater enslavement to new masters. More ominously, in *Poland*, Rousseau doubts that the meaning of the practice of freedom is truly understood. He makes the remarkable claim that the cost accompanying its acquisition and maintenance dwarfs the manifold burdens imposed by tyrants. Freedom ought to terrify more than oppression does, and if people were astute they would flee from it "in terror."

How can Rousseau's admonition be explained? Through an exploration of the politics of virtue, I would argue. Indeed, Rousseau is candid about the austerity and deprivation associated with civic life. The demands of citizenship are rigorous in the republic he commends. Minimally, the common good must take priority over a complex of compelling but narrow interests, inclinations, and insistences, an achievement that is exhausting and exacting, an achievement made possible by an affective commitment both necessary and problematic. Thus I plan to take Rousseau at face value—up to a point. A new twist on terror can be given to his warning, however, which might send even Rousseau himself reeling in horror. Enter the politics of enmity.

The frequent broadsides Rousseau levelled at Hobbes's conception of the state of nature are well known. Refusing Hobbes's equation of nature with war, Rousseau locates the advent of hostilities with the burgeoning of society. Nature, once upon a time a nomadic condition of relative peace, is not responsible for what plagues humankind. And so human being is not necessarily condemned to the permanent threat of perpetual war thanks to an irascible nature. The world may indeed be Hobbesian, but it need not be so. Rousseau imagines what Hobbes can scarcely conceive.

Leaving aside the fairness of Rousseau's criticisms of Hobbes, perhaps Rousseau's refusal can similarly be refused. Has Rousseau really effaced the specter of Hobbes from modern political thought? Rousseau's social and political prescriptions aim, minimally, to replace a condition damned by a precarious struggle for survival with a democratic order that champions genuine peace and security. With the introduction of the contract people have "exchanged to their advantage an uncertain, precarious mode of existence for another that is better and safer; natural independence for freedom; the power to harm others for their personal safety; and their force, which others could overcome, for a right which the social union makes invincible."[4]

Nevertheless, what I would like to suggest is not so much that Rousseau fails in his endeavor, but, given the pride of place accorded to his virtue politics, what he delineates is something other than what he claims to deliver.[5] Though contested largely on different terrain, Rousseau's republic inaugurates a state of war every bit as much as Hobbes's commonwealth resigns itself to one. Moreover, unlike the war Hobbes theorizes, where the introduction of the contract leads to its overt cessation, the logic of Rousseau's compact entails both perpetual escalation and the eternal return of a new, more insidious series of conflicts. Virtue wars, in short. While Rousseau may deem (some) "conflict" salutary, even ennobling, the wars his texts launch too often degrade, defile, and destroy. Contra Rousseau, there is no good war.[6]

The conceptual approach sketched above, I believe, contrasts importantly with alternative interpretive schemes to *The Social Contract* which are rooted in the empirical, as it were—readings which are admittedly encouraged by the text itself. A brief comment, then, seems in order to distinguish properly the approach taken here.

The Social Contract, the story goes, is a document of moral and political canons.[7] It raises the hopes of all who were invisible and inaudible under the ancien régime. By promising a political order based on principles of justice, Rousseau gives voice to generations of victims untold and anonymous.

The Social Contract, accordingly, theorizes the logic of legitimacy. Taking laws as they might be, Rousseau indicts the governments of eighteenth century Europe for constitutional bankruptcy. He provides a model against which regimes, despotic and constitutional alike, can be measured henceforth: the principles of the contract "although they may never have been formally pronounced . . . are everywhere the same, everywhere tacitly recognized and accepted."[8]

By thus focusing on the legitimacy problematic, it would seem that while *The Social Contract* possesses the rhetorical pyrotechnics, morally speaking, to incinerate actually existing states, it ignores the question of historical transformation. Hence movement to the legitimate state Rousseau describes is from a hypothetical state of nature rather than a contemporary regime of dubious merit. Starobinski scolds Rousseau for this deft theoretical maneuver and the problems it allows him to skirt. Rousseau, on this reading, had no interest in or was incapable of moving beyond the morally pure realm. He had no interest in history. He could only condemn.[9]

While the value of the utopian tradition in political thought can be acknowledged by those attributing membership in it to Rousseau, an air of disappointment nonetheless surrounds such readings, as if to say: How could Rousseau dash human hopes after having raised them so?

Whether the utopian interpretation does Rousseau justice is an open question. While recognizing its prevalence, I prefer to dissect the logic and gauge the fallout of Rousseau's political conceptions rather than dismiss their worldly viability or Rousseau's interest in it. Here theoretical concern centers on his conceptual achievements and shortcomings.

Virtue and Enmity

Rousseau's virtuous republic has much to recommend it. The conduct of politics is to be governed by general principles of justice and fairness where the law is an expression of the common good people share. Citizens devote themselves to things political and public. In national emergencies or crises, such as war, citizens are ready and anxious to make the ultimate sacrifice, life, to ensure the republic's survival. Yet even as they tend to public affairs, citizens are mindful of their familial—and other private—obligations and responsibilities. A proper balance is negotiated. Citizens are routinely to comport themselves according to the highest standards of good and evil, right and wrong. They try to realize what is most noble and distinctive in themselves, and encourage the same in others, for that is the way to the good life. The republic embodies a way of life which conforms with established moral values recognized to be true. Members have respect for the order of things, both transcendental and earthly, and a humble sense of their place in the world.

Rousseau's virtue politics, then, cuts against the grain of the obsessive individualism that marks, perhaps defines, the modern age. Politics as usual names a thinly veiled war of all against each in which private concerns dominate public deliberations and public life is transmuted into a vehicle for personal enrichment. Politics is scorned because it specializes in greed, acquisition, and avarice. In this connection, consider the familiar maladies of a commonwealth built around the rational pursuit of self-interest. People learn to take advantage of ambiguities built into the structure of law to further their own agendas. They pride themselves on their ability to find and forge legal loopholes. People secretly evade laws to enjoy a profit in which no one else can share. Such stealth accords with the estimation they bestow upon and the privilege they concede to themselves and deny everyone else. People blatantly violate laws with which they disagree or find inconvenient, alert to the potential consequences, which they deem acceptable risk. People routinely conduct themselves indifferent to the wider social ramifications of their actions. They let others worry about such things.

Consider, similarly, the social and political classes Rousseau despises. The rich and the ruthless, the ambitious and the arrogant monopolize the levers of power. They ascend to positions of political and economic dominance because they let nothing and no one deter them. The remainder of society figures crudely, if at all, in their considerations. The carnage they sometimes leave in their wake actually makes the game that much more enjoyable and pleasurable to them. Rousseau assumes, of course, that we are all susceptible to these kinds of temptations.

Rousseau, then, is no innocent. A virtue politics places considerable demands on its participants, which for Rousseau is a recommendation rather than a criticism. In *Emile*, he provides an interesting account of the conceptual nature of virtue.[10] Tracing its etymology to the word strength, Rousseau argues that virtue entails struggle. It names a permanent, perpetual practice or endeavor. Only beings who are by nature weak cultivate virtue. Through countless acts they are able to overcome their inherent weaknesses. Struggle defines existence, victory names the outcome sought. Virtue is thus to be lauded, because it is arduous, susceptible to repeated failure. The verbs deployed to describe the practice of virtue salute it: conquer, master, command, tame, discipline.[11] Thus Rousseau proudly compares human being to God. God, Rousseau observes, is good. But He is not virtuous. He cannot be.[12] Since He is good without effort He cannot experience virtue. Human beings are asked to do that which God cannot. Thus it is, according to Rousseau, that virtue is a "much profaned word." It exacts a heavy toll.

Noticeably absent here from Rousseau's reflections on virtue is the question of love. Love animates and informs Rousseau's virtue politics. The citizen is defined by his love for the republic and its institutions. Yet as Rousseau revealed in the second *Discourse*, love is an inherently ambiguous phenomenon. Love allows us to perform noble deeds and heroic actions, perhaps even sacrifice our own lives in extreme circumstances. A spouse willingly gives his life to save a partner. A parent unthinkingly trades her life to spare a child. A patriot will drop everything and risk all if the homeland is in danger. Love enables us to transcend the constricted horizons of our own worlds and to rise above the clamorings of nature. The "I" becomes indistinguishable from the "we." Love can thus render humanity not just manageable but divine. Love allows us to reach heights not otherwise attainable.

But love awakens other and dangerous dispositions. Jealousy and rage are equally its products. Love can easily blind us to all considerations save the objects of our affections. There is no trick to which we will not stoop, no tactic we will be unwilling to employ in its name. The crime of passion is a crime of love. The "I" endures within the "we" and detects threats to its rightful domain everywhere. If we find ourselves invested in property (thus expanding the borders of our worlds), what of "emotional property" like our beloved or the nation?[13] Then pity the soul who stands in the way of love. Again no sacrifice will be too great in this wretched competition. We can thus easily sink below the level of the beast, unable to hear the gentle, moderating voice of nature as we slaughter whatever lies in our paths. Love makes it all possible. Rousseau captures well its duality:

> a terrible passion which braves all dangers, overcomes all obstacles, and which, in its fury, seems fitted to destroy the human race it is destined to preserve.[14]

Love contains ambiguity at its core. Both good and evil emanate from it. A kindly and generous disposition turned in one direction can become, if turned in another, aggressive and cruel. Each of these elements comes from love. You cannot engender one without enabling the other as a possibility to be released sooner or later. The singularity that announces love's ultimate glory also foments petty insecurities, jealous fits, and murderous frenzies if its singularity slackens, disappears, or multiplies.[15]

Rousseau's republic of virtue courts the dangers of love. Enmity (hate) is not the underside of love to be shunned or rejected. Hate is the test of love. In politics, love and hate are to be positive, active partners which united are stronger than in isolation. Each is to be cultivated. To love virtue is to loathe vice. To love justice is to detest injustice. To love freedom is to deplore domination. To love equality is to hate inequality. To love the common good is to scorn private interest. To love right is to despise evil. To love the law is to abhor its transgression. To love duty is to denounce irresponsibility. To love service is to contemn idleness. To love the republic is to abominate its enemies. There is no ambiguity in Rousseau's idealized moral universe. Dichotomies define it. Rousseau writes:

> Long ago, Greece flourished in the midst of the cruelest wars. Blood flowed freely, and the whole country was covered with men. It seemed, says Machiavelli, that in the midst of murders, proscriptions, civil wars, our republic became more powerful; our citizens' virtue, their mores, their independence did more to reinforce it than all the dissensions to weaken it.[16]

Rousseau's virtue politics is a high-stakes gamble. A republic rooted in enmity, especially fundamentalist enmity, cannot easily contain the deadly compounds of which it is composed. Absent an ethical appreciation for the constructed, contestable, dependent, relational character of identities and institutions, practices and truths, enmity can destroy the republic it might otherwise serve in some capacity.[17]

Moral Enmity

Even though Rousseau's republic was founded to enable and realize the best in the citizen and the citizen was crafted to live and flourish in the republic, the virtuous citizen endangers it. With the social compact based on mutuality and reciprocity, on the ability of citizens to keep promises, Rousseau wonders and fears whether citizens will be able to sustain the commitments that bind the social body. What is it that leads Rousseau to question the fidelity of citizens? The permanent, perpetual moral struggle facing them.[18] While pinpointing a fundamental rift marking his republic, Rousseau simultaneously reveals the profound implications of a citizen failing to meet his obligations.

> Indeed, each individual can, as a man, have a private will contrary to or differing from the general will he has as a citizen. His private interest can speak to him quite differently from the common interest. . . . [H]e might wish to enjoy the rights of a citizen without wanting to fulfill the duties of a subject, an injustice whose spread would cause the ruin of the body politic.[19]

Rousseau bifurcates the individual into man and citizen. A different will corresponds to each. The citizen, possessing a general will, ponders the common good and dedicates himself to equality and the freedom it ensures. The man, possessing a particular will, focuses on his own welfare and promotes what benefits him alone. He is his only reality. Later in the essay Rousseau sets these wills further at odds, claiming that the private will does more than coexist with its obverse. It acts incessantly against the general will, the intimation being that it will not rest until it has succeeded in overturning the rightful order of things. Virtue is manufactured in the tension between the contending wills.

The identity of the citizen is secured by working on the resistances of the private self. The virtuous citizen first converts private will into resistance against its public will and then converts resistance into moral energy. He never succeeds fully and the residue left behind always provides new energy for the moralization of will. Resistance by itself, in turn, is insufficient. It is to be moralized. The private will is not another voice which enjoys or is entitled to equal standing with its counterpart. There is no moral equivalence here. The particular will represents the enemy within, that which threatens the viability of the political order.[20]

The struggle which transpires in the citizen has widespread ramifications. If the private will manages to subordinate the public will, the state is already lost. The seeds of its destruction have been sowed. In short, the fate of the republic hangs in the balance as each citizen wages a virtue war within himself. What is the dynamic at work here? Surely Rousseau cannot be suggesting that with the capitulation of one citizen to self-interest the republic, then and there, has met its ruination? I believe he is.

To Rousseau the voice of particularity is an Hobbesian creation. To some, nothing is more pleasurable than enjoying the benefits of political membership while contributing nothing to its upkeep. One thereby reaps a double advantage. For example, who would not be tempted by the possibility of benefitting from military security while avoiding actual service? Who would not be tempted to pay another to serve in his place, especially during time of war?

Can any state prevent this phenomenon from arising? And what if it does arise? Suppose that an order acknowledges that social parasites are a permanent problem. Does it not still make sense for resolute citizens to continue to do their fair share and obey the law as always? Would not citizens in the long run be harming themselves if they were to abandon their commitment to the general will? Emulating evil makes no sense. No doubt the majority of citizens will continue to act honorably even in the face of isolated acts of defection from the common good. What worries Rousseau is that the number of citizens who abandon their commitment can accumulate steadily, surreptitiously, until one day the fundamental character of the order has been transmogrified. Dissolution can happen before everyone's eyes and yet go unnoticed. For Rousseau, the only way to avoid such a destiny is to stop it before it starts. Hence he alerts, subtly, the citizen to the stakes involved in the clash of voices each experiences. It is ignored at your, at our, peril.

Thus, a republican order prizes most deeds that move the individual beyond the narrow confines of the personal toward the wider world of the community. "The better constituted the state, the more public affairs dominate private ones in the minds of all citizens."[21] Knowing what is at stake can make participation in the fate of the republic thrilling. If the citizen can rise to the occasion, he will have single-handedly saved the republic (as will have his fellow citizens): he did not set into motion the sequence of events leading to its eventual destruction.

Thus, when Rousseau declares that each individual can have a particular will differing from the general will he must exercise as a citizen, does he not in effect announce that no difference is to be recognized as such in the public domain? Given that the general will is singular and demands unanimity, whatever is opposed to it is assigned to the morally inferior realm of the particular. What may look like an ethic of accommodation, I would suggest, is actually a code of cruelty. As Rousseau seems to allow for divergence from officially sanctioned norms, he simultaneously eliminates it from the world of the political. The public identity he seeks to install in each citizen is the one true identity to fit the order.[22]

Rousseau's persistent petitioning of the Greeks may further reveal the virtue burdens placed on the citizen. The ancient Greeks are among Rousseau's models. They conducted the business of freedom in the public square: it was their number one priority. They were able to do this thanks to a network of support and servitude. Responsibility for the physical necessities of life lay elsewhere: women and slaves. Rousseau raises a disturbing question. "What! Freedom can only be maintained with the support of servitude?" His immediate response does not reassure: "Perhaps." He explicitly denies that freedom justifies slavery. He insists that Sparta, regrettably, was compelled by force of circumstance to realize its own freedom at a heavy price to others. While institutionalized slavery is illegitimate, Rousseau's assessment of Sparta can be applied, mutatis mutandis, to the intrasubjective world of the citizen. "There are some unfortunate situations when one cannot preserve one's freedom except at the expense of others, and when the citizen can only be perfectly free if the slave is completely enslaved."[23]

Consider how this might describe each citizen's relationship to himself. Sovereignty climaxes the moment the citizen truly masters himself. The language of mastery is fitting. The passions and ap-petites that govern humans in the natural scheme of things do not marvelously, magically disappear with the onset of the republic. Moreover, new needs arise with the social state every bit as stubborn as those nature bequeaths. To will the law, the citizen must dominate those elements within which militate against the general will, whether their source is prior to or attendant upon the introduction of the republic. Is the price of sovereignty an undeclared war between those elements of the citizen pursuing generality and those elements engaged in a continual counter-attack in the name of the so-called particular? Apparently.

> Repose and liberty seem to me incompatible; it is necessary to choose between them.[24]

Rousseau induces the citizen to wage this war by providing a con-text in which he can prevail, and by hinting at the spoils of victory. The war need not be conducted alone. But it is a war.[25]

While repressing insatiable, unreasonable, self-indulgent appetites and impulses may be unproblematic, Rousseau's war in the self may exact a heavier toll than first appears. Consider the procedural logic followed in the assembly. When citizens vote on potential laws, they must determine whether or not it conforms to their general will. In the assembly, the majority vote declares what that will is. Appear-ances aside, citizens are not really being asked to affirm or reject the laws proposed. Given that the general will is always right, those in the minority who mistakenly identified the general will are deemed wrong. Rousseau concedes a leap of faith is necessary here, for citizens are to assume that the majority vote can be trusted. While the discre-pancy between majority and minority might be the occasion for poli-tics, for opposition and challenge, the matter is closed. Rousseau in-sists that those who were mistaken were in the grip of a delusion. Their private will was attempting a coup. It failed. Fortunately. For the citizen to accede to the majority, he must suppress any doubt or disbelief regarding the outcome of the vote even though it is equally plausible that the minority was right.[26] If the citizen were to act on such a conviction, the state would intervene and force him to be free. Yet on what grounds are those in the minority to be declared victims of their private will? Automatically dismissing the position of the minority and attributing it to the intrusion of the private will demeans and dispenses with those in opposition. The need for politics is obviated. As dissent converts citizens into malefactors, the general will itself becomes simultaneously a source of unity and division.

What happens once the assembly has concluded its formal legislative work? While those opposed to the original contract were excluded from it, citizens in the minority must be made virtuous. Rousseau's texts indicate that once the votes are counted, the work of the defeated has just begun. "[W]hen the opinion contrary to mine prevails, that proves nothing except that I was mistaken, and what I thought to be the general will was not."[27] Unlike the citizen in the majority, who has managed to hierarchize his will, for the moment anyway, the citizen in the minority must set to work on himself and redouble his efforts to overcome his internecine struggle. Rousseau sets in motion an imaginary yet productive self-loathing. "If my private will had prevailed, I would have done something other than what I wanted."[28] Notice the grammar of responsibility. Rousseau speaks in the first person singular. Perhaps nothing infuriates like knowing that one should, indeed could, have acted otherwise—particularly on critical moral and political matters.[29] Rousseau can creatively employ self-recrimination by transforming it into the determination to do better the next time. Disappointment and shame are powerful tools of improvement—if used judiciously, selectively, discriminatingly.

What of citizens in the majority? What do they do next? The sovereign must remain steadfast. The general will which directs the forces of the state "is not that of a past time but of the present moment." It must be checked, rechecked, and checked again to ensure its dominance. Monitoring can never cease, for at any given moment the citizen might betray himself and the republic. Surveillance is normalcy in a world in which time is an infinite series of present moments.

Each citizen, then, prior to entering the public realm, turns inward and communes with himself. He is left to himself to resurrect the horrors of the past and potential ills of the future. The victims of personal dependence recall prostitution's humiliation and the benefits the contract provides.[30] Likewise, would-be perpetrators of domination prepare for public display. They must reach deep within themselves to rouse the voice of conscience that makes their crimes abhorrent even to themselves. Both groups must selectively remember. Further, those who have been victimized must not succumb to fantasies of revenge, while those who have a will to dominate must put a leash on themselves. Each must exercise a form of self-restraint. The one is to forgive pain, the other to forget pleasure. Rousseau locates responsibility for the well-being of the polity in the citizen. This is where the battle for the republic is truly joined. As Rousseau's virtuous republic relocates politics to the interior struggles of citizens, they become self-policing.[31] What could be more ideal?

Rousseau reminds citizens to meet their civic obligations. What is troubling is the dogmatic attribution of responsibility for failure to those in the minority. Rousseau is not necessarily wrong to do so, but can he always be right? The point here is not that freedom has been denied in Rousseau's republic. Rather, it has been simplified such that some of its costs, some of its injuries, are hidden, even denied.

A politics which excessively champions unity—or slowly collapses the two—tends to treat what otherwise might be considered worthy contributions to the republic (doubt, debate, dissension, disruption) as symptoms of disease and disorder in need of treatment, correction, cure. In Rousseau's republic, the possibility that the general will could issue a second judgment equally general, or multiple judgments, is ignored. Thus the general will, as it expresses freedom, produces tragedies, too.

What Rousseau (conveniently) collapses under the rubric of the private will names but one challenge to the virtuous republic. Suspicions are raised, though, as Rousseau summons one threat after another to the integrity of the general will. If the virtuous republic is obviously superior, whence its impressive roster of enemies? Has Rousseau identified actual threats? Or does the general will knowingly engender endless enemies as it tries to install itself? If so, will the virtuous republic continue to make war in perpetuity? If so, it becomes a very dangerous place indeed, for the logic of escalation is boundless.

If Rousseau finds the particular will to be threatening, if the citizen himself is an enemy to the republic of virtue, so is woman—or the effeminate. To which I now turn.

Gender Enmity

Rousseau imagines the following scene in the Paris apartment of a single woman. The idol, stretched out on a couch, commands a small army of men who pay homage to her beauty. They willingly comply with her dictates. But they do so uneasily. As the idol wags her tongue and bats her eyes, the men wander about the room restlessly. They look out of windows, poke the fire, flip the pages of books, glance at pictures, pace back and forth across the room, sit, stand, sit again. They chafe at being confined in these "voluntary prisons." Yet there they are—knowing that they should be elsewhere; knowing that they have duties needing attention; knowing that they are wasting valuable time and energy. And there they will remain, divided will and all. What is a body to do?[32]

For Rousseau, woman as wife and mother is indispensable to the health and well-being of the republic. The political order could not come into being or persist without her. Yet woman in public, woman as professional, woman in a nontraditional role, woman as would-be man is seen as inimical and life-threatening to the very same republic. Unless and until woman stays in her place—the domestic sphere—the very idea of a republic is dubious.[33]

Woman, then, represents as great a danger to the common good as the particular will. At times, she seems to constitute another, more alluring version of it. Rousseau routinely reduces woman to nature, passion, body, impulse, unreason.[34]

From the idol to the actress, woman is a temptress. She plunders the strength and resolve the virtuous citizen needs to tend to the republic. In her wake, rather than reflecting on the requirements of the common good, he dreams of his next encounter with the fundamentally forbidden. Who wants to deliberate with one's fellow citizens when clandestine pleasures await? Woman enslaves man through the deployment of sex. She can and will "effeminate man and mitigate his taste for his real duties."[35]

Ostensibly Rousseau bemoans the fact that women are not content to play their assigned roles. Modern women, in particular, are resentful of the various opportunities available only to men. These women seek to claim the same advantages.[36] If they cannot enter the world of men, they will force men to enter theirs. How? By transforming them into women. "As for us, we have taken on entirely contrary ways; meanly devoted to the wills of the sex which we ought to protect and not serve, we have learned to despise it in obeying it, to insult it by our derisive attentions; and every woman at Paris gathers in her apartment a harem of men more womanish than she."[37] Rousseau insists

[handwritten marginalia: origin of "real womanhood" & myth of Victorian age]

that a republic requires men and men are an endangered species fast disappearing.

Given this representation, if woman were to participate in the political arena, she would threaten the purity of the proceedings. No longer would reason and reflection rule. Appetite would reign supreme— and it would not be for the common good. Since man has his own trouble with passion, he does not need woman aggravating matters. Man, at least, is capable of a hard-won self-restraint. In short, while woman is defined both as essential and as inimical to the republic of virtue, it is the threat she allegedly poses that obsesses Rousseauian arrangements.

Rousseau makes selective pronouncements on woman in the course of his meditation on theater, the *Letter to d'Alembert,* where he portrays a way of life in tune with republican values.[38] Since the responsibilities of woman in the republic entail a domestic, retired life,[39] she must possess certain qualities, acquire certain capacities to be able to perform her multiple roles. Without a doubt, woman makes critical contributions to Rousseau's republic. As mother she is responsible for the government of the home, which includes overseeing the education of children. The next generation of citizens (not to mention mothers and wives) must be imbued with the proper values in timely fashion. A greater trust could not be placed in her hands. So much can go wrong so easily with the raising of children. As wife, she has multiple duties. Inter alia, she must provide a haven for her citizen-husband where rest and relaxation can be found after he returns from the taxing business of work and politics. Looking after both the family fortunes and the commonweal is arduous and risky. Without various compensations at home, he will be publicly useless.

Thus man and woman have designated roles to play in assigned spheres of life in Rousseau's republic. Each contributes equally, if differently, to the common good of the state. Thus questions, to say nothing of disputes, of superiority or equality between man and woman are irrelevant and pointless, according to Rousseau. Given the lean, spare sovereign politics practiced in the republic of virtue and the significance of the ambiguous arts of government in which both are implicated, Rousseau's assessment of his division of labor is not unsurprising.

Rousseau assembles a substantial arsenal of arguments to support his social and political arrangements, but Nature is the centerpiece.

Nature, he claims, dictates the roles man and woman are to play. What could be more obvious than the plethora of signs it provides to prove its intent, including the talents native to each? Despite its degradation, Nature still inscribes its handiwork. Nature wants, Nature protects, Nature safeguards, Nature speaks, Nature indicates, Nature imposes, Nature prescribes. The history of civilizations offers corroborative evidence. Can it be a coincidence, Rousseau asks, that all societies have organized themselves in identical fashion regarding man and woman? More specifically, Rousseau invokes the ancients for historical and rhetorical support. They invented sexual correctness. In Greek life, women led retired lives. They ventured into public infrequently; they never did so with men; on those rare occasions they were permitted to attend the theater, they were relegated to the less desirable seats; and they were forbidden, upon penalty of death, to appear at the Olympic games. "Whatever she may do, one feels that in public she is not in her place."[40] Rousseau thus tries to capitalize on the nostalgia for the ancients his texts tirelessly foster. It is only the fashionable cosmopolitan philosophy of the day that dares countermand the order of Nature and split the otherwise unanimous voice of humankind.[41] Rousseau claims, no doubt anticipating the controversy his scheme will provoke, that if woman were to object to the dual role structure as an "unjust man-made inequality, she [would be] wrong" on all three counts.[42]

Regardless, Rousseau adds in a revealing supplement, even if nature did not dictate distinct roles, it would be good for the republic if duties were divided according to sex. Though Rousseau raises the possibility that the domestic lot and chaste sexuality of woman might be the product of education or social convention, he just as quickly disposes of it as a potential objection by insisting that both are in the best interests of society. The matter becomes moot. For him.[43] Rousseau, then, denies that a system of rigid sex roles is the product of prejudice. Rather, it is the embodiment of reason itself.[44] (He later argues that the role he assigns woman is "common to all the peoples of the world," though perhaps this should arouse suspicion in Rousseau rather than confirm his judgment. How is it that civilization, indicted for maximum feasible ignorance and corruption, is correct on this one matter?)

What is curious about Rousseau's discourse on woman is that while defending the position he has identified as intrinsic to the world, he discloses its artificial and constructed character. For Rousseau, it is obvious that "man and woman are not and ought not to be constituted in the same way."[45] The logical conclusion to draw is that each must be educated to suit his and her constitution. But Rousseau's formulation exposes the workings of the educational process. The moral imperative precedes and promotes the creation of the reality reported. That is, because man and woman ought not to be constituted in the same way, they are not. Nature is not cause but effect. As Mary Wollstonecraft pointed out, woman is the most artificial of creatures. What Rousseau did to Hobbes must now be done to Rousseau himself. As for the demonstration of the truth about the sexes, with Rousseau it never ends. If it were the design of nature he claims, would it need such fervent articulation to gain assent?

Despite the critical roles woman is to play in the republic, despite the republic's responsibility for creating woman to fulfill these roles, Rousseau denies her political rights and privileges. Woman cannot but resent the impossible position in which she has been placed. Rather than promote peace and stability, Rousseau's arrangements seem poised to self-destruct as a disruptive force at the moral heart of the republic has been formed, one whose fate belies its democratic principle. Moreover, as woman is excluded from the public sphere, might not the family compete with it for primacy? Woman, denied direct participation in politics, would have no real experience of its value and significance. Would she accord it the respect it demands? Surely Rousseau can anticipate such possibilities? Perhaps, then, Rousseau's provocations are deliberate? Perhaps he intends for man and woman to be at odds in his republic of virtue?

Rousseau's virtuous citizen, it seems, requires the difference of woman. The masculine male citizen Rousseau designs defines itself against the retired life of the normalized female and defends itself against the eroticized life of the professional or public woman.[46] To fulfill the duties of the civic life Rousseau imposes on man, he must not only tame dangerous and destructive passions within. He must also overcome inclinations toward idleness, passivity, and private considerations. Thus woman is to be domesticated, her desires controlled, shown her place. Woman becomes the worldly embodiment of what the male citizen struggles to control and overcome within himself—his "feminine" others. As Linda Zerilli points out, the figure of woman is Rousseau's scapegoat.[47]

Rousseau's republican fantasy life climaxes in the *Letter to d'Alem-*

bert. To reassert and reestablish textually the proper sexual and political order of things, Rousseau imagines an intimate encounter in which man actively asserts himself, freed from the stupefying dominion of the female gaze operative in the salon. In a remarkable passage, even for Rousseau, he concocts a domestic morality exercise in which woman features prominently. Her duty, we learn, extends beyond bearing, raising, and educating children, and taking care of her husband. Rousseau insists that the connection between man and woman—and his rightful rule over her—is most effectively established if obstacles are encountered, even deliberately placed between them. Only then is the relation brought to life, supplied with the vitality it needs to last. Obstacles do not, despite appearances, generate distance. Rather they induce proximity.[48] Rousseau records violence as intrinsic to the virtuous, masculine male as he experiences the thrill of triumph, the satisfaction of desire in the act of intimacy. By forcibly taking his wife, he not only exercises exquisite control over his passions, he need not stray outside the home to find excitement and sate a passion for adventure and conquest. Rape is a family value in his virtue politics:

> It is not yet enough to be loved; desires shared do not alone give the right to satisfy them; the consent of the will is also needed. . . . To win this silent consent is to make use of all the violence permitted in love. To read it in the eyes, to see it in the ways in spite of the mouth's denial, that is the art of he who knows how to love. If he then completes his happiness, he is not brutal, he is decent.[49]

By forcing himself on woman, Rousseau's account suggests, man not only confirms and solidifies his power but actually serves the chasteness it appears he has just violated. Otherwise, woman might have casually abandoned her modesty. By raping woman and thereby reaffirming her subordinate position, the masculine male requires her to defend that which she is supposedly ready to disregard: her virtue. What a moment ago she was ready to discard she will now defend. He attacks in his, her, and the republic's moral interest. For Rousseau, rape is a ritual of enhancement. "What would become of the human species if the order of attack and defense were changed?"[50] Rousseau asks. And what would become of the republic?[51]

For Rousseau, the interior war conducted by each citizen has a worldly counterpart. The projection of desire and depravity onto woman provides the citizen welcome resistance. Does the relation with woman, where man rules the family and politics is denied, give him the confidence that as citizen he can conquer his own voices of particularity?[52] Rousseau fears that infidelity can ultimately produce a family in which its members become "secret enemies" of one another.[53] But what kind of family, what kind of republic does fidelity itself produce?

Rousseau's virtue politics places heavy burdens on citizens. Engaging the private and the effeminate are full-time vocations. The republic's enemies seem to be proliferating at an alarming rate. As Rousseau's campaign to make the world safe for virtue continues, new fronts are opened. Just as his forces appear stretched (too) thin, new enemies energize the cause. Now it is time to consider Rousseau's patriot.[54]

Foreign Enmity

Patriotism, love for la patrie, figures large in Rousseau's moral and political universe.[55] Perhaps first and foremost, it entails love of the republic, specifically, the institutions and laws which constitute a free people. The patriot is one who prizes and celebrates freedom, and defends it when called upon to do so. The patriot rushes to the assembly in the performance of his civic duties, whether to cast a vote in the assembly on behalf of the general will or to stare down a potential tyrant who thinks it his calling to rule the state. Should the country go to war, he is ready to sacrifice his life for the republic which made his own life possible in the first place. He is also ready to sacrifice for that which makes his homeland unique: its people, history, culture, traditions. Bonds formed of blood, belonging, and borders move patriots. For Rousseau, Cato is a patriot, Socrates is not.

The patriot, sadly, is a rare and vanishing breed. It has been trampled under the onslaught of Enlightenment. On the accomplishments of his day, Rousseau observed with lament in the first *Discourse*: "National hatreds will die out, but so will love of country."[56]

Not surprisingly, then, Rousseau deplores the fate of modern European states. In *Poland*, he pinpoints one of the sources diluting the stock of each of its various tribes. The demise of nationally based education has enabled a hybrid identity to emerge: the European.

Rousseau's analysis? Identity no longer stems from difference. The continent suffers from a shortage of what is sui generis:

> A Frenchman, an Englishman, a Spaniard, an Italian, a Russian are all practically the same man.
>
> Today, no matter what people may say, there are no longer any Frenchmen, Germans, Spaniards, or even Englishmen; there are only Europeans. All have the same tastes, the same passions, the same manners, for no one has been shaped along national lines by peculiar institutions.[57]

Continentals behave in uniform fashion. Public discourse is monotonously similar. Social and political understandings are interchangeable. Rousseau identifies a psychological symptom of this deadening sameness. No matter where they find themselves "they [men] feel at home in any country."[58] Europeans are the same because they are enslaved by the pretentious concerns of the private and commercial worlds: pleasure, money, license, consumption, indulgence, intrigue.

According to Rousseau, without a political identity, the edge of nothingness approaches. Lack of a homeland to which one is intimately, intensely, irreducibly connected is a condition worse than death.[59] Rousseau draws attention to a modern irony: as the normative value of the individual rises, life correspondingly descends into narrow, suffocating dimensions.

La patrie is to be the agent of redemption and rescue the age from its deadly trajectory. Thus Rousseau individuates states and homogenizes citizens. Eliminate difference within the republic, foster and exaggerate it without. These twin projects presuppose and engender one another. The specter of the other, at home and abroad, is integral to the republican cause. A calculated xenophobia promotes unity. "Everything foreign to the constitution should be carefully banished from the body politic."[60] The territorial borders demarcating the homeland furnish an apt metaphor for identity politics. They are to be clearly drawn so that transgression, infiltration, or invasion can be detected early and easily. Should boundaries be crossed, rapid response and pursuit is employed to restore their integrity. An order ready to repulse assault from without is poised to resist challenge from within. And vice versa.

Rousseau links patriotism to national security.[61] Only a state with a strong patriotic tradition can withstand the diplomatic and military machinations of enemy states. So Rousseau counsels the Poles on the Russian threat. Conquest of territory does not necessarily amount to conquest of a people. Even if Polish borders were overrun, Poland could endure. If it is prepared. "The virtues of her citizens, their patriotic zeal, the particular way in which national institutions may be able to form their souls, this is the only rampart which will always stand ready to defend her."[62] Rousseau, recall, boasts that Poland can take its liberty with it on horseback as it flees any Russian advance.

Rousseau draws on an elaborate network of tribal mechanisms to instill patriotic fervor, mechanisms deemed frivolous or trivial in the modern age. Public games, festivals, rituals, spectacles, ceremonies are designed to produce appropriate sentiments:

> [L]et eulogy be given . . . to those virtuous citizens who have had the honor to suffer for the fatherland in the chains of the enemy. . . . [C]onstantly recall this great memory before the eyes of the public.[63]

Rousseau admires Lycurgus in part because of his masterful psychological stratagems through which the priorities of citizens were reordered: "He kept the fatherland constantly before their eyes in their laws, in their games, in their homes, in their loves, in their festivals; he never left them an instant for solitary relaxation."[64] The habitual performance of duty for duty's sake pales before the passionate love of country which fears no sacrifice and brooks no obstacle. Patriotism produces its own state of intoxication.[65] "Loving the fatherland, [citizens] will serve it zealously and with all their hearts."[66]

Why does Rousseau fervently celebrate la patrie? It plays a role in the life of a people which nothing else can duplicate. Could it not be supplanted by another mode of coordination? Not according to Rousseau. He presumes that a republic devoid of passion cannot last and there is no passion like patriotism, especially in a republic like Rousseau's where practices of citizenship are inert. "[P]assions are the principal instruments of our preservation. It is . . . as vain as it is ridiculous to want to destroy them."[67] What about interest or reason?

Rousseau scorns the resort to interest as a coordinating force in a well-ordered society.[68] Self-interest routinely avails itself of multiple courses of action, both productive and destructive to the republic. Insofar as interests are pursued instrumentally, the republic is always subordinate to them even if, at times, it might be given priority. Likewise, the notion of the common good is unlikely to energize the self-centered, save perhaps under some extraordinary circumstance.[69] It is too vague, abstract, remote, immaterial.

The force of reason is no better. It cannot generate the moral energy required for subjects to experience genuine attachment to the polity. Connection to and distance from the republic both seem equally respectable through its sterile optic. It may, for example, counsel a cosmopolitan or universal sensibility which emphasizes the rights of humanity at the expense of one's fellow citizens. Much like the Christian assessment of national loyalty, reason cannot understand the strong commitment to pencil marks drawn arbitrarily on the maps of the world which signify so much to the patriot. What matters cartographic correctness?

The dispositions attending love of country, which invigorate the life of la patrie, can also sap and destroy it. At times of crisis, for example, enemies both real and potential run rampant. Imaginary enemies, unfortunately, emerge as well. Reflect on what might happen to the dynamic of sovereignty given a national emergency. Law freely willed is designed to guarantee the freedom of the republic. It embodies the general will which makes citizens free. If citizens disagree on what constitutes the general will on a given matter, the majority prevails. Since the general will is constant, those in opposition to the majority are in error. What they "thought to be the general will was not." They must recognize the mistake and align themselves with the majority. Failing to do so on ordinary matters in mundane times, they will be forced to be free. Otherwise they become pariahs in the state. On vital matters, in tense times, they might well be forced to flee. The logic is frighteningly simple. In Rousseau's moral universe, if you oppose that which protects a free way of life, you are by definition unpatriotic.[70] You have sided with the forces of corruption, of evil, of the foreign, of death. You become the enemy within, no matter how sincere your opposition may be. In Poland, you might be identified with Russia; in Corsica, with France. In the republic of virtue patriotism demands, ultimately, unanimity and uniformity. This is its litmus test. These pressures, ordinarily at work in the republic, easily become exacerbated and exaggerated in times of storm and stress. Patriotism is incompatible with politics.

Patriotism invariably turns ugly. Hatreds often lie just beneath the surface of social and political life, called into action under appropriate circumstances. They are poised to erupt with proper provocation or pretext. Targets may vary from crisis to crisis, from generation to generation. Aside from specific actions which endanger, threaten, or actually injure, hatreds can stem from the sheer existence of people with a different set of moral, political, economic, or religious institutions and values.

The practice of patriotism, rooted in the dangerous, volatile disposition of love, cultivates and incites forces which can convert care and generosity into blind hatred, transform creative energies into destructive furies, reduce the plurality of norms and values to a single republican model of conformity, and ultimately unravel as well as bind the fabric of the polity. Patriotism, the force without which Rousseau's republic supposedly cannot be, simultaneously portends its demise. If patriotism sustains commual life, it can take it as well.

Now consider Rousseau's preference for Cato over Socrates. If public space were conceived as a site of settlement and opposition, consolidation and disruption, consensus and dissent, then forms of political action otherwise deemed problematic could contribute to the unity of the state. There are times when what any republic requires most is disobedience, whether or not it is initially condemned by a majority of citizens. Disobedience can bring to light injustices and injuries otherwise cloaked. It can also remind a republic of the principles it embodies but may have neglected or forgotten. By peremptorily categorizing as enemies some members of the community, the republic deprives itself of potentially valuable contributions. Socrates would not be long for Rousseau's republican world.

Civil Wars

Rousseau's republic of virtue composes myriad conflicts throughout the state. The calm facade characterizing Rousseauian social and political structures—whether national assemblies, familial relationships, friends gathering, or public festivals—conceals a perpetual storm of contending forces battling for hegemony. To Rousseau, some conflict can prove salutary. Borrowing a page from Machiavelli, he distinguishes between divisions that are beneficial to a republic from those which are harmful to it. The one contributes to solidarity, the other to corrosion. "If there were no different interests, the common interest, which would never encounter any obstacle, would scarcely be felt." Rousseau's stance is purely instrumental. Difference is tolerated as long as it proves itself contributive to a singular expression of the common good. Mastery and harmonization are sought: "Everything that destroys social unity is worthless."[71] By and large, however, Rousseau is wary of difference.

Rousseau perceives a dual threat from difference, whether it is the private will, the feminine, the Christian, the foreign.[72] First, the mere existence of an another form of life, an alternative perspective, or a contrapuntal understanding, is problematic to Rousseau's virtue politics. It is a reminder that doubt and disbelief live in some quarters, that the truth of things is in dispute. Thus difference may undermine the self-confidence of the general will. If some citizens are not persuaded by Rousseau's virtue politics, it might lead others to question their own conclusions. Though believing themselves to be living right, perhaps they are mistaken. With the demands Rousseauian virtue places on citizens, uncertainty is a plague which could spread if not checked immediately. Should it spread, the republic would surely die, we are led to believe.

Second, a differential politics might openly pursue courses of action which menace the established form of virtue. Hence Rousseau's fear of the theater. Ribald plays, for example, can seize the imagination and induce patrons to identify with scoundrels who mock morality. For Rousseau, to identify with someone is to become that person—if only briefly at first. Identification with a scoundrel, even for a moment, threatens to dissolve the virtuous identity Rousseau privileges.[73]

Here Rousseau's republic must proceed with caution. To counter the threat of difference, the republic may inadvertently expose the price at which its integrity is secured—a price, on reflection, some are not willing to pay or inflict. Difference, then, can trigger a chain reaction the outcome of which may be fatal to the republic. Preserving the singularity of Rousseau's virtue politics at the expense of some of its principles may be anathema to citizens. Would it then be capable of sustaining itself in its preferred form or of preserving fidelity to its duties? Perhaps this explains why the law needs the transcendental assistance of the civil religion.

In short, that which is different can be not only inimical but life-threatening. In Rousseau's republic, sites of "politics" resemble not so much the agon or playing field, but a mute battleground. The various arts of government employ whatever means are necessary to deal with difference.

> Indeed, it is only evildoers of all classes who prevent the citizen from being free. In a country where all such men were in galleys, the most perfect freedom would be enjoyed.[74]

Responsibility for political failure is assigned to malfaiteurs. The freedom of the state is perfect because to break the law you willed is also to will the punishment for breaking it. You owe your life in prison to yourself. You can thus be free while sitting in a cell. Apparently, filling the nation's prisons to capacity would not be a source of embarrassment or an indication of failure to Rousseau, but a sign of success, a source of civic pride. It enables an order to proudly display its holy word, libertas, on the face of its penal institutions and on convicts' chains.[75] Prisoners are neither out of sight nor quite out of mind. Difference is to be controlled, contained, coerced, crushed.

If, however, we are not designed to live a life in conformity with the dictates of a virtue politics, such a politics must be imposed. And that which is imposed not only encounters resistance, it engenders it. This is a formula for subjugation followed inevitably by violence, for resistance can be defeated but not destroyed regardless of the resources devoted to it. Even if difference can be stifled in one place, it always manifests itself elsewhere. At best difference can be displaced. That which is different recurs eternally, with the forces of extermination in hot, if futile, pursuit. Rousseau himself provides an example.

On Cruelty

The Social Contract chapter entitled "The Right of Life and Death" explores juridical relations in the state. As Rousseau considers the application of the death penalty to criminals, the preservation of the republic is his utmost concern. Despite the mention of murderers, the term "criminal" is elastic and left conveniently undefined by Rousseau. All lawbreakers so-called are collapsed into one. "Besides, *every* offender who *attacks* the social right becomes through *his* actions a *rebel* and *traitor* to his *homeland;* he *ceases to be* one of its members by violating its laws, and *he* even *wages war* against it."[76] Accompanied by rhetorical fanfare, here the relation of sovereign to subject has been militarized. With a violation of the laws, the community has entered a state of hostilities that it did not declare but to which it must respond. It constitutes an attack on the body politic. In Rousseau's account, the violator is an agent of insurrection who must be tried and convicted for his self-evidently treasonous crime. Even the republic is linguistically transformed—it receives the more intimate moniker of homeland:

> Then the State's preservation is incompatible with [the offender's], so one of the two must perish, and when the guilty man is put to death, it is less as a citizen than as an enemy.[77]

To what law does Rousseau refer in the above passage? Any law? Constitutional law alone? Or does Rousseau leave this insufficiently clear in the text such that the two begin to merge? Also, why the near hysteria? Can the polity suffer neither challenge to nor breach of its laws without going to the brink in self-defense? Rousseau insists that the social contract is a sacred right. Here its defense knows no apparent limitation.

The vituperative tone of the chapter jars the reader. Law, the product of convention, is always subject to revision or revocation. Thus it is subject to challenge. Rousseau's extraordinary treatment ups the ante for the citizen tempted to challenge or transgress its proper boundaries. Between compliance with the laws and death for disobedience there is apparently no space for public discord or protestation. The democratic sovereign seems to have taken on the cast of its monarchical forebears, procedural improvements aside. Rousseau apparently assumes that in a well-regulated republic, there will be little need of punishment because there are few instances of crime. Crime requires criminals and the latter are in critically short supply—though an order must never run out entirely. Offenses are thus uncommon. Because they are uncommon they become spectacular. To violate the law is to violate the sacred, delicately balanced civil order. To restore the balance, the punishment need fit the crime. The sovereign has spoken and "the voice of the people is in fact the voice of God."[78] These are the teeth behind the forced to be free formulation. The ultimate form of constraint is the coffin.

Later in the chapter, after rejecting the recourse to corporal forms of punishment as indicative of moral failure, Rousseau seems to qualify the will to execute virtue criminals when he insists that even the most wicked of people can be redeemed. "One only has the right to put to death, even as an example, someone who cannot be preserved without danger."[79] Rousseau's inflated, incendiary rhetoric, however, makes this codicil nonsensical, for the criminal has been converted into a public enemy no longer entitled to membership in the community of rights.[80] In wartime conditions, if need be, the enemy is to be terminated with extreme dispatch and prejudice. The state of war launched by the figure of the lawbreaker merely brings to the surface that which is waged quietly underneath. Whether war is open and hot or covert and cold, death is always nearby in Rousseau's republic of virtue.

Rousseau certainly seems comfortable, even pleased, with his penal prescriptions. Those opposed to the regime of virtue, perforce reduced to manifestations of evil, are left to rot in tranquility in the republic's jail cells. Does the indignant and unforgiving Rousseau of these pages square with the Rousseau who rails against slavery and domination, monarchy and degradation, aristocracy and arrogance? Does his virtue politics not reproduce, mutatis mutandis, what he denounces in his theoretical predecessors and opponents? At least in part?

The chapters of *The Social Contract* addressing the maintenance of sovereign authority, seldom attended to by Rousseau's readers, may help answer these questions.

According to Rousseau, the importance of the people assembled cannot be overestimated. Only it can enact laws which express the general will. For Rousseau, however, the prospect of any eighteenth-century European people assembling is frightening.[81] Do not let such a fire-breathing monster anywhere near the awesome powers of the sovereign. Nonetheless, even while lamenting the deplorable state of the contemporary world, Rousseau's ontological confidence shines through his historical pessimism. He remarks that "[t]he limits of the possible in moral matters are less narrow than we think." "Let us consider what can be done on the basis of what has been done." How can these apparently unRousseauian claims be understood? If a distinction is made between what is historically likely or probable and what is ontologically possible, Rousseau's assessment contextualizes the cruelty to which I alluded above. If corruption can be replaced by virtue, what stands in the way? Not divine punishment or curse. Not nature. Rather "[i]t is our weaknesses, our vices, our prejudices" that prevent the transformation that could cure what ails contemporary political arrangements. The attributive adjective "our" is critical here. According to Rousseau, responsibility for failure lies not with a self-defeating virtue politics, but with the ways of life of those who are supposed to implement it. We are capable of realizing the virtue Rousseau demands. By definition, if we fail to do so, it is our fault. We are selfish (weak), perverse (vice-ridden), ignorant (self-interested). Thus, even if Rousseau's republic of virtue seems fantastical, blame cannot be attributed to the scheme itself. If humankind has made itself relatively unfit for virtue, it is in no position to assail the expectations it cannot meet as a result of its own malfeasance. Self-destructiveness is no excuse. Nor is it to be rewarded by lowering standards.[82]

The Return of the Repressed

Rousseau's own assessment of the social compact puzzles. Granted, pride and pause, confidence and concern are compatible in an evaluation. Rousseau, however, redefines ambivalence. Even as he celebrates the birth of a new day dawning, *The Social Contract* is tormented by the presence of a tragedy which the text both reveals and unconsciously works to conceal:

> Although in this state he deprives himself of several advantages given him by nature, he gains such great ones, his faculties are exercised and developed, his ideas broadened, his feelings ennobled, and his whole soul elevated to such a point that if the abuses of this new condition did not often degrade him beneath the condition he left, he ought ceaselessly to bless the happy moment that tore him away from it forever.[83]

But Rousseau is unable eternally to bless the happy moment. The text imparts a disturbing secret. Through the miracle of the contract, simultaneously humankind finds itself elevated to incomparable heights and reduced to equally unspeakable depths. The latter actually results in human being finding itself beneath the condition it left: a state of war.[84]

The charge is stunning. What could possibly be worse than a state of war, let alone surpass its vitiation? Rousseau's intimations are disturbing; they are also opaque. He hints at phenomena not intermittent but unexpectedly routine, at phenomena not singular or unique but multiple and commonplace. Perhaps the passage refers to the newfound capacities for controlled violence available to the state, which dwarf the sum of individual efforts at the exercise of force? Perhaps it refers to the technological innovations Europe generates which unleash untold destructive capability in warfare? With the state and science combined, conflict even in the chaos of the later stages of nature might seem amateurish, even tame, by comparison. When the competition among imperial states is added, the world seems on the brink of self-annihilation. Perhaps it refers to the new condition of subjects in the civil state? Security and vulnerability are flip sides of the same coin. Despite the freedom from personal dependence, subjects must now interiorize essentially political conflicts and police themselves accordingly. They are thus exposed in ways they could not imagine in the state of nature. In certain respects, the new order of things embodies perfectibility gone perverse.

Rousseau, I believe, could have cited any of these possibilities to provide clues to the interpretation of this troubling passage. He did not.[85]

And so another reading comes to mind, one that complicates the relative sense of satisfaction Rousseau's assessment of the civil state recommends. What if the introduction of the contract produces its own virulent forms of disorder? What if opposition and discord have been thoroughly institutionalized by the republic's success? Moreover, if Rousseau misunderstands the origins of the resistance he deplores, the resources devoted to removing it will continually escalate in scope and severity. To eliminate the ineliminable is to court moral and political disaster. This is a debasement of which Rousseau does not speak.

A tragic conception of politics lurks here, but a bookkeeping trick—which deftly changes the subject—seals possible textual irruption. In the paragraph following the one just quoted from *The Social Contract*, Rousseau calculates roughly what is gained and what is lost through the advent of the social compact. He compares the civil state with the state of nature which preceded it. Hardly a fair comparison. Who would dispute the benefits of transcending a condition the continuation of which, according to Rousseau, would bring only death to the human race? In any case, potentially unanswerable questions about the new social condition have been effaced. A space of ambiguity in the text has been obscured.

Perhaps tragedy can be refined in Rousseau's republic. Consider the cruelty of which the general will, at its best, is capable. Remember that the general will treats all citizens equally. That is, it benefits and burdens, favors and obligates identically. No citizen has to do what other citizens do not. It makes no exceptions. This ethic preserves the freedom of the republic and prevents politics from becoming an instrument of domination. It is laudable in intent. In chapter two, we considered a set term of mandatory service in the militia as meeting the stringent requirements of the general will. All citizens benefit from national security. All contribute to it.

What of the conscientious objector (just one of the innumerable deviants the specialty and responsibility of Rousseau's republic of virtue)? How would the general will treat a citizen who refused his turn in the militia? If he were granted an exception, the generality of law would be lost. The conscientious objector would benefit from life in the state without contributing his full share to its operations, the parasitism Rousseau fears could ruin the republic. Alternative service could be an option. What if the objector played a secondary or supportive role behind the lines, so to speak? File clerk. Corpsman. Then he would meet the service requirement for all citizens even if the specific form it took differed. The military cannot work without many cogs. Would not that be permissible?

But what if the conscientious objector refused all service, arguing that to play a supportive role helps make possible the violence and slaughter he opposes? What is the law to do now in the face of total refusal? A citizen has broken it willingly and rejected other service options. Rousseau remarks that it is only malefactors who prevent the citizen from being free and that they should be locked up accordingly. One definition of malefactor is lawbreaker. The conscientious objector has indeed broken the law—in a most public way. He has refused to protect the republic which protects him and makes his refusal possible. The dictates of the state, the principles of the republic, require that he be sent to prison. If he were locked away, according to Rousseau, the general will would be true to its egalitarian ethos, and freedom would then be perfected. But is someone of deep moral conviction, who in other ways is an exemplary citizen, a person the republic can lock up and still consider itself just? The punishment would be legal, of course. It would probably be severe as well. States take their security seriously. For Rousseau, the conscientious objector is the equivalent of a traitor. Would punishment be cruel? It would seem to be. The state would be requiring of the citizen something he cannot give without doing grave violence to himself and then punishing him for his convictions, for his inability to comply. Moreover, what would be the consequences of locking up such a man? What kind of example would that set?[86]

To complicate matters, what if a citizen, deeming it unjust or unnecessary, actively opposes a war the republic finds itself waging? What if he is convinced—and convincing others—that it will guarantee not the republic's destiny but its destruction? What if he insists that it violates the principles in which the republic professes to believe? What if the citizen finds enough support to damage but not defeat the war effort? What is Rousseau's republic to do here if it cannot persuade the citizen that he is mistaken? Even if it could afford leniency with the conscientious objector, what about such political opposition? Rousseau's position is clear: "the citizen is no longer the judge of the risk to which the law wills he be exposed." Given the safety that the state provides, the life of the citizen becomes "a conditional gift of the State."[87]

Here Nietzsche's ethic of enmity challenges Rousseau's republic of virtue. In calling for the spiritualization of hate where conflict and struggle are endemic, Nietzsche articulates a mode of engagement that not only eschews the destruction of enemies, it requires an appreciation of their profound value, their necessity. Prudence and forbearance toward enemies is thus stressed. As Schmitt points out, a political opponent, including an enemy, need not be deemed morally (or otherwise) evil.[88] Not the citizen who contests the fundamental laws of the republic. Not the citizen who challenges the fundamental decisions it renders. What might this mean for Rousseau?[89]

Given Rousseau's claim that reciprocity and respect are integral to citizenship, a Nietzschean spiritualization of enmity resonates with the more protean elements of his thought. If the republic of virtue were more generous toward its enemies, it might discover that it did not have as many as it once suspected. Generosity might then spread in the republic where it was once anathema to even consider it. Citizens who disturb and defy the republic can love it as much as those who observe and obey it. To the citizen who resists the war, for example, Rousseau's republic might owe a profound debt. If the cause of the republic is just, other citizens will come to its defense, and soon enough opposition that once inflamed "loyalists" can be taken in stride as the requirements of communal living turn out to be looser than assumed. If the cause be unjust, other citizens may also resist, and the republic might be spared a disaster it would otherwise have suffered. If the republic remains adamant and the citizen refuses to yield and is willing to face the consequences, surely he has met the criterion of Rousseauian citizenship? He, too, is willing to give his life for the republic, if need be. The gift may be somewhat unconventional, but it is thoughtful, generous, dauntless. Because the state has threatened his life, because he risks everything in his refusal, the state should itself refuse—not just decline—to take his life. Perhaps it ought not to sanction him at all. While a fête at public expense may be excessive, the republic can respect his integrity, even think of him as exemplary in his way.

What, then, of the fate of Rousseau's virtuous republic? Ironically, if the republic were not so invested in its own love (and thus hate), love of the republic might be enhanced. Acts of generosity can work to strengthen the commitment of citizens as they are accorded the regard they have come to expect. Citizens may well applaud rather than resent an ethic of forbearance, recognizing the fortitude and restraint it demands. It is anything but a sign of weakness. They may also realize, secondarily, that in other circumstances they (or someone they know or love) might enjoy similar treatment. Citizens may not applaud it, of course; some may condemn it. But if a republic can embrace tragic conflicts, it might afford itself one of the noblest practices and experiences of liberty, and contribute to the kind of fragile unity that can endure—because it requires constant crafting.

Perhaps, as Rousseau's republic is pushed by those who disquiet and disrupt it, it might find itself moving on its own toward accommodation with once and future enemies. In the meantime, Rousseau might still prefer to deny or evade cruelties lodged amidst the abundant successes of his exquisitely ruled republic. In the *Geneva Manuscript*, he envisions the culmination of political life as follows:

that [the citizen] will become good, virtuous, sensitive, and finally—
to sum it all up—rather than the ferocious brigand he wished to
become, the most solid support of a well-ordered society.[90]

Should Rousseau be allowed the last interpretive word? Paul de
Man insists *The Social Contract* cannot be read without feeling the
exhilaration of a firm promise of grand things to come, a promise
nourished by a presumption of resolution which allows Rousseau to
dispense with having to show (redundantly) that what he deems politically and morally necessary is also possible. De Man may be right
when he claims that *The Social Contract* "persists in performing
what it has shown to be impossible."[91] But what if Rousseau's
democratic republic promises nothing but tragedy through the introduction of a politics of virtue and enmity? It would then actually
deliver what it promises, while obscuring the result.

NOTES

Preface

1. Nietzsche writes: "The Greeks, thanks to their moralistic super-ficiality, misunderstood [the tragic]. Even resignation is *not* a lesson of trag-edy, but a misunderstanding of it." *Will to Power*, trans. Walter Kaufmann and R. J. Hollingdale (New York: Vintage Books, 1968), #1029, 532–33.

1. On Tragedy

1. Paul de Man, *Blindness and Insight* (Minneapolis: University of Min-nesota Press, 1983), 112–13. No doubt this approach has been facilitated by Rousseau's confessional writings.

2. The interpretive reversal is true of critics apparently well-disposed to Rousseau. De Man cites Jean Starobinski. Judith Shklar could be mentioned as well. See *Men and Citizens* (Cambridge: Cambridge University Press, 1985), 2, where she writes: "In Rousseau's case utopia was a perfect way to express ideas that were dictated by personal imagination and by a profound need for self-revelation and self-vindication."

3. By reducing them to contradictions, for example. Consider the fine study of Rousseau by Arthur Melzer, *The Natural Goodness of Man* (Chicago: University of Chicago Press, 1990), 3–4: "And indeed, we seem to find no fewer than four major contradictions in his works. . . . In general, it seems to me that to be judged successful, a statement of Rousseau's system must be able to resolve [these] contradictions."

4. Governed by similar concerns Heidegger, in *What Is Called Thinking* (New York: Harper and Row, 1968), 76–77, offers general interpretive advice.

He recommends encountering (as opposed to running counter to) a thinker and thinking the unthought contained in his or her works. What might it mean to think the unthought? Here a number of possibilities arise. To articulate that which is dangerous and therefore repressed because it jeopardizes sacrosanct values or prized accomplishments. To excavate what is presupposed but has been subsequently forgotten or denied because of its suspected ramifications. To explore an alternative which cannot be seen or emerge fully amidst a range of possible alternatives which obscure it. To formulate that which is not thinkable with the resources provided by the dominant terms of discourse. Tragedy is Rousseau's unthought.

5. Jean-Jacques Rousseau, *The First and Second Discourses*, trans. Roger D. and Judith R. Masters (New York: St. Martin's Press, 1964), 92. The reference here is to the second *Discourse* (hereafter SD).

6. Consider the following aphorism from Nietzsche: "*Limits of our hearing.*—One hears only those questions for which one is able to find answers." Friedrich Nietzsche, *The Gay Science*, trans. Walter Kaufmann (New York: Vintage, 1974), #196, 206 (hereafter *GS*).

7. "Terribleness is part of greatness: let us not deceive ourselves," Nietzsche counsels. Friedrich Nietzsche, *The Will to Power*, trans. Walter Kaufmann and R. J. Hollingdale (New York: Vintage Books, 1968), #1028, 531 (hereafter WP).

8. GS, #304, 244.

9. In *The Genealogy of Morals*, Nietzsche considers more explicitly the costs and consequences of moral and political "doing" and struggle. He posits a law of life, if you will: creation presupposes destruction, demands it even. "It may occur to some reader to ask me, 'Are you constructing an ideal or destroying one?' I would ask him, in turn, whether he ever reflected upon the price that had to be paid for the introduction of every new ideal on earth? . . . [T]he raising of an altar requires the breaking of an altar." Here Nietzsche offers a reminder that moral and political ideals frown upon competition or challenge. Truth rarely brooks dissent. Ordinarily resistance signals only that the work of truth is not yet complete. Pretenders to the throne, then, face a bloody road if they are to prevail. With Machiavellian calm Nietzsche anticipates the inescapable place of conflict and struggle, violence and tragedy in politics. Friedrich Nietzsche, *The Birth of Tragedy and The Genealogy of Morals*, trans. Francis Golffing (New York: Anchor Books, 1956), 228. The quote is from *Genealogy* (henceforth TGM).

10. WP, #40, 25.

11. This "epistemic" issue is a source of dispute between de Man and Derrida. Consider what the latter says on the issue of progress in Rousseau: "He *would like to say* that progress, however ambivalent, occurs *either* toward the worse, *or* toward the better, either for better or for worse. . . . But Rousseau *describes what he does not wish to say:* that 'progress' takes place *both* for the worse *and* for the better. At the same time." Jacques Derrida, *Of Grammatology*, trans. Gayatri Chakravorty Spivak (Baltimore: Johns Hopkins University Press, 1976), 229, emphasis in original. I am sympathetic to Derrida, though I resist his argument that Rousseau's own doctrine provides the

best evidence against it and that he "chose" to remain blind to such knowledge. In my view, he could not see what I call the tragic because the ontological parameters operative in his texts prevent it.

12. Jean-Jacques Rousseau, *On the Social Contract*, trans. Judith R. Masters (New York: St. Martin's Press, 1978), 64 (hereafter SC). This text also contains the *Geneva Manuscript* (hereafter GM).

13. An account of failure need not be restricted to so-called utopian enterprises. For every Plato there is an Aristotle, for every Rousseau a Hobbes, for every Hegel a Marx. Hobbes, for example, writes of the prospects for his Leviathan: "And now, considering how different this Doctrine is, from the practise of the greatest parts of the world, especially of these western parts . . . and how much depth of Morall Philosophy is required . . . I am at the point of believing this my labour, as uselesse, as the Common-wealth of Plato." Thomas Hobbes, *Leviathan* (New York: Penguin, 1968), 407.

14. This is Judith Shklar's reading of Rousseau. See *Men and Citizens*, vii, e.g.

15. SC, 103–4.

16. SD, 110.

17. When Rousseau writes in the opening of *The Social Contract* that he takes men as they are and laws as they might be, I take this to be an ontological claim of promise more than a grim historical assessment: it points to the vast potentiality of human being emphasized in part one of the second *Discourse*.

18. Tragedy is an elusive notion. It is a term tossed about loosely, meaning many things to many people. What is it that makes something tragic? Many terrible things happen routinely, but not all of them are tragic. What separates one class from the other? More often than not, the tragic is thought to be singular, rare, an aspect of life, thankfully, that need not be confronted regularly by anyone. Tragedy, it is held, can be accommodated because it is unique. Its place in the order of things thus shifts from center to margin, however grudgingly. Tragedy, it would seem, can and must be kept in perspective.

19. In *Geneva Manuscript*, 162, and *Considerations on the Government of Poland*, 217, respectively, Rousseau speaks of "attempt[ing] to draw from the ill itself the remedy that should cure it," and of "extreme evils which call for violent remedies, and which we must try to cure at any price." Starobinski notes the ambivalence in Rousseau's political interventions, but Rousseau's hesitancy is historical, not ontological. It has to do with current capability not permanent possibility. Perhaps it is this presumption to which Starobinski, Rousseau's greatest critic, succumbs in his essay "The Antidote in the Poison." He writes: "Although Rousseau blames human history for having developed the alienating faculties of reflection, amour-propre, abstraction, imagination, and intellectual dependence, he expressly warns against any attempt to turn back the clock. The development that has made us unhappy must be carried even further: reflection must be perfected, amour-propre put to work, the imagination channeled. Alienation must be made reciprocal and complete. This is our only chance of rediscovering in a new (political and moral) form our original (natural and animal) wholeness." It seems to me that

Starobinski has left unchallenged the ontological dimension of Rousseau's thought. The claim I make is that refinement of conventions cannot cure the "evils" of conventionalization. Or, the remedy is not to be found in the ill—it is the ill. Jean Starobinski, *Blessings in Disguise; or, The Morality of Evil*, trans. Arthur Goldhammer (Cambridge: Harvard University Press, 1993), 118–29. *Poland* is contained in Jean-Jacques Rousseau, *Political Writings*, trans. Frederick Watkins (Madison: University of Wisconsin Press, 1986).

20. Keith Ansell-Pearson, in *Nietzsche Contra Rousseau* (Cambridge: Cambridge University Press, 1991), 6, also seems to overlook the ontological. "Nietzsche is well aware of the tragic ambiguity which characterizes Rousseau's meditations on history. Historical existence is necessarily tragic because there can be no *final* redemption for humanity in its rage against time, as it is the law of life that everything will die and perish." I would argue that there can be no prior redemption which then dissolves with death.

21. SD, 157, 173, 175.

22. "What dawns on philosophers last of all: they must no longer accept concepts as a gift. . . . Heretofore one has generally trusted one's concepts as if they were a wonderful dowry from some sort of wonderland. . . . This piety toward what we find in us is perhaps part of the moral element in knowledge. What is needed above all is an absolute skepticism toward all inherited concepts." Nietzsche, WP, #409, 220–21.

23. SC, 131.

24. GM, 162.

25. Jean-Jacques Rousseau, *Emile*, trans. Allan Bloom (New York: Basic Books, 1979), 277 (hereafter E). Rousseau also pursues such fundamental questions in *Reveries of the Solitary Walker*, trans. Peter France (New York: Penguin Books, 1979), third promenade, where he identifies the reflections of the Savoyard Vicar as "more or less" his own (55). While the two should not be identified, neither can they be divorced. It seems that Rousseau doubts the truth he wishes the Vicar to hold without doubt. But the Vicar has doubts too. For an alternative account, see Mary Nichols, "Rousseau's Novel Education in the *Emile*," *Political Theory* 13, no. 4 (November 1985), 535–58.

26. Ibid. The Vicar also writes (268): "The only thing we do not know is how to be ignorant of what we cannot know. We would rather decide at random and believe what is not than admit that none of us can see what is. We are a small part of a great whole whose limits escape us and whose Author delivers us to our mad disputes; but we are vain enough to want to decide what this whole is in itself and what we are in relation to it." Ironically, while the Vicar exposes this human practice he also seems to be one more instance of it. Does his assertion merely provide better cover for his own position?

27. Famously Rousseau opens the first book of *Emile* with a sweeping accusation, the scope and severity of which may eclipse the significance of the ontological thesis preceding it: "Everything is good as it leaves the hands of the Author of things; everything degenerates in the hands of man." Rather than treat the assertion as simply providing grounds for condemnation or complaint, Rousseau announces the created character of the universe, one

made of sound, solid material. The historical cannot negate the ontological. The world is pregnant with possibility. E, 37.

28. The presumption manifests itself in the language Rousseau deploys. He speaks of "the fundamental problem which is solved by the social compact," an agreement which is made "without reservation." He claims to ground his reflections in "men as they are and laws as they might be." He refers to legislation reaching "its highest possible point of perfection" and the union of the state being "as perfect as it can be." He conceives of the legislator as "giving" those laws to a people which best fit them. He speaks of the "discovery" of the best rules of society, and he maintains that there is no "true" renunciation or loss involved in the transition from nature to politics. He insists that the art of politics, aping God's creative powers, can prolong the life of the state "as far as possible" with only some unforeseen accident threatening its premature demise. Vocabulary betrays ontology. The need for metaphysical comfort may now be so deeply embedded in languages, institutions, philosophies, and bodies that it defies discernment. It is implicitly installed in the established terms of discourse more than it is explicitly argued against a robust set of challenges to it. SC, 53, 68, 67, 64, 75, 99.

29. *Leviathan*, 363.

30. SC, 53.

31. See SD, 104, 140, 168, and SC, 56. As William E. Connolly astutely observes, *Political Theory and Modernity* (Oxford: Basil Blackwell, 1988), 58, Rousseau's "metaphors suggest it without insisting upon it."

32. SD, 104.

33. E, 281.

34. Ibid., 268–69.

35. SC, 53. Regrettably, they are not accepted and recognized by everyone.

36. SC, 53; GM, 168.

37. WP, #583, 314. The war Nietzsche proposes is an ethical one. He opposes that which enables this and that (theoretical) crusade. He thus declares war on war.

38. Michel Foucault, "The Order of Discourse," trans. Ian McLeod, in *Untying the Text*, ed. Robert Young (Boston: Routledge and Kegan Paul, 1981), 65. Treating political thought in this fashion has its share of critics. Does ontological critique pursue outmoded ways of thinking and thereby entangle itself in a realm it wishes to leave behind? By concentrating on "antiquated" religious questions does it not short shrift more fundamental questions of race, class, and gender? Perhaps. But this supposes that religious wars are over, a supposition I do not share. God lives, infecting social and political discourse. The spirit of fundamentalism thrives in secular culture. Theory may don secular garb, but appearances can deceive. If the demands driving fundementalist discourses are susceptible to rejection if articulated publicly, they can survive only if smuggled into a theory to lead a closeted life. Subterfuge as a last resort. Exposure, then, may be the precursor to dissolution.

Besides, ontological critique does not exhaust the theoretical enterprise, nor does it claim to do so. It does suspect that theories contain a repository of violences passed on largely unnoticed through generations of thought because they are encrusted in common languages. It thus assumes certain continuities in the multifarious orders of thought that traverse the histories of the west.

39. SC, 64.

40. An "Hobbesian" monarchical commonwealth of rationally self-interested actors, which is likely to mimic the state of war it prevents; or a representative democracy where elected officials by definition traffic in the public freedom while working for the good of the people, for example.

41. Of course, other kinds of politics do this too.

42. Here I am indebted to William E. Connolly, *Identity\Difference* (Ithaca: Cornell University Press, 1991), 64–69.

43. SC, 69.

44. Agonistic respect may implicitly underestimate the intransigence of moral and political conflicts. Bonnie Honig's generous reading of the impulse in virtue theories to seek an end to politics as contest ("the desire to decide crucial undecidabilities for the sake of human goods that thrive most vigorously in stable, predictable settings") may be an ingenious way to invite them to rethink their self-conceptions and ultimately moderate some of their foundational insistences. Might they take the bait, so to speak, and try to live up to the redescription Honig offers them? The permanent political conflict she affirms may thus require proponents of virtue to concede precisely what their identity and survival as they understand them require them to deny: that the truth is not one and it cannot prevail. Bonnie Honig, *Political Theory and the Displacement of Politics* (Ithaca: Cornell University Press, 1993), 201 (henceforth PTDP).

45. See William E. Connolly, *The Ethos of Pluralization* (Minneapolis: University of Minnesota Press, 1995), 29, 104, for example. Even if such a strategy does backfire, one way to proceed, as Connolly himself points out, would be to try again. The cultivation of agonistic respect is a long-term project requiring much patience and discipline.

46. Thus Chantal Mouffe's counsel that opponents consider themselves adversaries rather than enemies is likely to seem unpersuasive to a fundamentalist. Chantal Mouffe, *The Return of the Political* (London: Verso, 1993), 4 (henceforth RP).

47. WP, #55, 35.

48. Cf. Honig, PTDP, 3–15.

49. Mouffe's insistence that "those who do not accept the democratic 'rules of the game'" are rightly excluded from the political community may not provide as much assistance as first appears. Fundamentalists in the United States, for example, routinely, sincerely espouse fealty to basic democratic principles. Readily they work within established institutions and time-honored practices. Yet they pursue, with success, moral and political agendas that are repressive and undemocratic. Can it be said that they accept the rules of the game? The placement of preconditions on political participation, while laudable, may prove ineffective. RP, 4, 129, 132, for example.

50. TGM, 208.

51. Law can also be used as a "weapon against struggle" among contending forces and factions. Law that is general—as in Rousseau's republic—tends to curtail or eliminate contest. How does this work? Recall Rousseau's description of the legislative enterprise. The first to propose a law does so confident that others are ready to endorse it (allegedly because its need has been universally seen and felt). Once passed, politics is concluded since the matter is resolved. Rousseau, of course, warns citizens of the temptation to think that once a set of fundamental laws has been passed their work is over and done with, that they need not concern themselves with politics again. Yet Rousseau's vision of politics may succumb to another version of this enticement. On each matter before the sovereign, the people can be content that its work is complete, total, decisive, conclusive, definitive. It can rest assured that the contingency of the political has been tamed. Rousseau thus overestimates what law can accomplish by underestimating the obstacles it must overcome and the damage it does as it is secured.

52. If no political community could withstand such regular self-scrutinization, laws could be reviewed on a selective basis. The greater the majority, the greater the need for review since the injuries attending a law backed by a powerful consensus are more likely to be hidden from view or ignored. Laws passed by narrow margins would not need this kind of guarantee. They are likely to be revisited as a matter of course.

2. On Nature

1. Thanks are due to Bonnie Honig to whom I am indebted for the musical metaphor. Later in the chapter, she pushed me to think more deeply about the nostalgia problematic.

2. Rousseau's indignation should be a clue, for the venom and vitriol he expresses are ultimately incompatible with a thoroughly tragic sensibility. To have an appreciation for tragedy is to have a heightened appreciation for the intransigence of limits and liabilities. Such an appreciation in turn disables the formation of irredeemable moral and political expectations the frustration of which can lead to considerable rancor.

3. Jean-Jacques Rousseau, *The First and Second Discourses*, trans. Roger D. and Judith R. Masters (New York: St. Martin's Press, 1964), 137–38. The quote is from the second *Discourse* (hereafter SD). The first *Discourse* is henceforth FD.

4. FD, 46–47.

5. SD, 107, 117.

6. Ibid., 105.

7. Ibid.

8. Ibid., 117.

9. Rousseau's reference to the statue of Glaucus illustrates this possibility. Rousseau writes that human being as nature formed it has "changed its *appearance* to the point of being *nearly* unrecognizable." Similarly, he speaks of the difficulty of separating "what is original from what is artificial in the

present nature of man." SD, 91, 92–93, emphasis added. Starobinski observes that while Rousseau may formally question the status of the state of nature, there is no doubt that he comes to believe in its historical certainty. Jean Starobinski, *Jean-Jacques Rousseau: Transparency and Obstruction*, trans. Arthur Goldhammer (Chicago: University of Chicago Press, 1988), 14–15 (henceforth JJR).

10. FD, 53–54.

11. Starobinski explores this theme without parallel. See his *JJR*, 15–23.

12. Though Rousseau is decidedly ambiguous about the reality of his state of nature, whether or not it actually existed is ultimately undecidable, perhaps irrelevant. For Rousseau even a fiction can be true.

13. SD, 104.

14. Ibid., 137. Appeal to a primordial past seems insulated from the ravages of critique. First, even if full possession is ruled out in advance, the joys of wanting may be intensified by denial of its realization. Second, no memory entices like the one that selectively, unconsciously forgets, making it simpler to equate earlier with superior, different with better. There is great insistence in nostalgia which makes puncturing its mystique problematic.

15. Ibid., 129. Cf. 150–51, where Rousseau makes a nearly identical claim for a much later period in history.

16. Ibid., 140.

17. *Rousseau's Political Writings*, ed. Alan Ritter and Julia Conaway Bondanella (New York: Norton, 1988), 191–92, emphasis added.

18. Rousseau claims misery would result as well. Just as the savage would be an alien in civil society, so civil man could never live in the state of nature. "What reflection teaches us on this subject, observation confirms perfectly: savage man and civilized man differ so much in the bottom of their hearts and inclinations that what constitutes the supreme happiness of one would reduce the other to despair." It seems that Rousseau does not appreciate the upshot of his own *Discourse* since neither, strictly speaking, can exist in, let alone experience, the world of the other. SD, 178–79.

19. SD, 201.

20. Ibid., 158–59.

21. Ibid., 102.

22. Ibid., 177.

23. Ibid., 80: "Once people are accustomed to masters, they are no longer able to do without them. If they try to shake off the yoke, they move all the farther away from freedom because . . . their revolutions almost always deliver them to seducers who only make their chains heavier."

24. For Starobinski, only solitude remains available to Rousseau. "The Discourse on Inequality," in *JJR*, 303.

25. SD, 151.

26. Here I would like to cite Wendy Brown's "Wounded Attachments," in *States of Injury* (Princeton: Princeton University Press, 1995), 52–76.

27. While the third movement finds its inspiration in Rousseau's discussion of passion and law, Rousseau himself cannot be considered the author of this movement.

28. Though this is how Rousseau understood it. William E. Connolly presents Rousseau's argument in this way in *Political Theory and Modernity* (Oxford: Basil Blackwell, 1988), 47–53 (henceforth PTM).

29. SD, 134, 173.

30. Ibid., 134.

31. Ibid., emphasis added.

32. Ibid.

33. Ibid., 137.

34. A tragic sensibility involves more than assessing the ambiguity of an achievement. Rousseau remarks in a footnote to the *Discourse* that even in the best of contemporary orders there "always arise more real calamities than apparent advantages." It might be assumed, therefore, that the task of politics is to augment what is admirable to the utmost and deplete what is deplorable to the proverbial vanishing point. Indeed Rousseau mentions in the same footnote that wise governors "will know how to prevent, cure, or palliate that multitude of abuses and evils always ready to crush us."

The tragic is more intractable than juggling a balance sheet. In *any* polity, that which is indispensable is simultaneously pernicious. The relevant equation is not either/or. It is both/and. Phrased discursively: the project of peace facilitates war; the will to morality itself is immoral; the pursuit of justice promotes its own injustices; the cause of equality generates new inequalities; the demand for virtue engenders the proliferation of vice; the quest for identity and inclusion fosters difference and exclusion. Ironically, the legitimate republic produces the opposite of what it celebrates in the course of the effort to secure it. Ultimately, a world minus these material features cannot be conceived. And so I understand the question of limits differently than does Rousseau and challenge what he deems to be, in theory, possible.

35. Rousseau's verb choices in the passage cited are revealing: to spread and multiply.

36. Jean-Jacques Rousseau, *On the Social Contract with Geneva Manuscript and Political Economy*, trans. Judith R. Masters (New York: St. Martin's Press, 1978), 63, 66. The quotes are from *The Social Contract*.

37. Jean Starobinski, "The Political Thought of Jean-Jacques Rousseau," 223–24, in *Rousseau's Political Writings*.

38. Cf. Connolly, *PTM*, 53, 57, who allows Rousseau to retain key conclusions I want to take away. Connolly writes: "Rousseau, I think, responds to these issues by pointing to a *possible* world in which human reason and freedom are perfected and degeneration does not occur. If the fall can in principle be avoided . . ."

39. Starobinski, "The Political Thought of Jean-Jacques Rousseau," 224.

40. If Rousseau is trying to rewrite Genesis, he seems to have misread it. For believers, paradise lost is catastrophic. No matter the possibilities for life afterward, the post-Paradise world pales by comparison. Paradise names that which is unique: without like or equal. The loss of the state of nature, however, need not be lamented at all. Who would miss, let alone want to return to, a condition that was not even recognizably human? Even if it were possible to return, Rousseau would reject it. Thus it is difficult, pace Starobinski and

Connolly, to read the text—as opposed to Rousseau's intentions—in this way. No paradise was lost here.

41. SD, 142–43. For Rousseau, it should be noted, these "harsh" conditions produce positive effects: "a robust and almost unalterable constitution." On Rousseau's evolutionary account, difficult aspects of nature contribute to a process of development and in the process lose their problematic character. For Rousseau what is "harsh" is good. Period. Accordingly, as the human animal becomes accustomed to the training nature provides, a kind of tough love, human and world become one. This is as it should be. Is there a telos at work here?

42. Ibid., 121, 128, 135, 219.

43. Joel Schwartz, in *The Sexual Politics of Jean-Jacques Rousseau* (Chicago: University of Chicago Press, 1984), 16–22, offers an alternative reading of Rousseau's understanding of "sexuality in the state of nature," arguing that Rousseau "does not suggest that there might be cases of rape in the state of nature." Schwartz's presentation nevertheless belies both the intent he assigns to Rousseau as well as the upshot of his own argument. First, the politics of the state of nature seems to drive the (insistent) depiction of it. In Schwartz's words: "If the state of nature is to be peaceful, the character of sexuality there must be such as not to occasion conflict." Second, one of the passages from the second *Discourse* critical to Schwartz's interpretation can be read differently—and to subversive effect. Here is the quote Schwartz selects: "men must feel the ardors of their temperament less frequently and less vividly . . . Everyone peaceably waits for the impulsion of nature, yields to it without choice with more pleasure than frenzy: and the need satisfied, all desire is extinguished." Schwartz claims "there is peace between men and women because their sexual unions result from mutual desires." Perhaps, but desire is not always mutual. Then, even if the wait is "peaceable" (the scare quotes are Schwartz's), the moment of impulsion is not necessarily peaceful, as Rousseau's description suggests. Choice is absent, frenzy is not. And if pleasure becomes associated with that very same frenzy? Rousseau concludes: once "the need [is] satisfied, all desire is extinguished." A curious verb choice indeed. Fires are extinguished; weak desires fade or dissipate. Schwartz himself seems to backslide when he writes that Rousseau's delineation of desire "allows him to deny *or at any rate to minimize* the extent to which *sexual disputes* would cause *outbreaks of violence* in the state of nature" (emphasis mine).

44. SD, 142: "But difficulties *soon* arose . . ." (emphasis mine).

3. On Founding

1. *The Republic of Plato*, trans. Allan Bloom (New York: Basic Books, 1968), 369a, 472a, 427b, 458a.

2. Thomas Hobbes, *Leviathan* (New York: Penguin, 1968), 81–82.

3. John Rawls, *A Theory of Justice* (Cambridge: Harvard University Press, 1971).

4. Jean-Jacques Rousseau, *On the Social Contract with Geneva Manuscript and Political Economy*, trans. by Judith R. Masters (New York: St. Martin's Press, 1978). The quote is from *The Social Contract*, 53 (hereafter SC). The other two texts will be referred to as GM and PE.

5. See Jean-Jacques Rousseau, *The First and Second Discourses*, trans. by Roger D. and Judith R. Masters (New York: St. Martin's Press, 1964), 162-63 (which are from the second *Discourse*), where Rousseau salutes Lycurgus for attending to structural deficiencies and razing the old constitution before building a new one.

6. Republic, 546a.

7. SC, 98-99.

8. Ibid., 100.

9. Ibid., 52.

10. Ibid.

11. This is the appropriate word for Rousseau.

12. The death throes of the state of nature threaten humankind with extinction. The imperatives of self-preservation fasten the attention of those implicated onto their own immediate interests. The threat of mutual annihilation compresses the time available for action. Loftier considerations are disqualified in advance, for the world hovers on the brink of self-annihilation. Neither the formation of an authentic republic nor law-abiding citizens— admittedly problematic projects under auspicious circumstances—are in the offing.

13. Ibid., 69. A similar paradox haunts the reformation of an already existing civil society afflicted with corruption.

14. Rousseau's expectations of the Legislator vary. Does he hesitate on the timing of the Legislator's intervention, as F. M. Barnard suggests? Or are there two distinct Legislators present in Rousseau's work, one who founds a people and a second who provides a people already founded with the laws it needs, as Hilail Gildin would have it? See F. M. Barnard, *Self-Direction and Political Legitimacy: Rousseau and Herder* (Oxford: Oxford University Press, 1988) and Hilail Gildin, *Rousseau's "Social Contract"* (Chicago: University of Chicago Press, 1983).

Perhaps the (apparent) discrepancy can be resolved by examining what the Legislator does regardless of the instant he arrives. Witness the "historical" accounts in *Poland*. Whether the Legislator appears at the inception of a people or at a later date when laws are devised, he performs the same tasks. Lycurgus not only provides laws to a people previously constituted, he attends to their mores as well. Thus Lycurgus actually founds the people he seems merely to address legislatively. It would appear that a people cannot become a people by an inaugural act, contract or no contract. A people comes to be thanks to the network of practices and the web of understandings that govern their quotidian lives. The Spartans, then, did not truly emerge as such until Lycurgus's intervention. For similar reasons Numa, not Romulus, is the true founder of Rome. No Legislator can just legislate insofar as no people can already possess the attributes necessary for legislation to take root. They have to be cultivated and coordinated with care. Rousseau seems to recognize this when he remarks that the work the Legislator does behind the scenes, where the mores, customs, and opinions of a people are contrived, truly defines his task.

15. SC, 68.

16. Shklar's identification of the Legislator with politics, if preventive, seems odd. The Legislator at his best preempts politics altogether. The Legislator signifies not the presence of politics but its absence. See Judith Shklar, *Men and Citizens* (Cambridge: Cambridge University Press, 1985), 165ff.

17. SC, 76. Speaking of the particular component of founding, he continues: ". . . the Hebrews long ago and the Arabs recently have had religion as their principal object; the Athenians, letters; Carthage and Tyre, commerce; Rhodes, navigation; Sparta, war; and Rome, virtue."

18. Ibid., 70.

19. Ibid., 75. The verb is *assigner*. Jean-Jacques Rousseau, *Oeuvres Complètes*, vol. III, ed. Bernard Gagnebin and Marcel Raymond (Paris: Gallimard, Bibliothèque de la Pléiade, 1964), 392.

20. Ibid., 76.

21. Here Rousseau's reading of history informs his analytic intervention. He insists in the second *Discourse* that the history of state building reveals serious mismanagement. Architectural blunders were the rule. Edifices were placed on foundations riddled with cracks. Collapse was inescapable.

22. Ibid., 65.

23. Perhaps the monumental task assigned the Legislator determines the attributes he comes to possess.

24. Ibid., 68. Foundings must be executed precisely the first time for another reason. If changes must be made to the original creation, the status of the founding is thrown into doubt. How can a gift from God (via the Legislator) be anything other than the embodiment of perfection? If perfection is beyond its reach, how can it be a divine offering? The need for change problematizes, then, the attributes accorded the republic's basic arrangements. Founding is by definition extraordinary; it must be exempt from the defects of less remarkable creations. It is self-sufficient. As is. The necessity of alterations or amendments seems inherently dubious.

Even if the prestige of the Founding could be protected, the project of amendment still would have to answer an unanswerable question: if things were not done right the first time, as once believed, how can it be assumed with confidence that the second time will prove different? Perhaps the mistakes of the initial effort provide the requisite instruction. Errors having been identified, they will not be repeated. But if the first set of arrangements was misconceived, despite certitude about its correctness, perhaps the second is equally deficient, insight garnered from experience in the interim notwithstanding. Faith in founding itself is shattered if and when it fails to live up to expectations.

25. It is perhaps in the tension between the two poles that the force of the Legislator lies. Neither human nor divine, the Legislator can appeal to twin

but complementary sources of authority, each incomplete by itself, each buttressing the other.

26. Ibid., 68.

27. Jacques Derrida, "Declarations of Independence," trans. Tom Keenan and Tom Pepper, *New Political Science* 15 (1986), 7–15. The paradox Derrida delineates confronts any who would get together to establish a new political order. On what legal basis are they authorized to do so?

28. Ibid., 69.

29. Rousseau assures readers that few can plausibly assume the voice of God or legitimately pose as the interpreter of the Word. "Any man can engrave stone tablets, buy an oracle, pretend to have a secret relationship with some divinity, train a bird to talk in his ear, or find other crude ways to impress the people." Frauds will be exposed as soon as they speak, their own words betraying them. Even if an imposter could fool the people into accepting laws that are not in their interests, the deception would prove self-defeating. The temporary triumph of a fraudulent Legislator would fade rapidly before the inexorable awakening of the people.

30. GM, 183.

31. The oldest laws become the best laws not just because the people tacitly reaffirm them by not revoking them when they could do so, but because they stem from the originary divine genius of the Legislator.

32. SC, 69. Commentators tend to be harsh with Rousseau regarding the Legislator. See Margaret Canovan, for example, "Rousseau's Two Concepts of Citizenship," in Ellen Kennedy and Susan Mendus, eds., *Women in Western Political Philosophy* (New York: St. Martin's Press, 1987), 82. The place of God in an order is a complicated question. It cannot be reduced to pure manipulation or hoodwinking.

33. SC, 110.

34. Paul Ricoeur points out that Machiavelli posed with unrivaled clarity the problem of violence at the inception of an order. Ricoeur, "The Political Paradox," in *Legitimacy and the State*, ed. William Connolly (New York: New York University Press, 1984), 259. For Hobbes, opposition is uncomplicated. In *Leviathan*, 231, for example, he writes: "For if he voluntarily entered into the Congregation of them that were assembled, he sufficiently declared thereby his will (and therefore tacitely covenanted) to stand to what the major part should ordayne."

35. SC, 52.

36. Ibid., 110.

37. Bonnie Honig's reconstruction of Hannah Arendt's discussion of the American founding, with the assistance of Derrida, confronts the same legitimacy quandary. As Honig argues, Arendt "seeks in the American Declaration and founding a moment of perfect legitimacy." Hence Arendt's emphasis on the performative character of both acts. But to secure the purely performative character of the founding, Arendt must eliminate its constative aspects. Honig points out that Arendt fails to recognize that her beloved "We hold" is not purely performative; it is constative as well. Yet in my view, even if the status

of the "We hold" were conceded to Arendt as she would like, her problems would not be over. The perfection and purity she seeks would still be unavailable. The "We hold" cannot be the unproblematic self-constituting act of founding Arendt seeks because even pure performatives reek of violence. The formation of every "we" simultaneously constitutes a "they" excluded from the would-be community. The exclusion rests on arbitrary grounds and is secured necessarily by violent means. No act of founding can be a simple "free coming together" inasmuch as it generates its own opposition and resistance. So-called pure performatives (Rousseau's contract minus the Legislator) can be as despotic as any constative Arendt fears and loathes. Bonnie Honig, *Political Theory and the Displacement of Politics* (Ithaca: Cornell University Press, 1993), 96–115 (henceforth PTDP).

38. Rousseau's Legislator is a likely source of opposition. Though unable to employ violence to found the political community, the Legislator may be the source of that violence which alone can conclude the contract. It is the Legislator's unique ability, it would seem, to inspire and inflame the emotions of the people. But not everyone can be so moved to give his assent to the laws. Though the Legislator has no formal means of power at his disposal, Rousseau is silent on the question of others acting on behalf of the Legislator and the would-be state. Once he articulates his vision, it would be remarkable indeed if those who were convinced of his truths did not respond to those who denied them. In addition to being politically problematic, is not opposition to the contract simultaneously an offense against God? If so, can it be allowed to pass? Or does it demand response? The Legislator may not begin with an army but one might form around him and his system of laws. The Legislator deploys religion as a force of unification, but can he really control its reception? Besides, must it not divide to be able to unite?

39. The Founding paradox, it would seem, cannot be answered satisfactorily at the moment of Founding. Honig writes: "Every system is secured by placeholders that are irrevocably, structurally arbitrary and prelegitimate. They enable the system but are illegitimate from its vantage point." Honig's formulation contains a curiosity. What warrants the drift in the second sentence from prelegitimate to illegitimate? Or, what exactly makes Sieyès's circle vicious? Does such ex post facto judgment betray our temporal presumption, bringing moral valuation to bear on events decided before the system (law), the precondition of judgment, even existed? That is, how can the absence of authority be problematic in a world without it? If founding violence is inescapable, whether constative or performative, perhaps what proves ethically decisive is the response to it in the subsequent life of the republic. (Is it acknowledged? compensated? redressed? denied? repeated?) Regarding dastardly founding deeds, perhaps a republic must needs aspire to be worthy of their greatness. Perhaps that is all it can do.

40. SC, 110.

41. Ibid.

42. Ibid.

43. Niccolò Machiavelli, *The Prince*, trans. Russell Price (Cambridge: Cambridge University Press, 1988), 9, 11, 33, 55, 58. I borrow the phrase "economy of violence" from Sheldon Wolin, *Politics and Vision* (Boston: Little, Brown, 1960), 220–24.

44. SC, 61. I return to this theme in the concluding chapters.

45. Ibid., 110.

46. Ibid.

47. Even if membership in the order were possible later, the foreigner would enter on unequal terms. The disparity in power would be so extreme that the condition of equality would be lost. If the basic structure of the republic is nonnegotiable, the notion of consenting to an irresistible, immovable object somewhat strains credibility.

48. Ibid.

49. Cf. PE, 220.

50. SC, 110.

51. Cf. SC, 74.

52. Jean-Jacques Rousseau, *Political Writings*, trans. and ed. Frederick Watkins (Madison: University of Wisconsin Press, 1986), 163. I use this volume for the *Considerations on the Government of Poland* (hereafter P).

53. Exodus, 32:10. The Gideon International, Nashville, 1985.

54. P, 163.

55. Exodus, 3:14.

56. *The Prince*, 20.

57. P, 163–64.

58. Ibid., 164.

59. Ibid., 163.

60. SC, 48, 71.

61. P, 164.

62. Ibid., 164–65. Numa, whom Rousseau considers "the true founder of Rome," rather than Romulus, similarly transformed defiled beings into citizens.

63. *The Prince*, 20.

64. P, 164.

65. Niccolò Machiavelli, *The Discourses*, trans. Leslie J. Walker (New York: Penguin, 1970), 486.

66. Exodus, 21: 12, 14–17, 23–25, 29; 22: 19–20.

67. *The Discourses*, 132.

68. Jean-Jacques Rousseau, *Emile*, trans. Allan Bloom (New York: Basic Books, 1979), 238 (hereafter E).

69. Ibid.

70. In SC, 113, Rousseau mentions the dearth of reliable data on the early days of Rome. He suspects that most of what is communicated about it are "fables." He bemoans the relative ignorance surrounding the most instructive part of a people's history: its origins. Since peoples are no longer being formed, Rousseau writes, no new information can be gathered to illuminate the

phenomenon. For the birth of states, conjecture is the theoretical weapon of choice.

71. One might consider the following: In *The Natural Goodness of Man* (Chicago: University of Chicago Press, 1990), 235–36, Arthur Melzer remarks on "the Legislator's deceit" and the use of "fraud" about which Rousseau writes "admiringly"; Roger Masters in *The Political Philosophy of Rousseau* (Princeton: Princeton University Press, 1968), 365–67, speaks of the wicked, vicious, and lawless actions of the Legislator; Hilail Gildin, in *Rousseau's "Social Contract,"* 69–72, also cites the pretense and fraud of the Legislator by which the people are "duped."

72. SC, 68.

73. Ibid.

74. Paul Ricoeur argues persuasively that the virtual character of the act of consent provides Rousseau's contract with its unifying power. If it were an historical event, it would lose its invincibility. "The Political Paradox," 254.

75. P, 163.

76. Ibid.

77. Ibid.

78. SC, 113.

79. P, 163.

80. For Rousseau, the cause-effect dynamic is the reverse. The Legislator adds a mystical dimension to the life of the republic. Though present at the creation, his death threatens the viability of the order he brought into being. His prestige may endure for a generation or more, but since he is literally unavailable to preside over his progeny, his name must be kept alive. Eventually death eliminates eyewitnesses to the original miracle. Over the lifetime of a state the magic surrounding the Legislator, attributable to his "superhuman eloquence and vigor," diminishes if left uncared for by the republic. The once transparent wisdom of institutional arrangements tends to suffer from the creeping opacity that comes with age. Annual celebration and remembrance, however, provide an opportunity to restore and renew the order by revisiting ancient deeds and acknowledging the continuing legacy of debt to them. GM, 182–83.

81. Consider Rousseau's treatment of a contemporary Legislator. It was common practice for ancient city-states to turn to foreigners to establish their laws. More recently the practice was successfully duplicated by the Italian Republics and the city of Geneva. Invoking the Swiss republic, Rousseau lavishes praise on Jean Calvin for his part in the legislative enterprise. Rousseau equates the austere genius of Calvin with his activity as a founding father. The terms of his affection, however, reveal how a founder comes to be: "Whatever revolution time may bring about in our cult, as long as love of the homeland and liberty is not extinguished among us, the memory of that great man will never cease to be blessed." For Rousseau, the fate of Geneva perpetually governs the memory of Calvin, as if he alone were responsible for its success or failure. The causal chain is assumed and the projection of present success onto past efforts escapes unnoticed. If love of homeland and liberty

were extinguished, would Calvin's status change? Would he revert to a religious icon? Or a mere footnote to history?

82. SC, 67.

83. Honig's opposition is to "the attempt to 'put the law *above* man,' to secure the law of laws from all (political) intervention." Likewise she describes Derrida's resistance as the refusal "to allow the law of laws to be put, unproblematically, *above* man." Are such political ambitions too modest (despite the resistance anticipated)? What of the attempt to place the law of laws beyond *most* political intervention? What of the effort to put the law, *problematically,* above man? Are these to be opposed too? What is the effect here of working within the terms of the constative discourse? Is this one of the nihilistic habits Nietzsche counsels us to eschew? Does testifying to the "resistibility of the constative anchor" still leave it (more or less) intact? Or lend it a legitimacy that needs to be foreclosed? PTDP, 109–10, emphasis in original.

84. SC, 106–7.

85. By no means is the annual assembly without value. One of Rousseau's concerns is to discourage the ambitions of government and to preserve the integrity of the sovereign. Ritual reaffirmation keeps would-be constitutional criminals at bay. The more the sovereign flexes its muscles, the stronger it is. The government will be hesitant to move against a formidable opponent.

4. On Government

1. Bernard Manin, "On Legitimacy and Political Deliberation," trans. Elly Stein and Jane Mansbridge, *Political Theory* 15, no. 3 (August 1987), writes: "Rousseau considers politics to be essentially a simple matter" (347). I would argue that this is to be the result more than it is the presumption of Rousseau's interventions.

2. In the case of *Considerations on the Government of Poland* (henceforth P), which is contained in Jean-Jacques Rousseau, *Political Writings*, trans. and ed. Frederick Watkins (Madison: University of Wisconsin Press, 1986), see 190, 192, 195, 204, 205, 267. Watkin's text also includes *Constitutional Project for Corsica* (henceforth C).

3. Jean-Jacques Rousseau, *On the Social Contract with Geneva Manuscript and Political Economy* trans. Judith R. Masters (New York: St. Martin's Press, 1978), 75: "In Europe there is still one country capable of legislation; it is . . . Corsica. . . . I have a feeling that some day this little island will astound Europe." The quote is from *The Social Contract.* Henceforth these texts are referred to as SC, GM, and PE, respectively.

4. Rousseau uses the word in various contexts: he speaks of modern republics (SC, 68), modern men (SC, 54; P, 264), modern ideas (SC, 102), a modern spirit (P, 217), and hints at a modern age, in *Emile,* trans. Allan Bloom (New York: Basic Books, 1979), 42, 194 (henceforth E).

5. P, 191–92, 193–95.

6. Willmoore Kendall approaches *The Social Contract* and *Poland* in this fashion. In the introduction to his translation of *The Government of Poland* (Indianapolis: Hackett Publishing Company, 1985), Kendall speaks of finding "the correct one" (xvii) reading of Rousseau based on an understanding of his intentions. Kendall outlines three possibilities for the relationship of *Poland* to *The Social Contract* to explain the "glaring discrepancies" between the two texts: Rousseau changed his mind; Rousseau pretended to a conservatism he did not really hold to please the Catholic governors of Poland; Rousseau re-enacts the relationship of Plato's *Republic* to Plato's *Laws*, that is, a relationship of theory to practice that cannot—or cannot yet—be a relationship of "one-one correspondence." If either of the first two possibilities is true, then the work, according to Kendall, stands or falls as a treatment of Poland's ills and is thus not terribly interesting; it is even a failure. If, however, the third possibility is the right answer, as Kendall believes, then the *Poland* becomes a text crucial to understanding Rousseau as a whole and the plight not of Poland but of modern man. It then becomes "a pearl of great price" (xviii). While it might appear that I fall into Kendall category number three, we differ on the reading of *The Social Contract* that undergirds his interpretation. It is much too rich to be read as "pure theory" as Kendall is wont to do. Moreover, Kendall misses the many forms of rationality at work in these texts, a point which I try to clarify below.

7. In *Corsica*, 321, Rousseau even refers to a comparison of charity hospital administrations in Paris and Lyons. Judith Shklar's reaction to *Poland* in *Men and Citizens* (Cambridge: Cambridge University Press, 1985), 14–15, is mixed. Given Rousseau's failure to address "eighteenth century warfare [and] the military policies of Poland's mighty neighbors," she accuses Rousseau of a "pseudo-realism." On the other hand, she notes the intricate and endless detail of the text, but given her reliance on the sovereignty problematic, she dismisses *Poland* as "the most visionary, pejoratively utopian, of his works." Why Shklar's judgment seems to me hasty should become clear below.

8. Michel Foucault, "Governmentality," which appears in *The Foucault Effect*, eds. Graham Burchell, Colin Gordon, and Peter Miller (Chicago: University of Chicago Press, 1991), 103 (henceforth G). For a superb account of Foucault's thought regarding, among other things, practices of freedom, see Thomas L. Dumm, *Michel Foucault and the Politics of Freedom* (Thousand Oaks: Sage Publications, 1996).

9. G, 92; PE, 211.

10. G, 95.

11. For the art of government to be understood, perhaps a distinction needs to be formulated between socialization and governmentality. From ancient city-states to the modern nation, political communities must inculcate their citizens. To socialize involves enabling citizens to live their lives within established parameters and patterns by familiarizing them with a basic set of understandings and by providing them with essential capacities and skills the exercise of which is their responsibility. Socialization does not narrowly determine the kind of life to be lived. It makes one possible. Socialization is thus

open-ended (to some degree). Governmentality, on the other hand, names a more determinative form of power. Relentlessly, it pursues a "series of specific finalities" or ends, and in so doing extends the public domain and renders it increasingly transparent. Governmentality is thus integral to a micropolitics of the self and the order which is not a persistent theme in premodern thought.

12. G, 110.

13. While the word "things" interests Foucault, the word "dispose" warrants notice as well. The first reveals the object and scope of government, the second indicates its ontological underpinnings. The presumption behind the disposal project is that things (whether nature, wealth, geography, persons, social relations) are susceptible to—obviously in need of—purposive manipulation. The term dispose may even suggest responsiveness to governmental intervention.

14. PE, 211, 214, 215, 216–17. Here I would like to distinguish my effort to problematize and politicize the art of government from the defense of liberty undertaken by Isaiah Berlin. Berlin privileges freedom negatively—as freedom from. He theorizes in the name of an area or space to be cordoned off from the intrusions of authority or state power. Berlin deems a minimum space of personal freedom or non-interference indispensable to preserve and promote, or at least not to deny and degrade, the essence of human nature. Berlin's conceptualization of (negative) liberty rests on a number of contestable assumptions about the workings of power and the character and formation of subjectivity. It would be anachronistic to assume that power emanates first and foremost from the state, and dangerous—because illusory—to conceive of the subject as that which ideally ought to be protected from power in order to develop its natural faculties and thus pursue the basic and beloved ends of life. Rather, subjectivity stems from power, productively construed. In the case of Rousseau power works via the multifarious practices of government diffused throughout the state and society. The point is not to reject in toto the art of government and its results. My concern has more to do with the way in which the exercise of power which shapes selves and orders escapes critical attention and thus possible challenge and resistance. In Rousseau's texts, practices of government are depoliticized. Berlin's analysis of liberty may produce a similar effect. Isaiah Berlin, "Two Concepts of Liberty," in *Four Essays on Liberty* (Oxford: Oxford University Press, 1969).

15. SC, 67, 76, 102, 107.

16. Ibid., 54.

17. Ibid., 96.

18. Ibid., 81.

19. Ibid., 67.

20. In *Emile*, 42, similarly, Rousseau writes of "the mobility of human things," of the "restless spirit of this age which upsets everything in each generation," and he observes that "[w]e are approaching . . . the age of revolutions." Here Rousseau seems to anticipate political upheaval (he doubts that the old regimes of Europe will survive much longer), but his remarks can be

read as ontological commentary as well. If a form of life is conventional, the traditions, customs, and prejudices that once cemented things become problematic. What, then, can bind society? What new means of order will emerge to hold things together?

21. SC, 121.

22. It is in this context that Rousseau offers a rare comment on contemporary political matters. One response to overwhelming size is the resort to representation. He scorns the English people for thinking they are free after they have collectively cast their votes for parliament. According to Rousseau, here the exercise of freedom eliminates it. The act of consummation doubles as an act of annihilation. Pace Rousseau, the irony is not that "[g]iven the use made of these brief moments of freedom, the [English] people certainly deserve to lose it." Rather, the paradox is that they cannot do otherwise as they are subject to forces beyond their control. It would seem that we are all "English" now.

23. SC, 80.

24. In *Poland* Rousseau moves from the hypothetical to the historical to make the same point. The modern age must contend with recalcitrant phenomena, many of which do not bode well for the possibility of a participatory democracy. The increasing territorial size of states and their growing populations are particularly problematic. One of his first recommendations to Poland: shrink the nation's boundaries and split the country into pieces so that the latter can be governed according to republican principles. Rousseau even jokes that Poland's avaricious neighbors may succeed in doing this service for it, "which would no doubt be a great misfortune for the dismembered parts; but it would be a great boon to the body of the nation." P, 182.

25. SC, 83.

26. Ibid., 80.

27. Ibid., 78.

28. For alternative accounts, see, for example, Arthur Melzer, *The Natural Goodness of Man* (Chicago: University of Chicago Press, 1990), who approaches Rousseau through a separation of powers framework. Melzer's account is of interest (213–20) where he concentrates on Rousseau's new science of government and its "quasi-mathematical" theorizing; it loses force, however, where it restricts questions of government to a central state apparatus and presumes a solely negative conception of power to be operative in Rousseau's texts.

Most accounts of Rousseau overlook or disparage his reflections on government. I will mention but a few: Stephen Ellenburg, *Rousseau's Political Philosophy: An Interpretation from Within* (Ithaca: Cornell University Press, 1976); Hilail Gildin, *Rousseau's "Social Contract"* (Chicago: University of Chicago Press, 1983); Louis Althusser, *Montesquieu, Rousseau, Marx*, trans. Ben Brewster (London: Verso Books, 1982), and Carole Pateman, *The Problem of Political Obligation* (Berkeley: University of California Press, 1985). Ellenburg's treatment of government is trapped within the sovereignty problematic: he thus refers to the state apparatus as the "nongoverning government"

(255). Gildin's analytic treatment of *The Social Contract* probes the text for internal consistency. That government might be more complicated than commonly assumed is not considered. In addition, since the focus of the work is Rousseau's classic text, *The Social Contract*, *Poland* and *Corsica* are more or less invisible. As for Althusser, he is dismissive of the project of government per se (see ch. 6). Rousseau, in short, cannot handle "real problem[s]." Althusser too often dismisses an emaciated version of Rousseau. Pateman (152) inadvertently sums up much of the secondary literature when she writes, critically, that "Rousseau's 'government' is a purely administrative body."

29. SC, 104.

30. See P, 169, 177, 211, 256 and C, 285, 309, 311, 313, 317, 323, 329. In the French Rousseau speaks of "au bien public," "l'ordre et la tranquillité dans l'Etat," "l'aggrandissement possible de la nation," and "multiplier la population," and "la force et la prospérité de l'Etat" in Jean-Jacques Rousseau, *Oeuvres Complètes*, vol. III, ed. Bernard Gagnebin and Marcel Raymond (Paris: Gallimard, Bibliothèque de la Pléiade, 1964), 1028, 993, 928, 961.

31. PE, 216.

32. P, 159; see also 181, 182, 170.

33. PE, 215; E, 120.

34. PE, 216, emphasis added. The verb is *pénétrer* (Pléiade, III, 251). Rousseau's ontological rendering of human nature undergirds the governmental arts. Conceived in terms of its latent possibilities, human nature lends itself to political intervention and fashioning. Perfectibility and free will, the dynamic duo of human endowment, open up possibilities for movement and activity in any of a number of different directions. While Rousseau prefers to relate the intrinsic features of nature to the realization of a higher essence, these features also bear on less lofty, more material projects.

35. Ibid., 217; P, 162–63. See also *Letter to M. d'Alembert on the Theater*, trans. Allan Bloom in *Politics and the Arts* (Ithaca: Cornell University Press, 1968), 67 henceforth LD. And see PE, 227, where Rousseau "marvels [at] the governments of antiquity, which did more with parsimony than ours with all their treasures. And it is from this, perhaps, that the common meaning of the word economy is derived, referring more to the wise handling of what one has than to the means of acquiring what one does not have."

36. This is often overlooked in both celebrations and critiques of Rousseau. For an instance of the latter, see Richard Flathman's essay "Citizenship and Authority: A Chastened View of Citizenship," in Flathman, *Toward a Liberalism* (Ithaca: Cornell University Press, 1989), 76, 100.

37. PE, 216, emphasis added.

38. Ibid., 218.

39. SC, 65. Rousseau's discussion of crime and criminals has drifted. Wickedness is a broader category, not confined to the law. Recall that the sign of good governance is "number and population." Every body counts. SC, 95–96.

40. The practices of government developed in Rousseau's texts do not, I believe, reveal a totalitarian temperament. Rousseau is not Messianic. Nor is

he responsible for the excesses of the French Revolution. I refer here to the work of J.L. Talmon, *The Origins of Totalitarian Democracy* (New York: Frederick A. Praeger, 1960). The very terms of Talmon's treatment of Rousseau are employed to dismiss, not engage, him.

41. P, 236.

42. Ibid., 167. Rousseau's work in *Poland* thus betrays a rationality centered on the question of state power: assessing, inter alia, the forces both real and potential under its command, the resources at its disposal, the means for augmenting each, and the potency of the states with which it is unavoidably entwined. The manufacture of force or strength to designated levels ultimately grounds the raison d'être of the state. See P, 268–69, where Rousseau criticizes Christian powers for not following reason of state: "Nothing could be more frivolous than the political science of courts. Since it has no certain principles, no certain conclusions can be drawn from them; and all this fine theorising about the interests of princes is a child's game which makes sensible men laugh."

43. Ibid., 237, 238.

44. Ibid., 237.

45. Ibid., 236.

46. Ibid., 237–38. See LD, 105.

47. P, 239.

48. Ibid.

49. Ibid., 240.

50. Rousseau understood that dress was more than a sign circulating in a system of signs; it works its way inward as well.

51. The concern with dividing entities into manageable units is reflected as well in Rousseau's counsel to divide Poland's internal borders into more manageable geopolitical units. See P, 182–83.

52. Ibid., 242.

53. Ibid., 244, 245. Lest this reading of Rousseau seem more severe than it is, cf. PE, 220, where Rousseau scorns sacrificing the life of one for the safety of all. He is no mere utilitarian.

54. Ibid., 241.

55. Ibid.

56. Ibid., 224.

57. Ibid. Though Rousseau does not say it, he might well have: to him money is feminine.

58. Cf. his attitude to Corsican informational reports (C, 286).

59. P, 226. Cf. E, 321.

60. Ibid., 223.

61. Ibid., 227–33.

62. See P, 227–33; C, 318–19.

63. SC, 101.

64. Ibid., 102.

65. C, 316.

66. C, 316.

67. P, 232.

68. SC, 74.

69. Ibid., 68.

70. P, 229.

71. Ibid., 229. Cf. PE, 218.

72. Ibid., 233, emphasis added.

73. The displacement of sovereignty is reflected in Rousseau's language. The collective body rotates linguistically from people to inhabitants to population to life as statistical object. Selves alternate among citizens, parts, forces, and units of strength. Rousseau flip-flops among these alternatives as if they were interchangeable.

74. C, 278.

75. Ibid., 281.

76. Corsica is haunted by the collapse of its precarious unity. Rousseau fears a return of the repressed: factions which once sacrificed self-interest to cooperation in the name of national independence may again turn their considerable forces upon one another if and when the "danger that has united them grows distant." Internal warfare would compromise external defense as resources were diverted to and drained by internecine conflict. Corsica's conquerors have successfully practiced the time-honored art of any competent invader: divide and rule. As a result Corsican identity has been altered over the course of occupation. It has become composite. Conveniently, then, the figure of the foreigner as menace is used to consolidate the tattered Corsican identity. Real threat and possible reconquest drive Corsican identity politics as it seeks to secure the unity and harmony to which, Rousseau claims, this island people is ordinarily drawn. As in *Poland*, the art of government turns to identity politics, here a kind of nationalist sensibility. Enemies abound both at home and abroad. I return to this theme in the concluding chapter.

77. C, 281.

78. Ibid.

79. Cf. what Rousseau writes in P, 231: "The inevitable and natural result of a free and just government is increased population. The more you perfect your government, therefore, the more you will multiply your people even without intending to do so."

80. C, 313.

81. Ibid., 310.

82. Ibid., 282.

83. Ibid., 282–83.

84. Ibid., 283.

85. Ibid.

86. Rousseau loves organic metaphors—perhaps because they obscure the violence of integration.

87. Ibid., 317.

88. Ibid., 289.

89. LD, 128.

90. Ibid.

91. Ibid., emphasis added.

92. Here again governmentality reveals the extent of its concerns, targeting what people do alone or together, in private, when no one is looking.

93. Rousseau's ontological presumption of resolution obscures, sometimes eclipses, the technologies and mechanisms that manufacture subject-citizens out of selves. These processes are seen by Rousseau to express and complete selves unproblematically. The opposition, resistance, dissent, and difference they produce is either denied, disparaged, or demonized.

94. LD, 128, emphasis added.

95. Ibid., 130.

96. P, 172.

97. LD, 131.

98. Jürgen Habermas, *The Structural Transformation of the Public Sphere*, trans. Thomas Burger with the assistance of Frederick Lawrence (Cambridge: MIT Press, 1989), 98–99.

99. LD, 108.

100. Ibid., 99.

101. Ibid.

102. Ibid.

103. Ibid., 105.

104. Ibid., 108.

105. Ibid., 105.

106. Rousseau, of course, reconfigures these binaries as his political prescriptions dictate. Woman is not always weak and soft, for instance.

107. Ibid., 101.

108. Ibid., 88–89.

109. Ibid., 105.

110. Ibid., 106.

111. Here Linda Zerilli may underestimate the circles for women ("They too have their little societies."). Challenging Derrida's assessment of *Letter to d'Alembert*, she argues that Rousseau's dream is not of a mute society per se, but of "a society without female voice, one in which woman remains within her proper function as a sign." As Zerilli points out, the function of the female gaze is to enhance the self-conception of man; yet the women's circles also form part of the republic's panoptic and disciplinary architecture by which they shrink men back down to size, so to speak. They help produce and regulate the virtuous moral and sexual (and hence political) code of the republic by the reach of their voices. Linda Zerilli, *Signifying Woman* (Ithaca: Cornell University Press, 1994), 39.

112. LD, 67, 69, 74.

113. Ibid., 105.

114. Ibid., 69.

115. See also SC, 46, 48.

116. LD, 16.

117. Ibid., 33–34.

118. Ibid. Culpability lies also with the nature of the institution itself. The theater is designed to garner applause and praise. As such, it is not likely to conform to virtue or portray "the true relations of things." According to Rousseau, for example, tragedy valorizes the reprehensible and comedy ridicules the venerable.

119. Ibid., 20.

120. Ibid.

121. Ibid., 52.

122. Ibid.

123. SC, 99.

124. Ibid., 107, 76, 54.

125. Shklar, *Men and Citizens*, 181. But Shklar exaggerates when she writes that citizens "are not called to make or remake laws."

126. SC, 106–7.

127. Ibid., 108. This can explain why the sovereign assembly meets only at prearranged times determined by date. Other than convocation due to crisis, any other gathering of the assembly on its own is illegitimate. The assembly does not name a continuing site of public deliberation but an intermittent space which exists (opens) only at these selected times.

128. Ibid., 108; GM, 174.

129. SD, 159.

130. SC, 61.

131. Ibid., 109.

132. GM, 174.

133. Braced with a tragic conception of politics, citizens would attend the assembly, but they would not rush to it. Given its gravity, there would be hesitation, trepidation, regret at the wounds and injuries necessarily inflicted as power is exercised.

134. SC, 83.

135. Ibid., 76–77.

5. On Enmity

1. I refer here to the narrative in *The Social Contract*, not the second *Discourse*.

2. Jean-Jacques Rousseau, *On The Social Contract with Geneva Manuscript and Political Economy*, trans. Judith R. Masters (New York: St. Martin's Press, 1978), 53. The quote is from *The Social Contract*. Hereafter these three texts will be referenced individually as SC, GM, and PE respectively.

3. Carl Schmitt, *The Concept of the Political*, trans. George Schwab (Chicago: University of Chicago Press, 1996), 27 (hereafter CP).

4. SC, 64.

5. Here I part company with Tracy Strong, *Jean-Jacques Rousseau: The Politics of the Ordinary* (Thousand Oaks: Sage Publications, 1994), 103, 86–87, 189, who seems determined to deny the Hobbesian aspects of Rousseau's

thought. Indeed Rousseau's deployment of death's spectre can be subtle, but it retains a privileged place in his republic nonetheless.

6. Judith Shklar, in *Men and Citizens* (Cambridge: Cambridge University Press, 1985), 73 (hereafter MC), describes Rousseau's thought thus: "[W]hether we seek goodness or civic virtue, the will must engage in defensive war against all those of our desires that would destroy our inner peace." The formulation betrays the nature of Rousseau's virtue politics by projecting evil intent onto the aggressive desires which do not know their place. Does not such a Manichean perspective take for granted a possibility, inner peace, still in need of demonstration? Shklar repeatedly concedes this theoretical point to Rousseau (21, 167, 183).

7. Shklar, MC, 168, captures this dimension of Rousseau's thought succinctly. Speaking of sovereignty, she writes: "By taking this fear- and awe-inspiring power, so wholly associated with monarchical government, and attributing it to the people Rousseau was able to tell simple men in a phrase how immense he thought their rightful claims were." Shklar insists, however, that this is "not a new sovereignty in any intelligible sense."

8. SC, 46, 53.

9. Compare Shklar, MC, 1 ("[Rousseau] was . . . utterly uninterested in history, past or future, the last also to judge and condemn without giving any thought to programs of action."), 3 ("The utopian form was ideally suited to convey [Rousseau's] concern for the contrast between what is and what ought to be. With it came the characteristic indifference to history."), and 30 ("Rousseau was intent upon only one thing: judgment. To reveal the failures of actuality and to condemn the unpardonable was enough."). For similar analyses see Jean Starobinski, *Jean-Jacques Rousseau: Transparency and Obstruction*, trans. Arthus Goldhammer (Chicago: University of Chicago Press, 1988), 30, and Bernard Yack, *The Longing for Total Revolution* (Princeton: Princeton University Press, 1986), 76–81.

10. Jean-Jacques Rousseau, *Emile*, trans. Allan Bloom (New York: Basic Books, 1979), 444–45 (hereafter E).

11. The context of virtue must be attended to with care. Virtue cannot be cultivated regardless of circumstance. Even the best intent in the world is unreliable. An act of will alone is insufficient to secure virtue. A Sisyphean fate dooms all. The social compact provides a stable frame within which salutary dispositions and sound habits can be nurtured in citizens. Even so, making citizens, Rousseau advises, cannot be accomplished in a day. Insofar as it is the work of a lifetime, the work should begin as early as possible. Without exaggeration, Rousseau counsels states to begin training citizens in infancy. From the moment a baby's eyes first open and its sex is announced, political education commences. "Not only does philosophy demonstrate the possibility of these new directions, but history provides a thousand stunning examples." PE, 222.

12. E, 444–45.

13. Think of the complex of crimes committed in the name of property that Rousseau cites.

14. Jean-Jacques Rousseau, *The First and Second Discourses*, trans. Roger D. and Judith R. Masters (New York: St. Martin's Press, 1964), 134. The quote is from the second Discourse. Hereafter the first Discourse is referred to as FD.

15. I am indebted here to William E. Connolly, *Political Theory and Modernity* (Oxford: Basil Blackwell, 1988), 50–51.

16. SC, 96.

17. For a masterful elaboration of these themes, see William E. Connolly, *The Ethos of Pluralization* (Minneapolis: University of Minnesota Press, 1995).

18. SC, 54–55.

19. Ibid., 55.

20. Ibid., 64.

21. Ibid., 102.

22. Admittedly the sovereign establishes limits which allow people to enjoy goods and freedom the use of which is irrelevant to the community. Crucially, though, the community "alone is the judge of what matters" (SC 62, 63–64.) I would like to thank Alan Keenan for reminding me of such passages in Rousseau.

23. Ibid., 103.

24. P, 161.

25. Rousseau deems a civil religion indispensable if good citizens and faithful subjects are to flourish. He denies its tenets are religious dogmas, but the denial dissolves as they are presented. While Rousseau concedes that the sovereign has no competence in heavenly matters, for this is God's proper domain, the text furtively suggests that the ultimate fate of citizens can be predicted with some degree of certitude. Allegedly the sovereign is concerned only that individuals be good citizens here and now, but a connection is insinuated into the civil religion linking earthly conduct to heavenly future. Listen to the threat and the promise, however veiled, lodged in the dogmas as Rousseau recites them: "The existence of a powerful . . . divinity; the afterlife; the happiness of the just; the punishment of the wicked; the sanctity of the social contract and the laws." The dogmas begin with a declaration of God's power, which is followed immediately by the promise of an afterlife where, it would seem, the good are to be rewarded and the evil held to account, based on their fidelity to the sacred republic and its institutions. Citizens who obey the law can anticipate heavenly compensation. Everyone else can look forward to eternal damnation: violation of the law involves more than the transgression of mere human convention. Though none of this is explicit, the virtue campaigns receive otherworldly encouragement.

26. It is one thing to abide by majority rule, quite another to affirm that whatever it does is ipso facto right (as opposed to legal).

27. SC, 111.

28. Ibid.

29. E, 278–79.

30. SC, 64. Cf. Shklar, MC, 186.

31. The civil religion also contributes to the transparency of the state.

Rousseau does not naively assume that citizens simply will do what they have sworn. He insists, with an almost eerie calm, that citizens who appear not to subscribe to the civic faith to which they have sworn allegiance should be executed by the state. In other words, if someone who once "publicly acknowledged" the dogmas behaves *as though* he does not believe in them, he should be eliminated.

Here inquisition is not the test of belief. Nor does confession play a legal role. Subjects will be judged according to commonly observable conduct. That Rousseau apparently sanctions behavior rather than belief ought not to provide too much comfort, however. Rousseau's juridical formula disciplines citizens effectively insofar as it calls on them to regulate themselves in a context lacking stable empirical referents. To ascertain whether or not a law has actually been traduced is no easy task. What procedures should be used to make such a determination? How decisive need evidence be? The questions stack up rapidly. But that is not what is being decided here. Violation of law is indeed punishable by the state, but here Rousseau treats another species of action altogether. Discrepant appearances are criminalized.

Rousseau's behavior challenge contributes to the panoptic forces at work in the republic. Where people act as born spies of one another, an accusation of infidelity could sprout from anywhere. The citizen has strong incentive, then, to watch himself intensely. How does one respond to a charge devastating in terms of severity yet potentially amorphous in terms of deed?

Even a subject's sincere belief that he is proceeding within the parameters of officially sanctioned conduct is no guarantee of political innocence. What one actually does, strictly speaking, is irrelevant. Interpretation is everything. As a safeguard the subject can do nothing but redouble his efforts—make sure that he is beyond beyond reproach. Absolute purification looms as the underside to a politics of virtue, which could degenerate into a nasty infinite regress, with the ironic result that the citizen ends up exactly where he started before the introduction of civil life: insecure, paranoid, without recourse. Have Rousseau's prescriptions eluded his control? Rousseau's republic demands that woman also tends to the politics of appearances. Included among her duties: to be and to be seen to be faithful, virtuous in the eyes of her husband and of the community.

32. Jean-Jacques Rousseau, *Letter to M. d'Alembert on the Theater*, trans. Allan Bloom in *Politics and the Arts*, (Ithaca: Cornell University Press, 1968), 101, hereafter LD.

33. Rousseau's writings on gender are complicated. I would like to mention a few representative secondary sources on the relationship of Rousseau and woman: Jean Bethke Elshtain, *Public Man, Private Woman: Women in Social and Political Thought* (Princeton: Princeton University Press, 1981), 157–70; Carole Pateman, *Participation and Democratic Theory* (Cambridge: Cambridge University Press, 1970), 24–27; Carol Pateman, *The Problem of Political Obligation: A Critique of Liberal Theory* (Berkeley: University of California Press, 1985), 154–58; Carol Pateman, *The Sexual Contract* (Stanford: Stanford University Press, 1988), 96–101; Joan B. Landes, *Women and the*

Public Sphere in the Age of the French Revolution (Ithaca: Cornell University Press, 1988), 67–71, 77–79; Lynda Lange, "Rousseau and Modern Feminism," in Carole Pateman and Mary Lyndon Shanley, eds., *Feminist Interpretations and Political Theory* (University Park: Pennsylvania State University Press, 1991), 101–5; Nannerl O. Keohane, *Philosophy and the State in France: The Renaissance to the Enlightenment* (Princeton: Princeton University Press, 1980), 421–26, 432–41, 445–49; Margaret Canovan, "Rousseau's Two Concepts of Citizenship," in Ellen Kennedy and Susan Mendus, eds., *Women in Western Political Philosophy* (New York: St. Martin's Press, 1987), 80–84, 89–90.

Many accounts of Rousseau err when singling out woman as victim in Rousseau's texts. Man is a victim of Rousseau's virtue politics, too, though not in the same way or to the same extent as woman. Rousseau forges social and political identities appropriate to each, one masculine, one feminine.

The point here disconcerts: the study of Rousseau is more problematic than many of these texts indicate. The violence in his republic of virtue is more widespread than they note. These texts are strong, however, in pointing out that Rousseau's treatment of woman is "tied, in deep ways, to the inner structure of his theory" (borrowing Elshtain's formulation). It is not an aberration, nor can it be corrected by mere inclusion.

For an account that is sensitive to the rhetorical aspects of Rousseau's discourse on woman, see Penny A. Weiss, "Rousseau, Antifeminism, and Woman's Nature," *Political Theory* 15, no. 1 (February 1987), 81–98.

34. Given his evolutionary account of human nature in the second *Discourse*, such ahistorical assessments constitute a remarkable turnabout.

35. LD, 117.

36. Consider, for example, Rousseau's republican critique of the actress. She signifies moral depravity. Though acting was one of the few professions available to women (and thereby a source of independence), Rousseau reduces the actress to prostitute. He insists that one who would sell herself for a performance in the theater cannot be expected to do otherwise outside it, especially when it comes to those dangerous passions it is her unique skill to inflame. The temptress strikes at the heart of the family: fount of virtue, site of property, guarantor of posterity. For a woman to assume an independent role in public is by definition to neglect, ignore, or refuse the duties she bears elsewhere. By her example she tempts others to contravene their duties too. Women, especially actresses, thus commit the greatest offense to good order "when they take on the masculine and firm assurance of the man . . ."

37. LD, 101.

38. A parallel discussion is undertaken by Rousseau in book five of *Emile*.

39. LD, 82, 87; E, 358, 361, 363.

40. Ibid., 88.

41. Ibid., 83.

42. E, 361.

43. LD, 87.

44. E, 361.

45. Ibid., 361.

46. LD, 102–3.

47. Linda M.G. Zerilli, *Signifying Woman* (Ithaca: Cornell University Press, 1994), 19. As Zerilli points out, standard queries about Rousseau's sexism largely miss the point that Rousseau does not "get to *women*. [He is] too captivated by his struggle with *woman*." Emphasis original.

48. LD, 84, 85, 87. See also E, 358 and SC, 61.

49. Ibid., 85.

50. Ibid., 84.

51. Analyzing Rousseau's military festival in *Letter to d'Alembert*, Zerilli discusses the role of the female gaze at this gathering. She notes that its function "is to reflect man back to himself at twice his original size." *Signifying Woman*, 38. It is all too successful and the results are soon felt.

52. PE, 210.

53. E, 361.

54. Religious enemies also menace the republic. Rousseau excoriates Christianity with a rhetoric that is pre-Nietzschean in its energy and scornfulness. The idea of a Christian citizen strikes Rousseau as ludicrous, a veritable contradiction in terms. One devoted to and obsessed with the post-apocalypse world yet to come cannot make a good citizen in an earthly republic. An authentic Christian, by definition, is indifferent to politics. Conceivably he might even wish to hasten the end of things finite. Christians may indeed fulfill any and all duties to the best of their abilities, but they would do so without passion or commitment. (Rather than rush to the assembly, they sprint to church.) In the case of war, for example, where defense of the homeland and national freedom are at stake, lack of conviction more or less guarantees defeat and the death of the republic. Yet to the Christian what matters geographical correctness? National boundaries are arbitrary and the only true kingdom worth defending is God's. The Christian lacks a political soul—a flaw indeed fatal. Politics, of course, can suffer from theistic indifference as well as enthusiasm. Nonbelievers are on Rousseau's enemies list, too.

55. See PE, 218, 224, e.g.

56. FD, 38.

57. P, 176, 168. Cf. E, 40.

58. Ibid., 169. The patriot, in contrast, is homesick. Should he venture to a foreign land he will experience at worst boredom, at best repugnance. Even pleasures of the flesh cannot tempt, let alone seduce, the true patriot. The identity Rousseau seeks to fashion must become natural to those encompassed by it. It must flourish "by inclination, by passion, by necessity." P, 169.

59. Ibid., 176. Death at least provides resolution.

60. Ibid., 168; C, 289.

61. P, 168.

62. Ibid.

63. Ibid., 170.

64. Ibid., 164.

65. Ibid., 176.

66. Ibid., 169.

67. E, 212.

68. Of course, Rousseau also subordinates interest while retaining it.

69. SC, 55.

70. Ibid., 64–65. I pursue the matter below in the cruelty section.

71. Ibid., 61, 128.

72. Difference can be lodged anywhere. It may be located external to the order (another people, a foreign enemy). It may be embedded in the state itself (the malefactor, the dissident). It may be interior to the citizen (one of the voices of particularity within).

73. LD, 45–46.

74. SC, 110.

75. Ibid.

76. Ibid., 65, emphases mine.

77. Ibid., 65.

78. PE, 213.

79. SC, 65.

80. Inflated because it allows no room for principled dissent, for one.

81. SC, 99.

82. Ibid., 99–101.

83. Ibid., 56.

84. Ibid., 52, 64. Rousseau discounts the possibility that the introduction of the contract exacts a price, relative to what it replaces, in return for its benefits. Human being is not faced with justifying society over nature, government over independence: "it is so false that the social contract involves any true renunciation on the part of private individuals." The text, again, diverts attention from the troubling portrait it sometimes draws of a social world in which ennoblement is accompanied by and in fact produces domination and cruelty.

85. Mark Hulliung, in *The Autocritique of Enlightenment* (Cambridge: Harvard University Press, 1994), 167, is one of the few Rousseau readers I know of to comment on this passage. He attributes Rousseau's remark to the way some societies, Sparta and Rome, produce remarkable human beings, while other societies, contemporary European ones, produce nasty, savage people who do things in groups they would never contemplate doing when alone. But what if we bring Rousseau's insight to bear on the best of societies. This is what accounts for Rousseau's "silence," I believe.

86. Carl Schmitt's theorization of democracy finds an ally in (his understanding of) Rousseau. Schmitt argues that a democracy rests on the principle of equality—that equals are treated equally. Schmitt's is a substantial understanding of equality, which might be rooted in race, religion, morality, or even civic virtue. He argues that democracy so understood presupposes homogeneity. Without it, democracy cannot be. According to Schmitt, contractual appearances notwithstanding, homogeneity constitutes the core of Rousseau's state and finds expression in the general will. Democratic power is then exercised to keep whatever threatens the homogeneity of the state at a

distance—what Schmitt calls the foreign, for example. "Democracy requires
. . . if the need arises . . . elimination or eradication of heterogeneity." If the
state is to endure, its unity must be preserved and protected, and it is precisely
the heterogeneous that threatens it. On Schmitt's reading, the disturbance
caused by the conscientious objector could not be tolerated, for it would divide
the state and imperil its unity. Schmitt, *The Crisis of Parliamentary Democracy*, trans. Ellen Kennedy (Cambridge: MIT Press, 1985), 9–14.

87. SC, 65.

88. CP, 27.

89. Friedrich Nietzsche, *The Twilight of the Idols and The Anti-Christ*,
trans. R. J. Hollingdale (New York: Penguin Books, 1968). The theme of spiritualization is taken from *Twilight*, 43–44.

90. GM, 163.

91. Paul de Man, "Promises (*Social Contract*)," in *Allegories of Reading*
(New Haven: Yale University Press, 1979), 275–76. Cf. Samuel Weber, "In the
Name of the Law," in Drucilla Cornell, Michel Rosenfeld, David Gray
Carlson, eds., *Deconstruction and the Possibility of Justice* (New York: Routledge, 1992), 232–57. Speaking of the *Geneva Manuscript*, Weber writes (242):
"As so often in this text, Rousseau, while ostensibly describing the reality of a
phenomenon, gives an account of its 'necessity,' not, however, of its *possibility*. On the contrary, the recurrent gap between the two is the '*mobile*' of *The
Social Contract*, the driving force that keeps its discursive machine moving."
(Emphases original.)

INDEX

Attunement, 27–30, 42–44

Berlin, Isaiah, 173

Calvin, Jean, 170–71
Circles, 106–10
Citizenship:
  and lawmaking, 82–84
  and politics, 17–20
  Rousseau's thin conception of, 19–
    20, 84, 108, 115–18, 133, 135, 141
Connolly, William E., 159, 160, 163–
  64, 181
Corvées, 96–97, 98–99, 102
Cruelty:
  faith and, 11–12
  and general will, 22, 38–39, 130–32,
    145–48, 150–51
  and God, 12, 17, 146
  logic of, 10–12, 131–32, 147–49
  ontology underlying, 12–16

De Man, Paul, 2–3, 153
Derrida, Jacques, 52–53, 70–71, 156–
  57
Death:
  and founding, 44–46, 56–57, 65, 68–
    69, 73–74
  and politics, 128, 145–47

Difference:
  dynamic with identity, 17, 57–58,
    62, 93–95, 100–103, 137, 139–40,
    177
  threat of, 143–45, 185
Discipline:
  agricultural, 100–103
  military, 92–93
  sexual, 101–2, 103–5
Domination, pleasures of, 10–11, 33,
  130–31, 144–45
Drinking, necessity of, 107
Dumm, Thomas L., 172

Enlightenment, Rousseau's critique of,
  25–26, 32–33, 95–96
Enmity:
  and the feminine, 133–39
  and morality, 128–33
  and Nietzsche, 151–52
  and patriotism, 139–43
  and religion, 184
  and virtue, 124–28

Foucault, Michel:
  on governmentality, 77–80
  and ontology, 15–16
Founding:
  myths, 66–71

Founding: (*continued*)
    and order, 71–74
    paradoxes, 47–55, 73–74
    and the people, 47–49
    and politics, 49, 71–73
    violence, 46, 55–61, 63–64, 168
Freedom:
    and corvées, 98–99
    and sovereignty, 75–76, 80–81, 115
    See also Sovereignty, impossibility of

General Will:
    and cruelty, 22, 38–39, 130–32, 145–
        48, 150–51
    and equality, 38–39
    limits of, 22–23
Generosity, politics of, 151–52
God:
    and creationist ontology, 12–16
    and cruelty, 12, 17, 146
    and Legislator, 51–52, 53–55, 66–67,
        70–71, 166–67
    and virtue, 126
Gossip, normalizing power of, 109–10.
    See also Panoptic technology;
    Transparency
Government:
    and making citizens, 84, 87–89, 93–
        95, 175, 178
    and order, 81–84, 85–89, 91–92, 105–
        6
    and politics, 76–77
    and population, 99–103, 177
    and sovereignty, 75–76, 80–81, 89,
        118–19
Governmentality:
    Foucault on, 77–80
    Rousseau's contribution to, 85–87

Hobbes, Thomas, 1, 10, 13, 29, 31–32,
    35, 38, 42, 45, 80, 122–23, 129, 157,
    167
Honig, Bonnie, 70–71, 160, 167–68, 171

Identity, dynamic with difference, 17,
    57–58, 62, 93–95, 100–103, 137,
    139–40, 177
Individualism, Rousseau's critique of,
    124–25, 128–30

Kissing, evil of, 112–13

Law:
    and order, 35–36
    paradox of, 35–40
    and passion, 35–39
    silence of, 23, 151–52
    violence of, 36–39
Legislator:
    fiction of, 66–71, 170
    and God, 51–52, 53–55, 66–67, 70–
        71, 166–67
    necessity of, 47–48, 50–51, 166
    paradox of, 50, 52, 55, 168
    theatricality of, 54–55, 69–70
    and violence, 53–55
Love:
    ambiguity of, 126–27, 142–43
    will keep us together, 127, 139–42,
        152
Lycurgus, 61–63, 141, 165–66

Machiavelli:
    and conflict, 127, 143
    and founding, 62–64, 66
Marriage festival, 103–5
Militia, training in, 91–95
Money, evils of, 95–96, 98
Moses, 61–66

Nietzsche, Friedrich:
    and enmity, 151–52
    and founding violence, 60
    and law, 23, 156
    ontology of, 4–7, 15, 156
Nostalgia, 28, 42–44, 162

Ontology:
    Nietzsche's, 4–7, 15, 156
    and political possibilities, 12–20,
        147–48, 159
    Rousseau's, 11–16
Order:
    and founding, 71–74
    and government, 81–84, 85–89, 91–
        92, 105–6
    and practices of punishment, 145–48

Panoptic technology, 93–94, 96–98,
    103–5, 108–111, 132, 182. *See also*
    Transparency
Particular will, threat of, 128–30

Passions:
  problem of, 35–39
  and theater, 112–13
Patriotism:
  and enmity, 139–43
  self-defeating character of, 94–95,
    142–44
Politics:
  and citizenship, 17–20, 50
  as contestation, 20–21, 23–24, 51–52
  and contingency, 49, 115–16, 119
  as ritual, 71–73, 116–18
Population, government of, 99–103, 177
Public service. See Corvées
Punishment:
  and order, 145–48
  practices of, 88–89

Rape:
  in state of nature, 41–42, 164
  in virtue politics, 138–39
Reason, public, 106–8, 110–13, 117
Ressentiment, 21–22, 32–35
Rousseau interpretation, 2–3, 155–58,
    163–64, 165–66, 170, 172, 174–76,
    178–80, 182–84, 185–86

Schmitt, Carl, 121–22, 151, 185–86
Shklar, Judith, 155, 157, 166, 172, 179,
    180
Social contract:
  ambiguities of, 59–60
  and exclusion, 56–59, 121–22
  fraud of, 32–33
  myth of, 56–57, 60–61
Sovereignty:
  and freedom, 75–76, 80–81, 115
  and government, 75–77, 80–81
  impossibility of, 83–84, 174
  and politics, 116–18, 130–31
Starobinski, Jean, 40, 155, 157–58, 162,
    163–64
State of nature:
  as conceptual weapon, 30–31
  and Hobbes, 29, 31
  impossibility of return to, 31–32
  and nihilism, 40–42
  original condition of, 27–28
  rape in, 41–42, 164
  as secular version of Genesis, 35, 40–
    42, 163–64

  violence in, 41–42, 164

Theater:
  and acting profession, 114, 183
  dangers of, 111–14
  and passions, 112–13
Tragedy:
  eternal return of, 26–27, 35–40, 73–
    74, 94–95, 133, 148–53
  and incommensurability, 20–24
  and Rousseau, 7–10, 35–39
  toward a definition of, ix–x, 4–10, 38,
    39–40, 157–58, 161, 163
Transparency:
  and circles, 109–10
  and civil religion, 181–82
  and public office, 97–98
  and theory of government, 87–88
  See also Gossip, normalizing power
    of; Panoptic technology

Utopian tradition, Rousseau's relation-
    ship to, 123–24

Violence:
  founding, 46, 55–61, 63–64, 168
  in state of nature, 41–42, 164
  of virtue politics, 10–12, 16–20, 22,
    36–40, 71–74, 94–95, 99, 107–8,
    116–19, 123, 127, 128–53
Virtue:
  and conflict, 16–20, 123, 145–48, 183
  and enmity, 124–28
  and God, 126
  promise of, 16–17, 122, 124–28
Voltaire, (mis)reading Rousseau, 30–31

War:
  as permanent condition in republic of
    virtue, 128–53
  in the self, 128–31
Woman:
  construction of, 135–37
  as indispensable to republic, 134–35
  as inimical to republic, 133–35, 137–
    39

Xenophobia, political use of, 139–40

Zerilli, Linda, 137, 178, 184